Publications of the Committee on
Taxation, Resources and Economic Development

11

*Proceedings of a Symposium Sponsored by the
Committee on Taxation, Resources and
Economic Development (TRED)
at the Lincoln Institute of Land Policy,
Cambridge, Massachusetts, 1978*

Other TRED Publications

Land Value Taxation

The
Progress and Poverty
Centenary

EDITED by

Richard W. Lindholm

Arthur D. Lynn, Jr.

Published for the Committee on Taxation,
Resources and Economic Development by
THE UNIVERSITY OF WISCONSIN PRESS

Published 1982

The University of Wisconsin Press
114 North Murray Street
Madison, Wisconsin 53715

The University of Wisconsin Press, Ltd.
1 Gower Street
London WC1E 6HA, England

First printing

Printed in the United States of America

For LC CIP information see the colophon

ISBN 0-299-08520-1

Publication of this book was made possible in part
by support from the Schalkenbach and the Lincoln foundations.

Contents

v

Contributors

Kenneth E. Boulding
Institute of Behavioral Science, University of Colorado

Weld S. Carter
Antioch, Illinois

Shawna P. Grosskopf
Department of Economics, Southern Illinois University

Marvin B. Johnson
Department of Agricultural Economics, University of Wisconsin – Madison

Mary Miles Teachout
Harvard Law School

Richard W. Lindholm
College of Business Administration, University of Oregon, Eugene

Roger G. Sturtevant
Urban and Regional Planning, University of Oregon, Eugene

Ronald B. Welch
Sacramento, California

George F. Break
Department of Economics, University of California, Berkeley

Alan R. Prest
Department of Economics, The London School of Economics

Mason Gaffney
Department of Economics, University of California, Riverside

Arlo Woolery
Lincoln Institute of Land Policy, Cambridge, Massachusetts

Matthew Edel
Department of Urban Studies, Queens College

Discussants

William S. Vickrey
Department of Economics, Columbia University

Hartojo Wignjowijoto
Massachusetts Institute of Technology

Preface

The year 1979 was the centenary year of *Progress and Poverty,* the first and most important work of that unique American analyst and philosopher, Henry George. Accordingly, it is appropriate to consider anew George's particular role in American tax thought. This book reports the papers and summarizes the discussions held at the 1978 Conference of the Committee on Taxation, Resources and Economic Development (TRED). The discussions here included take a careful look at the writings and conceptual positions of Henry George (1839–1897); they explore the usefulness of George's philosophy in dealing with the modern forms of the problems he considered a century ago.

The papers included were prepared by both general philosophical and specialized tax economists, as well as by practicing tax administrators from both Europe and the United States. Although the preparers of papers and their several discussants represent a broad spectrum of tax and economic thought, a general, if tentative, consensus develops. It is that George's land tax possesses significant utility as a source of government revenue, especially for local government. Therefore, wider use of land value as a tax base merits the attention of policy makers.

The United States continues to be a country of great progress with substantial pockets of poverty a century after George wrote of this in *Progress and Poverty.* George advocated wide and substantial use of a tax on land, combined with sharply reduced taxes on earnings and economic endeavor, in order to alleviate poverty and stimulate progress. Yet his followers have enjoyed only modest political, practical, and academic success. Currently spiraling land prices, general inflation, and the shortage of investment produce economic conditions that suggest a reappraisal of tax incentives and disincentives. The analysis of this book and the conference it represents, *Land Value Taxation in Thought and Practice,* will give added insight and confidence to those considering tax system design and the place of land as a tax base in that context. Both the 1978 conference and this book owe much to the stimulus and support of both the members of the Committee on Taxation, Resources and Economic Development and the Lincoln Institute of Land Policy. As the late Harold Groves once remarked, Henry George's contribution contains elements of truth that are of enduring importance. It is appropriate to recall this fact a century after the publication of his major work.

Eugene, Oregon   RICHARD W. LINDHOLM
Columbus, Ohio   ARTHUR D. LYNN, JR.
November, 1980

I. THE BASICS OF HENRY GEORGE'S PHILOSOPHY

Introduction

Professor Boulding identifies the ideas of Henry George that continue to flourish. For example, Boulding asserts without a doubt that George was certainly right when he perceived that economic rent is the ideal subject of taxation. The weakness of George's theory of the public sector is his failure to consider the impact that government spending can have on the productivity of the private sector.

George thought the public grants economy was best conducted through the tax system. The tax system in turn could be limited largely to a single tax on land. If such a system was instituted, production in the private sector would expand and the need for the public grants economy would decline.

The world society, particularly since the destruction of cities and industries during World War II, has become quite aware that know-how is the active factor in production. Land, capital, and labor are limiting elements. The landowner has only a partial control over the land he owns. It is only within the boundaries of legal rights that he can utilize the land as he wishes. In George's opinion land use made by many individuals would lead to greater productivity. Government ownership of land would, in George's eyes, lead to all the weaknesses apparent in absentee ownership.

Weld Carter, a long-time student and advocate of the philosophies of

Henry George, has written an analysis based largely on quotations from *Progress and Poverty*. Carter effectively provides a true understanding of George's writing skill and passion and describes George as reformer, economist, and writer.

An example of the manner in which George develops a basic concept is illustrated by the following quotation: "taxes on . . . land value cannot check supply, and although a tax on . . . land value compels the land-owners to pay more, it gives them no power to obtain more for the use of their land, as it in no way tends to reduce the supply of land." The language is forceful; in emphasizing supply as fundamental in the analysis, it is oriented toward the economic approach now being utilized by current economic writers. George is fundamental and modern.

The justice and equality of a land tax rests on the creation of land value through the community and not by individual effort. The pro-ductivity of the community creates the demand for land and its market value. This same community provides the legal and police protection necessary for the enjoyment of property. The land tax ". . . is the taking by the community, for the use of the community, of that value which is created by the community. It is the application of the common property to common uses."

1
Kenneth E. Boulding

A Second Look at *Progress and Poverty*

I read Henry George's *Progress and Poverty* (1879) as a student. I remember being delighted by the book, though not wholly convinced by George's argument. I have often said that it was the one book in economics with large passages which could be set to music. Rereading it has been an aesthetic as well as an intellectual pleasure. The sincerity, the passion, the genuine pride in progress and the anguish over its failure to extinguish poverty, and the single-minded attempt to fuse the intellectual rigor of classical economics with the challenge of what is essentially a Christian morality, gives Henry George a unique place not only in the literature of economics but in the English language itself. On rereading it, one realizes that something has gone out of the English language in the last hundred years — a vigor, a passion, a rotundity. It has become more angular, more cynical, and less capable of expressing intellectual passion. Returning to George is like reliving the loss of a friend — one would like to have known him.

It is a little strange that economics, the dismal science of utilitarian rationality, should have produced prophets. Even Adam Smith himself had a touch of prophecy. Behind his eighteenth-century rationality there is a deep passion for human betterment. Keynes was also touched by the fire of the prophet. However, Karl Marx and George represent, more than any others, the prophetic tradition in economics. Marx certainly is the Jeremiah breathing forth doom, without any clear vision of what would follow it. Henry George is a different kind of prophet, an Isaiah or an Amos, lashing out against those who put field and field together and invoking a vision of justice as a mighty stream (Isa. 5:8; Amos 5:24).

In the last hundred years it has been Marx, the Jeremiah, who has triumphed in a river of human blood from Russia to Cambodia. Over half the world Jerusalems have been destroyed and human freedom is in captivity. But hope is not dead and it is worth listening to other prophets. Furthermore, it might be said of George, as of many prophets, that he was not without honor, save in his own country. His impact on the United States has been small, reflected only in a few communities, such as Fairhope, Alabama, and in a mild success in Pittsburgh. His greatest successes were in Australia, Denmark, Jamaica, New Zealand, and South Africa. The impact of George, however, is not to be measured by the amount of taxation of ground rent and land values in the world.

It is quite possible that no book on economics in over two hundred years has been read by so many people or has aroused more interest, as *Progress and Poverty*. The number of people who have been stimulated to an interest in economic problems by *Progress and Poverty,* from George Bernard Shaw on, probably would be a surprisingly large number if it were known.

The Message

What, then, is the prophetic message of Henry George? In the first place, it is that progress is real, that there is human betterment over time, and that the human race is not irretrievably trapped in stable misery. This I think was why he hated Malthus, or at least the "vulgar Malthusianism" of academic economics, which attributed all human misery to uncontrollable fecundity and saw no way out of it. On the other hand, he was also passionately aware of the disappointing results of progress over poverty that went along with the maldistribution of its fruits. Progress not only did not eliminate poverty but sometimes even increased it. Of course, he identified the villain of the piece as privately appropriated land rent and increasing land values. In this, he was a faithful disciple of David Ricardo, whose analytical structure made a deep impression on him.

Unlike Marx, George is not against private property as such. Indeed, he strongly favors private property in those things which are the result of human activity, for this he believes encourages progress. He is much closer to anarchism than to communism, though he is not an anarchist. He recognizes the necessity of government, but believes that it provides only the framework of progress — progress itself emerges as individuals are motivated to administer their lives and property more effectively. He did not attack the basic institutions of capitalism, not even financial markets, because he sees in these an instrument of progress, as indeed Marx himself did. It is the appropriation of the fruits of progress by the landowner which he identifies as the only — but almost fatal — weakness of the system of private property. This he proposes to remedy by a very simple solution — a 100 percent tax on pure land rent, i.e., what is paid for the use of simple land area irrespective of improvements. This in itself he thinks would prevent rising land values, because land values could not rise if net rents did not rise.

Land Rents

There is perhaps a little confusion in the exposition here between rent as income and land as a stock of capital value. This confusion between stocks and flows goes quite deep in classical economics and indeed is a basic flaw in Marx's analysis, and was not really resolved until Irving Fisher. Nevertheless, Henry George does identify two rather different problems associated with private ownership of land. One might be called the "income problem," that the landowner is able to extract from society an income in the form of rent without giving anything in return in the way of personal services or activity. In Adam Smith's words, "the landlords, like all other men, love to reap where they never sowed" (1789, rpt. 1937, p. 49). This is clearly a grant, a one-way transfer, not an exchange, from society to the landlord. If this is regarded as illegitimate, it must be identified as exploitation.

The other problem is that of speculative rise in the capital value of land, in terms of what is paid for simple land area. We saw this in the Florida land boom of the 1920s and the nationwide boom in 1979. Speculative high land values, as George perceived quite rightly, rested ultimately not only on the capitalization of expected future rents but on the expected rise in land values themselves. George sees the speculation in land values as the major cause of the business cycle.

People buy land at inflated prices because they expect to sell it later at still more inflated prices. On the other hand, this is a process that cannot go on for very long. Prices cannot rise without getting too high. At some point the expectation of further increase ceases and there is a collapse. During the rise in land values, however, enterprise is discouraged, and human activity is diverted into essentially useless speculation, causing unemployment and a check to progress. George came to this conclusion, one suspects, by observing successive booms and busts in his native San Francisco.

Process of Change

By contrast with Marx, George was a prophet of peaceful change. He is an evolutionist rather than dialectician. He did not believe in class war, and thought perhaps too optimistically that the basic interests of capitalists and workers were identical and opposed to those of the landlords. But he thought that landlords could be dealt with by democratic processes and essentially peaceful change.

Indeed, in his more optimistic moments George saw his rent tax proposals as an almost universally positive-sum game. He thought that by shifting the burden of taxation from improvements, that is, buildings and soil investments, on to bare land itself, even the landowner would ultimately benefit; he would be stimulated to make improvements merely by their absence. He would therefore end up perhaps even better off than he was before. There are passages which suggest that there has to be a real struggle between the land owning interests and the rest of society, but at no time does Henry George lose faith in the ability of democratic and constitutional processes to handle this struggle. The dialectical elements of the process represent a fairly minor aspect of the process of desirable change. This approach is in great contrast to the Marxian emphasis on struggle as the essential element in social change and on violence as the "midwife of the society." One is reminded of Keynes' remark that if only Malthus (the Malthus of 1836, of course) instead of Ricardo had been the dominant influence on the succeeding hundred years how much richer and happier the world would be. One cannot help feeling that if only George rather than Marx had been the dominant influence on reformers in the last hundred years, again how much richer and happier the world would be.

In the last hundred years we cannot deny that George has failed. But one hundred years is a short time in human history. One hundred years from now things might look rather different. It is important, therefore, to evaluate the thought of George to determine what was basically right in it and what went wrong. George was certainly right in perceiving that economic rent is the ideal subject of taxation. Taxation represents the capture of a certain proportion of the surplus of society by the coercive powers of state. It can capture only what is genuinely economic surplus, that is, an individual's income which, when lost, will not reduce his or her productive activity. If the state tries to do more than this, the producer will reduce both activity and product. If taxation, the capture of a product by the state, does not interfere with progress or productivity, and if the resulting activity of the state as determined by its expenditure patterns likewise does not interfere with progress and productivity, the activity of the state becomes a remarkable positive-sum game in which we all benefit. If, however, taxation goes too far, and cuts into supply price, it diminishes the incentives for production and for progress. And if this goes far enough, a stagnant or even declining society could result. Historically, it would not be difficult to find examples of this, though one suspects that the defects of public expenditure in terms of creating insecurity and waste may be more important in explaining stagnation and decline than the defects of the tax system.

There is a deeper issue involved here, which George perceived rather clearly. He argued that economic rent is not only the ideal subject for taxation; there is a moral principle that it should be taxed and appropriated for the use of society at large rather than individuals. It is what might be called a "public distributional good." Private appropriation must be justified in terms of some other benefits, cultural or political, the size of which depends upon the nature of the class and political culture. Thus, landlords who improve their property may do more for progress than a state that does not. This may have been the case, indeed, in England in the eighteenth century, with a "Turnip Townshend" on the one hand and the appalling corruption of the government on the other. But this is a case that would have to be made in each particular society, and a careful study of human history is all too likely to reveal that the combination of unimproving landlords and an improving state is commoner than the reverse.

Grants Economy

A somewhat more general point that George highlights is that the tax system is by far the most appropriate instrument for correcting the distributional imbalances that may develop out of private property and a system of exchange. George advocates a special case of what might be called the "public grants economy."

The private grants economy, especially within the family, is an important agency for correcting the imbalances that develop in a pure exchange system; it supports those, particularly the children, the sick, the incompetent, and the aged, who cannot support themselves by producing goods or services for exchange. The family is still the major instrument of the grants economy; some 30 percent of national income is redistributed within the family to individuals who cannot produce things for exchange. However, the family is not sufficient, particularly as the horizons of society expand to the nation state and ultimately to the world. Since the grants economy, especially inheritance, goes through the family to such a large extent, it will produce inequalities which may be socially unacceptable, if the system is confined to the family. Therefore, there has to be a public grants economy to supplement that of the family and to correct the excesses of the inequality that a pure exchange and family grants economy will produce.

This public grants economy, however, is best conducted through the tax system, including negative taxes, that is, subsidies, as well as positive taxes. George thought that positive taxes would suffice; indeed he felt that a single tax on land rent and values would be sufficient (in his day more than sufficient) for the expenses of government. By removing the burden of taxation from productive activities and combining the exchange and the family systems, a distributional pattern was created that was sufficient to prevent the paradox of poverty and limits to progress. Milton Friedman's proposal for a negative income tax is a direct descendent of the George proposals. It is a little surprising that Friedman has not been more enthusiastic about land rent and land value taxation, which would seem to fit in well with his general philosophy.

Human Welfare Politics

The significance of this debate for human welfare is large. If what might be called the "neo-Georgist" philosophy is correct, that the distributional defects of the market and family system can be corrected institutionally with relatively minor changes in the tax and subsidy system, the whole case for revolutionary Marxism is undermined. Communism and centrally planned economies are seen as the wrong answer to what was a perfectly legitimate question; it is not a "progressive" step but rather an evolutionary setback which the human race will eventually have to overcome. It is hard to see how a revolutionary and dialectical philosophy can avoid falling into tyranny, whether this is the tyranny of violence as with Stalin and with the nightmare of Cambodia, or a tyranny of persuasion, as with the People's Republic of China. Communism has engendered real economic gains that cannot be denied, but it has done this at the cost of an appalling political retrogression, which can also hardly be denied; for many people this seems far too high a price to pay if the economic development and redistribution can be done more cheaply. The neo-Georgist view, therefore, would represent almost the only genuinely valid criticism of revolutionary Marxism in terms of Marxism's own ideals of human welfare and the abolition of poverty.

What then went wrong? Why has this been the century of Marx rather than of George, at such an unspeakable cost in human suffering and political retrogression? The answer may lie partly in the personal characteristics of George himself. Although he undoubtedly had a great deal of charisma and capacity for leadership, his program and symbolism failed to put together a sufficient majority. At least in democratic politics, one has to have 51 percent of the vote, and this requires toleration, living with strange bedfellows, and even a loose attachment to high principle. Perhaps George, because of his honesty and decency, was incapable of this accomplishment.

It is unfortunate that the expression "single tax" became the symbol of George's proposals, although this was in no sense essential to his theories and indeed is hardly mentioned in *Progress and Poverty*. In addition the insistence on the 100 percent taxation of land rent and land values is a grave weakness, primarily because it alienated small landowners and especially rural land owners. Moreover, the plan was technically unsound. Mistakes in assessment in a 100 percent tax of any kind can be quite catastrophic, when at the 50 percent tax level they may be quite bearable.

George's Program

Many of the failures of George's political campaigns and political rhetoric do go back, however, to certain inadequacies in his analysis, and these must be faced squarely if we are to develop a neo-Georgian movement. George's analysis was profoundly insightful. It foreshadowed many things which have happened in economics and social philosophy. It was based heavily on classical economics, especially those of Ricardo, and it shared many of the classical system's defects. George's thought exhibits both the strength and the weaknesses of the amateur in the best sense of the word, that is, the lover of truth carried away somewhat by love. His exclusion from academic life — for which indeed we have to blame the academics — isolated him from marginalist revolution which was going on in the 1870s, even though in an odd way he made some contribution to it, for John Bates Clark was influenced by George. We cannot blame George for having been born before national income statistics and the Keynesian revolution. It is perhaps unfortunate that he rejected Malthus so completely and instead accepted the current academic economists' negative evaluations of the Malthus of 1836 and the *Principles*. One hundred years later, Keynes' *General Theory* essentially was a rebirth of these views. We need therefore to reinterpret George in the light of a larger and more adequate evolutionary economics so that the acceptance of his profound insights will not be hampered by one hundred- or even two hundred-year-old failures of analysis.

Classical Theory Inadequacies

In the first place, we need to reevaluate the classical theory of production in terms of land, labor, and capital as factors of production, a theory that has come down to us from Adam Smith and is still standard in all the textbooks. I have argued that land, labor, and capital are in fact quite heterogeneous aggregates useful only in certain rather crude analyses of production, and that productive processes consist essentially of the production of phenotypes, such as the chicken or the house, from genotypes, such as the egg or the blueprint. Production is a process by which know-how, in the form of the genotype, is able to capture and direct energy for the transportation and transformation of material into the improbable structures of the phenotype or product. Know-how is the active factor; energy and materials are necessary limiting factors. To these three factors of energy, know-how, and materials we also should add space and time, for all processes of production require these. Space and time also may be limiting factors.

A fertilized egg needs space, a womb, and time to grow. Land, labor, and capital are each mixtures and aggregates of these five essential factors. Thus, land, as it enters the market, is defined primarily by area. What is bought and sold, or rented in this case, is the area within certain lines drawn by a surveyor and recorded on the map in some government office. This then becomes property through the institution of title. Property may be subdivided, in which case new lines are drawn and new areas identified.

Qualities of Land

The economic significance of what lies within a particular area depends on the energy and materials that lie within it, whether this is soil, rich or poor, foundation materials for building, such as rock, sand, or quicksand, fossil fuels beneath it, or even sunshine falling on it. It depends also on its location relative to other pieces of land and qualities. All these things together generate market value of land, together with the general know-how patterns of the environment. Thus, uranium-bearing land was not so valuable before we knew about nuclear power. For a parcel of land on Wall Street, the underlying soil, if there is any, is irrelevant, though the capacity of the material structure to bear buildings is important. The location is overwhelmingly important. In the case of an Iowa farm, the material of the soil may be all important and the location relatively unimportant, although adjacent structures such as roads or railroads, may have some significance. Time may also be an important factor in the case of land. Land *now* is not land *then;* it is defined by a time position as well as by space position. Indeed, it is this property which opens up the possibility of land speculation, because the value of a piece of land changes over time.

Land is significant economically; it has some kind of value, because particular spaces, times, materials, and energy sources are significant for productive human activity. Human activity, for instance, requires space. Land, incidentially, which is defined mainly on a two-dimensional surface, actually has important three-dimensional aspects, both towards the center of the earth and away from it. Clearly when we buy a piece of land we do not buy a pyramid stretching from the center of the earth to the extremities of the universe. It may be legally dissociated either from what is beneath it, as in the case of mineral rights, or what is above it, as in the case of air rights. What we are really defining in the case is always volumes rather than areas.

Land Use Decisions

The question for society, then, is who makes the decisions about the changes that should be made and the activities that should be pursued on a particular legally defined parcel of land? In land as in other things, property eventually resolves itself into legal definitions about whose decisions relating to a particular parcel of land are legal and whose decisions are not. Property is the definition of a bundle of everybody's rights and duties with respect to defined objects. If I own a piece of land, it means that the law defines what I can do with it and what everybody else can do with it. I can grow potatoes on it but not marijuana; I can build a house on it if the house conforms to building codes and is passed by the building inspector. I can keep somebody else from building a house on it, even theoretically from walking on it, that is, from trespassing. I have an obligation to pay taxes; if I do not, the land will be taken from me. I may not do certain things that would be nuisances to my neighbors. The list goes on in a vast elaboration of detail. If an organization such as a government or a corporation owns the land, decision-making rules about it will be set forth in an elaborate set of rules and codes. In the national forest, the forester may make decisions about cutting down trees, but he cannot build a house for himself on it or even rent it out for timber-cutting, unless he has permission from a considerable hierarchical array of superiors, leading ultimately perhaps to Congress.

Private Ownership

The case for private property in land is strongest when it is administered directly by the owner. This is why we have encouraged small home ownership on such a large scale in this country. There is something in the "magic of property" when that property is close to the proprietor, and when the failures of decision-making in regard to land are reflected directly in the welfare of the one who makes the decisions. Even here we still have to take account of externalities, decisions that the owner makes which affect neighboring owners. We try to do this by such institutions as zoning, building codes, and even laws against attractive nuisances such as unfenced swimming pools. Private ownership can become pathological when the ownership is absentee, whether it is an absentee landlord, as in the catastrophic case of Ireland, or even an absentee corporation or an absentee government. There is nothing in the public ownership of land which does not make the decision-maker an absentee, which is why I suspect that George wanted to keep decision-making about land in the hands of private ownership, although he wanted to tax off the economic surplus which might result.

The market for land can hardly help being imperfect, even though it does not necessarily result in monopoly. Land rent is not necessarily an income that results from monopoly power, though sometimes it is. Thus, if I own a parcel of Iowa corn land I could prevent anybody from growing corn there. My action would not noticeably affect the price of corn, nor would it affect the market value of the land; it would only mean that I might deprive myself of the maximum income from it. Here the theory of differential rent arises in all its glory. The economic significance of a parcel of Iowa corn land depends on the price of corn and of alternative crops. This in turn is going to depend on the supply curve of corn in some sort of equilibrium, the equilibrium price being that at which there is no net incentive to expand corn production. If corn can be grown only on a certain limited area of land, at some point the supply of corn may become inelastic. Then if the demand rises into that area of it, other corn land will obtain something like a monopoly price as a result of land monopoly. If, however, the demand is such that the supply of corn is highly elastic, there will be very little monopoly element in its price or in the price of land that grows it. I may have no more monopoly in my piece of corn land than I have in my stocks of harvested corn. Land on Wall Street, however, is highly inelastic in supply because of the location factor. A stockbroker can get an inexpensive office in the Adirondacks but he will be seriously inconvenienced by the location. He would probably do less business there than he would in a very expensive office in a Wall Street skyscraper. Land cannot fly down from the Adirondacks to the tip of Manhattan Island as the stockbroker can.

Land Speculation

This geographical immobility of land is what creates the enormous differences in both the rent and the value of equal areas in different places. The relative mobility of workers and capital goods makes it impossible to have the kind of differences in price per unit that we find in the case of land. The case for social appropriation of large land values, especially in the central cities, seems very strong. The diseconomies of land speculation are quite frequently evident, in the wastage of urban land, unused lots, the sprawl of cities, and the leapfrogging of business areas over those which are being held speculatively on the edge of central cities out to new centers. There is also the possibility, recognized by George, that speculation may drive up the price of land to the point where it seriously interferes with developmental processes and operates as a tax on progress.

There is, however, a case on the other side. First, land speculation is not fundamentally different from speculation in other areas, for instance, on the stock market. Here too we see perverse dynamic movements, as in the events from 1927 to 1929, which were clearly pathological from the point of view of the larger society. The role of speculation in stimulating inflation is a relatively recent phenomenon following the Keynesian revolution, which gave us a money supply indefinitely flexible upwards and speculative price rises in commodities and in land and financial instruments. These price increases are self-justifying, because the money supply rises under the pressure of the fear of unemployment and in turn justifies the speculative price. The phenomenon, however, is not peculiar to land, and there is a case for taxing all speculative augmentations of the value of particular assets.

Land as Capital

Land from the point of view of the accountant and the balance sheet is an asset just like any capital good. We cannot really separate it from the general discussion about the validity and the pathologies of the ownership of capital in general. George defended interest and profit on the rather curious grounds that they arose from the biological increase of living things. This view has seldom recommended itself to economists, but nevertheless it deserves to be taken more seriously than it has been in the past. George sees quite clearly that interest and profit arise from the growth of the value of assets, but he argues that this happens because calves grow into cows and saplings grow into trees, so that their owners increase their assets by simply waiting. This, of course, is a reflection of the time factor in the productive process; there is an elaborate body of theory about this, originated by Irving Fisher and Böhm-Bawerk in the Austrian School, which attributes interest and profit to impatience on the one hand and to the productivity of sheer waiting on the other. We have to wait, of course, not only for trees to grow but for power stations to be built, and waiting itself has a psychological cost, that is, impatience. It is not surprising that we pay more for newly marketed goods than we would for the same goods in the future. This is discounting, which is essentially the same phenomenon as interest and profit.

This raises one question: if rent is properly appropriated by society as a whole, why is not interest and profit? This is precisely the great Marxian question. Of course the Marxists criticize George on the grounds that he did not go far enough; they claim that rent is only part of surplus value, and all of surplus value, including profit and interest, should be appropriated to society as a whole. George's answer to this would undoubtedly be that, whereas rent can be expropriated without any damage to human activity, private property in capital is so much more productive than public enterprise that the return to capital does not really constitute surplus value. The problem here actually is an empirical one, as to whether private enterprise is in fact more productive than public, so that the return to capital represents a net addition to the product of society and hence cannot be regarded as exploitation. The answer to this question depends on the institutions of society. While one can take a rather dim view of centrally planned economies in light of the experience during the twentieth century, the possibility of social inventions that would allow centrally planned economies to be politically democratic and permit individual freedom, while also being efficient, cannot be ruled out entirely. However, I confess that I am extremely skeptical about the realization in any conceivable future of such social inventions.

Another question of great difficulty, relevant both to George and to Marx, is the social appraisal of the value of luck, uncertainty, and what might be called the "lottery of life." Every person who buys a lottery ticket clearly has a demand for inequality; oddly enough this persists even in the socialist countries. A perfectly just society in which everything bad that happened to one was one's own fault and could not be blamed either on anybody else or on bad luck could well be regarded by most people as a nightmare. We believe in offsetting bad luck up to a point; otherwise we would have neither insurance nor welfare. But this rarely goes to the point of believing in perfect equality. If we prevent people from having good luck, as in the case of land speculation, we would cut out a pattern of human activity, particularly in risk-bearing, for which there is clearly some demand. This is a difficult question that I cannot pretend to resolve, but it cannot be neglected in the evaluation of any program for social change.

Conclusion

Perhaps the movement that undermined George's influence more than any other was the rise of the progressive income tax, most of which took place after the publication of *Progress and Poverty*. In the opinion of most economists and men of affairs, this represented a method of redistribution, even the capture of economic surplus, which was more general than any land tax. Of course, the rise in the expense and function of government also made the idea of a single tax on land totally inadequate. Furthermore, George did not have the benefit of national income statistics, which seem to point to a rather minor (even declining) role for land rent in the total economy. To some extent this may be an artifact of the statistical processes themselves; there is a good deal of evidence that the national income statistics underestimate the importance of rent. Nevertheless, even though what George started may have been a special case, it is a special case of a very important principle. Furthermore, we are by no means out of the woods in regards to social policy towards land and land rent. It remains a source of socially appropriable economic surplus, and the whole relation of the market in land to the needs of society, however these are defined, remains an unsolved one. The great difficulty here is that every piece of land is unique. The regulation of land use by government becomes an almost insoluble problem, requiring an administrative structure far greater than it could conceivably be worth.

George's solution — to keep land in private hands and tax away its economic surplus — has the great attractiveness of administrative simplicity. It is a neglected part of the tool box of social policy. It should be taken much more seriously by economists, other social scientists, philanthropists, reformers, and politicians, even though we may end up with a solution much more complex than a single tax.

References

George, Henry. 1879. *Progress and Poverty*. New York: Appleton.
Smith, Adam. 1789. Reprint 1937. *The Wealth of Nations. 5th ed*. New York: Modern Library.

2 *Weld S. Carter*

An Introduction to Henry George

Henry George, American economist and philosopher, was born in Philadelphia in 1839 and died in New York in 1897. His major works are: *Progress and Poverty* (1879), *The Land Question* (1881), *Social Problems* (1883), *Property in Land* (1884), *Protection or Free Trade?* (1886), *The Condition of Labor* (1891), *A Perplexed Philosopher* (1892), and *The Science of Political Economy* (posthumous 1898).

Of all these works, *Progress and Poverty* first drew large-scale attention to George. This is the book to which George Soule alludes in his *Ideas of the Great Economists,* when he writes, "By far the most famous American economic writer, author of a book which probably had a larger world-wide circulation than any other work on economics ever written, was Henry George, author of *Progress and Poverty* (1879)" (1955, p. 81).

What was the basis of the fame cited by Soule? Was George's contribution transitory or was it lasting? Can it be ignored or is it an essential part of our economic and philosophic literature? The late John Dewey has said, "It would require less than the fingers of the two hands to

19

enumerate those who, from Plato down, rank with Henry George among
the world's social philosophers. . . . No man, no graduate of a higher
educational institution, has a right to regard himself as an educated man
in social thought unless he has some first-hand acquaintance with the
theoretical contribution of this great American thinker" (Brown 1928, p. 2).

The Importance of Land

George is largely remembered for the single tax. But the single tax
came at the end of a long trail as a means — *the* means, he said — by which
to remedy ills previously identified and diagnosed. Behind the single tax
lay a closely knit system of thought. To understand George, it is
necessary to go behind the single tax and explore that system for its
major characteristics.

Notable in George's work is the emphasis he laid on the relation of
man to the earth. "The most important of all the material relations of
man is his relation to the planet he inhabits" (1881, rpt. 1953, p. 61).

George might well be called a land economist, indeed, the foremost
land economist. For George, the basic fact of man's physical existence is
that he is a land animal, "who can live only on and from land, and can
use other elements, such as air, sunshine and water, only by the use of
land" (1881, rpt. 1953, p. 4). "Without either of the three elements, land,
air and water, man could not exist; but he is peculiarly a land animal,
living on its surface, and drawing from it his supplies" (1883, rpt. 1953,
p. 132).

So man not only lives off land, levying on it for its materials and
forces, but he also lives on land. His very life depends on land. ". . . land
is the habitation of man, the store-house upon which he must draw for
all his needs, the material to which his labor must be applied for the supply of all his desires; for even the products of the sea cannot be taken, the
light of the sun enjoyed, or any of the forces of nature utilized, without
the use of land or its products. On the land we are born, from it we live,
to it we return again — children of the soil as truly as is the blade of grass
or the flower of the field. Take away from man all that belongs to land,
and he is but a disembodied spirit" (1879, rpt. 1958, pp. 295–96).

Land and man, in that order! These two things are the fundamentals.
They are, for instance, the fundamentals of production. It is said that
without labor, certainly, there can be no production. Similarly, without
land, clearly there can be no agricultural production or mining production. It was just as clear to George that there could be no production of
any kind without land. There could be no factory production, no trade,
no services rendered, and none of the multitudinous operations of town
and city.

All these processes require land: a place, a spot, a site, a location, so many acres or square feet of the earth's surface on which to be performed. "In every form . . . the exertion of human labor in the production of wealth requires space; not merely standing or resting space, but moving space — space for the movements of the human body and its organs, space for the storage and changing in place of materials and tools and products. This is as true of the tailor, the carpenter, the machinist, the merchant or the clerk, as of the farmer or stock-grower, or of the fisherman or miner" (1897, rpt. 1953, p. 359).

The office building, the store, the bank, as well as the factory, need land just as do the farm and mine. Land is needed as sites on which to build structures. Likewise, businesses need land as the locations on which to perform their subsequent operations.

George adds: "But it may be said, as I have often heard it said, 'We do not all want land! We cannot all become farmers!' To this I reply that we *do* all want land, though it may be in different ways and in varying degrees. Without land no human being can live; without land no human occupation can be carried on. Agriculture is not the only use of land. It is only one of many. And just as the uppermost story of the tallest building rests upon land as truly as the lowest, so is the operative as truly a user of land as is the farmer. As all wealth is in the last analysis the resultant of land and labor, so is all production in the last analysis the expenditure of labor upon land" (1883, rpt. 1953, pp. 136 — 37).

The railroad needs land, not just for its terminals and depots but for its very roadbeds; whoever uses the railroad uses the land that the railroad occupies, as well as the improvements the railroad affords. The State needs land not only for parks and reservoirs but for schools and courts, for hospitals and prisons, and for roads and highways with which to link its residents together.

Our homes require land, whether the home is a country estate, a city apartment, or a room in hotel or tenement. Our diversions require land, whether for a ride in the country, a round on the golf course, a seat at the theatre, or a chair in the library or before the television set. "Physically we are air-breathing, light-requiring land animals, who for our existence and all our production require place on the dry surface of our globe. And the fundamental perception of the concept land — whether in the wider use of the word as that term of political economy signifying all that external nature offers to the use of man, or in the narrower sense which the word usually bears in common speech, where it signifies the solid surface of the earth — is that of extension; that of affording standing-place or room" (1897, rpt. 1953, p. 352).

In George's view, man's dependence on land is universal and endless,

". . . for land is the indispensible prerequisite to life" (1897, rpt. 1953, p. 256). "What is inexplicable, if we lose sight of man's absolute and constant dependence upon land, is clear when we recognize it" (1883, rpt. 1953, p. 133).

Here then is the main element, the distinctive characteristic, of George's work. In George's view, man's relation to the earth is his primary material relation. All other influences, therefore, must be appraised as to how they affect, or are affected by, this basic relation. It is perhaps this to which Soule refers when he says, of *Progress and Poverty,* "This book expounded a theory developed with superb logic" (1955, p. 81).

Land vs. Products: Their Differences

In addition, George differentiated sharply between land itself and the products – or wealth, as he termed them – which labor made from the land. "In producing wealth, labor, with the aid of natural forces, but works up, into the forms desired, pre-existing matter, and, to produce wealth, must, therefore, have access to this matter and to these forces – that is to say, to land. The land is the source of all wealth. It is the mine from which must be drawn the ore that labor fashions. It is the substance to which labor gives the form" (1879, rpt. 1958, p. 272).

George saw, as between land and products, certain elementary differences. "In every essential, land differs from those things which . . . [are] the product of human labor. . . . It is the creation of God; they are produced by man. It is fixed in quantity; they may be increased illimitably. It exists, though generations come and go; they in a little while decay and pass again into the elements" (1883, rpt. 1953, p. 204).

Speculation

Having noted these differences, George proceeded to use them as the basis for his examination of related areas of economics, such as speculation. When asked how speculation worked, George responded that a distinction must be made between speculation in land and speculation in products.

Writing of industrial depressions, he said, "When, with the desire to consume more, there coexist the ability and willingness to produce more, industrial and commercial paralysis cannot be charged either to overproduction or to overconsumption. Manifestly, the trouble is that production and consumption cannot meet and satisfy each other.

"How does this inability arise? It is evidently and by common consent the result of speculation. But of speculation in what?

"Certainly not of speculation in things which are the products of labor
. . . for the effect of speculation in such things, as is well shown in current
treatises that spare me the necessity of illustration, is simply to equalize
supply and demand, and to steady the interplay of production and consumption by an action analogous to that of a fly-wheel in a machine"
(1879, rpt. 1958, p. 267). In other words, the tendency of speculation in
products is to increase the demand for products and thereby increase the
price of products. This increased price will induce more production,
which, increasing the supply, will tend to lower the price. Throughout
this cycle, there has been a stimulating effect on production in general.

He continued, "Therefore, if speculation be the cause of these
industrial depressions, it must be speculation in things not the production of labor, but yet necessary to the exertion of labor in the production
of wealth — of things of fixed quantity; that is to say, it must be speculation in land" (1879, rpt. 1958, pp. 267–68).

How can this be? How can speculation in land cause industrial depression? George explains, ". . . that there is a connection between the rapid
construction of railroads and industrial depression, any one who
understands what increased land values mean, and who has noticed the
effect which the construction of railroads has upon land speculation, can
easily see. Wherever a railroad was built or projected, lands sprang up in
value under the influence of speculation, and thousands of millions of
dollars were added to the nominal values which capital and labor were
asked to pay outright, or to pay in installments, as the price of being
allowed to go to work and produce wealth. The inevitable result was to
check production . . ." (1879, rpt. 1958, p. 275).

The tendency of speculation in land is similar to that of speculation in
products; it increases the demand for land and thereby increases the price
of land. However, here the similarity ends. The supply of land is fixed; as
successive units of land become priced beyond the level at which labor
and capital can profitably engage in production, an increasing (though
artificial) scarcity of land develops. "The inevitable result was to check
production" (1879, rpt. 1958, p. 275).

So, according to George, another difference between land and products is that speculation in products tends to stimulate production,
whereas speculation in land tends to check production.

The Incidence of Taxation

Another area in which George applied these inherent differences
between land and products was the field of taxation. To determine the

incidence of taxation, George had to know what was to be taxed, products or the value of land. In each case he traced out the effect from the essential nature of the thing to be taxed: ". . . all taxes upon things of unfixed quantity increase prices, and in the course of exchange are shifted from seller to buyer, increasing as they go. . . . If we impose a tax upon buildings, the users of buildings must finally pay it, for the erection of buildings will cease until building rents become high enough to pay the regular profit and the tax besides. . . . In this way all taxes which add to prices are shifted from hand to hand, increasing as they go, until they ultimately rest upon consumers, who thus pay much more than is received by the government. Now, the way taxes raise prices is by increasing the cost of production, and checking supply. But land is not a thing of human production, and taxes upon . . . [land value] cannot check supply. Therefore, though a tax on . . . [land value] compels the land owners to pay more, it gives them no power to obtain more for the use of their land, as it in no way tends to reduce the supply of land. On the contrary, by compelling those who hold land on speculation to sell or let for what they can get, a tax on land values tends to increase the competition between owners, and thus to reduce the price of land" (1879, rpt. 1958, pp. 415–16).

Here, then is another derivative difference between land and products, according to George: taxation on products causes an increase in the price of products; taxation on the value of land causes a drop in the price of land.

Taxes: Their Effects on Production

However, what is the effect on production of taxes levied on products and of taxes levied on the value of land?

Of taxes levied on products, George said: "The present method of taxation operates upon exchange like artificial deserts and mountains; it costs more to get goods through a custom house than it does to carry them around the world. It operates upon energy, and industry, and skill, and thrift, like a fine upon those qualities. If I have worked harder and built myself a good house while you have been contented to live in a hovel, the taxgatherer now comes annually to make me pay a penalty for my energy and industry, by taxing me more than you. If I have saved while you wasted, I am mulct, while you are exempt. If a man build a ship we make him pay for his temerity, as though he had done an injury to the state; if a railroad be opened, down comes the taxcollector upon it, as though it were a public nuisance; if a manufactory be erected we levy upon it an annual sum which would go far toward making a handsome profit. We say we want capital, but if anyone accumulate it, or bring it among us, we charge him for it as though we were giving him a privilege. We punish with a tax the man who covers barren fields with ripening grain, we fine him who puts up machinery, and him who drains a swamp. How heavily these taxes burden production only those realize who have attempted to follow our system of taxation through its ramifications, for, as I have before said, the heaviest part of taxation is that which falls in increased prices" (1879, rpt. 1958, p. 434).

Turning to taxation levied on the value of land, George went on to say:

> For this simple device of placing all taxes on the value of land would be in effect putting up the land at auction to whosoever would pay the highest rent to the state. The demand for land fixes its value, and hence, if taxes were placed so as very nearly to consume that value, the man who wished to hold land without using it would have to pay very nearly what it would be worth to anyone who wanted to use it.
> And it must be remembered that this would apply, not merely to agricultural land, but to all land. Mineral land would be thrown open to use, just as agricultural land; and in the heart of a city no one could afford to keep land from its most profitable use, or on the outskirts to demand more for it than the use to which it could at the time be put would warrant. Everywhere that land had attained a value, taxation, instead of operating, as now, as a fine upon improvement, would operate to force improvement (1879, rpt. 1958, p. 437).

A few pages before this he had told us that, "It is sufficiently evident that with regard to production, the tax upon the value of land is the best tax that can be imposed. Tax manufactures, and the effect is to check manufacturing; tax improvements, and the effect is to lessen improvement; tax commerce, and the effect is to prevent exchange; tax capital, and the effect is to drive it away. But the whole value of land may be taken in taxation, and the only effect will be to stimulate industry, to open new opportunities to capital, and to increase the production of wealth" (1879, rpt. 1958, p. 414).

In other words, according to George, taxation of products checks production, whereas taxation of land values stimulates production.

The Ethics of Property

Any discussion of Henry George should include a consideration of his ethical ideas, for throughout his works the question of right and wrong is dominant. In *Progress and Poverty,* for instance, he struck this keynote: ". . . whatever dispute arouses the passions of men, the conflict is sure to rage, not so much as to the question 'Is it wise?' as to the question 'Is it right?'. . . I bow to this arbitrament, and accept this test" (1879, rpt. 1958, p. 333)

George wrote as a social philosopher. Therefore his preoccupation in the field of ethics was with the relations of man to man, rather than with man himself — with stealing rather than with thriftlessness. This necessarily involves the matter of property and ownership.

Once again, the student will find George's analysis to be based on the differences inherent in the two categories of land and products. "The real and natural distinction is between things which are the produce of labor and things which are the gratuitous offerings of nature. . . . These two classes of things are in essence and relations widely different, and to class them together as property is to confuse all thought when we come to consider the justice or the injustice, the right or the wrong of property" (1879, rpt. 1958, p. 337).

What is the moral basis of property?

Is it not, primarily, the right of a man to himself, to the use of his own powers, to the enjoyment of the fruits of his own exertions?. . . As a man belongs to himself, so his labor when put in concrete form belongs to him.

And for this reason, that which a man makes or produces is his own, as against all the world — to enjoy or to destroy, to use, to exchange, or to give. No one else can rightfully claim it, and his exclusive right to it involves no wrong to anyone else. Thus there is to everything produced by human exertion a clear and indisputable title to exclusive possession and enjoyment, which is perfectly consistent with justice, as it descends from the original producer. . . . (1879, rpt. 1958, p. 334).

Here is a justification for private property in products. But what of land, which is not produced by man? Is there any other basis from which a justification for private property in land might be derived? In addition, is there anything in the right of private property in products which precludes the right of private property in land?

George explains, "Now this [the right of the individual to the use of his own faculties] is not only the original source from which all ideas of exclusive ownership arise . . . but it is necessarily the only source. There can be to the ownership of anything no rightful title which is not derived from the title of the producer and does not rest upon the natural right of the man to himself. There can be no other rightful title, because (1st) there is no other natural right from which any other title can be derived, and (2nd) because the recognition of any other title is inconsistent with and destructive of this" (1879, rpt. 1958, pp. 334–35).

To substantiate the first reason he further said,

Nature acknowledges no ownership or control in man save as the result of exertion. In no other way can her treasures be drawn forth, her powers directed, or her forces utilized or controlled. . . . All men to her stand upon an equal footing and have equal rights. She recognizes no claim but that of labor, and recognizes that without respect to the claimant. If a pirate spread his sails, the wind will fill them as well as it will fill those of a peaceful merchantman. . . . The laws of nature are the decrees of the Creator. There is written in them no recognition of any right save that of labor; and in them is written broadly and clearly the equal right of all men to the use and enjoyment of nature; to apply to her by their exertions, and to receive and possess her reward. Hence, as nature gives only to labor, the exertion of labor in production is the only title to exclusive possession (1879, rpt. 1958, pp. 335–36).

As to the second reason he said:

This right of ownership that springs from labor excludes the possibility of any other right of ownership . . . . If production give to the producer the right to exclusive possession and enjoyment, there can rightfully be no exclusive possession and enjoyment of anything not the production of labor, and the recognition of private property in land is a wrong. For the right to the produce of labor cannot be enjoyed without the right to the free use of the opportunities offered by nature, and to admit the right of property in these is to deny the right of property in the produce of labor. When nonproducers can claim as rent a portion of the wealth created by producers, the right of the producers to the fruits of their labor is to that extent denied (1879, rpt. 1958, p. 336).

Private property in land, according to George, is unjust because it lets owners of land refuse access to land, and thereby threatens livelihood and life itself. Private property in land is also unjust because it enables owners of land to levy toll on production for the use of land; therefore it is robbery. So another difference between products and land, in George's view, is that private property in products is right, and private property in land is wrong.

The Ethics of Taxation

It was but a short step from the ethics of property to the ethics of taxation. George's position here was that as labor and capital rightfully and unconditionally own what they produce, no one can rightfully appropriate any of their earnings; nor can the State. On the other hand, land value is always a socially created value, never the result of action by the owner of the land. Therefore this is a value that must be taken by society; otherwise, those who comprise the social whole are deprived of what is rightfully theirs. Furthermore, to charge the owner for this value, in the form of taxation, is only to collect from him the precise value of the benefit he receives from society.

As to the justice of taxes on products, George spoke of ". . . all taxes now levied on the products and processes of industry — which taxes, since they take from the earnings of labor, we hold to be infringements of the right of property" (1881, rpt. 1953, p. 8).

Of the justice of taxes on land values, he said, "Adam Smith speaks of incomes as 'enjoyed under the protection of the state'; and this is the ground upon which the equal taxation of all species of property is commonly insisted upon — that it is equally protected by the state. The basis of this idea is evidently that the enjoyment of property is made possible by the state — that there is a value created and maintained by the community, which is justly called upon to meet community expenses. Now of what values is this true? Only of the value of land. This is a value that does not arise until a community is formed, and that, unlike other values, grows with the growth of the community. It exists only as the community exists. Scatter again the largest community, and land, now so valuable, would have no value at all. With every increase of population the value of land rises; with every decrease it falls . . . .

"The tax upon land values is, therefore, the most just and equal of all taxes. It falls only upon those who receive from society a peculiar and valuable benefit, and upon them in proportion to the benefit they receive. It is the taking by the community, for the use of the community, of that value which is the creation of the community. It is the application of the common property to common uses" (1879, rpt. 1958, pp.420–21).

The Single Tax

To recapitulate at this point: man is always dependent upon land for his life and living, both as the source of raw materials for his products and as the place on which to fashion, trade, service, and enjoy these products. Private property in land is inexpedient, for by inducing speculation in land in good times, it brings on bad times; however, private property in products is expedient because it provides the incentive to produce. Private property in land is morally wrong, first because it denies land to mankind in general, and second because it provides a primary way for nonproducers to levy toll on producers. However, private property in products is morally right, deriving as it does directly from the right of a man to himself. The taxation of land values is expedient because it stimulates production whereas the taxation of products is inexpedient because it checks production. The taxation of land values is morally right, for through it the community levies on the precise values the community has created. However, the taxation of products is morally wrong because it deprives labor and capital of their just earnings.

This chain of reasoning, demonstrating that both justice and expediency called for the same course of action, inevitably led George to a "simple yet sovereign remedy" (1879, rpt. 1958, p. 405). That remedy was: *"To abolish all taxation save that upon land values"* (1879, rpt. 1958, p. 406). This is the single tax, with which George's name is so largely associated.

Some Implications of the Single Tax

As is already evident, the single tax was more than a mere fiscal reform, because it dealt with questions of primary social morality, and with matters that permeated the entire economy. Yet George saw even broader implications than these.

If the conclusions at which we have arrived are correct, they will fall under a larger generalization.
Let us, therefore, recommence our inquiry from a higher standpoint, whence we may survey a wider field.
What is the law of human progress? (1879, rpt. 1958, p. 475).

George saw ours alone among the civilizations of the world as still progressing; all others had either petrified or had vanished. And in our civilization he had already detected alarming evidences of corruption and decay. So he sought out the forces that create civilization and the forces that destroy it.

He found the incentives to progress to be the desires inherent in human nature, and the motor of progress to be what he called mental power. But the mental power that is available for progress is only what remains after nonprogressive demands have been met. These demands George listed as maintenance and conflict.

In his isolated state, primitive man's powers are required simply to maintain existence; only as he begins to associate in communities and to enjoy the resultant economies is mental power set free for higher uses. Hence, association is the first essential of progress:

And as the wasteful expenditure of mental power in conflict becomes greater or less as the moral law which accords to each an equality of rights is ignored or is recognized, equality (or justice) is the second essential of progress.
Thus association in equality is the law of progress. Association frees mental power for expenditure in improvement, and equality, or justice, or freedom — for the terms here signify the same thing, the recognition of the moral law — prevents the dissipation of this power in fruitless struggles (1879, rpt. 1958, p. 508).

He concluded this phase of his analysis of civilization in these words: "The law of human progress, what is it but the moral law? Just as social adjustments promote justice, just as they acknowledge the equality of right between man and man, just as they insure to each the perfect liberty which is bounded only by the equal liberty of every other, must civilization advance. Just as they fail in this, must advancing civilization come to a halt and recede . . . " (1879, rpt. 1958, p. 526).

However, as the primary relation of man is to the earth, so must the primary social adjustment concern the relation of man to the earth. Only that social adjustment which affords all mankind equal access to nature and which insures labor its full earnings will promote justice, acknowledge equality of right between man and man, and insure perfect liberty to each.

This, according to George, was what the single tax would do. It was why he saw the single tax as not merely a fiscal reform but as the basic reform without which no other reform could, in the long run, avail. This is why he said, "What is inexplicable, if we lose sight of man's absolute and constant dependence upon land, is clear when we recognize it" (1883, rpt. 1953, p. 133).

References

Brown, Harry G., ed. 1928. *Significant Paragraphs from* Progress and Poverty. New York: Doubleday, Doran.

George, Henry. 1879. Reprint 1958. *Progress and Poverty.* New York: Robert Schalkenbach Foundation.

George, Henry. 1881. Reprint 1953. *The Land Question.* New York: Robert Schalkenbach Foundation.

George, Henry. 1883. Reprint 1953. *Social Problems.* New York: Robert Schalkenbach Foundation.

George, Henry, 1897. Reprint 1953. *The Science of Political Economy.* New York: Robert Schalkenbach Foundation.

Soule, George, 1955. *Ideas of the Great Economists.* New York: The New York Library.

Comment Centered on Land Speculation

William S. Vickrey: I fail to see how the land tax curbs speculation. What in effect happens is that a high land tax declares the government a partial owner of the equity in the land. It means that if the government is taking 50 percent of the rental with land value tax, the other 50 percent is available to the speculator. Then if the tax is capitalized in valuation, in the long run at any rate, the speculator can do as much speculation, only he will have to find twice as much land to speculate in.

It is true, at least in some sort of macro-economic sense, that if only one-half of the variation in the value of the land is captured by private interest the impact on the economy may be less. This is because one-half of the speculative profit or loss accrued in effect goes to the government, which doesn't react quite as vigorously to gains or losses as does the private individual.

I think you can say that it doesn't curb speculation per se, but, in fact, there may be more land involved in the speculation, because the speculator's dollar will go further in the acquisition of land for speculation. To the extent that the amount of land available for speculation is limited, you may limit the macro-economic impact of speculation. However, this is pretty tenuous reasoning at best.

I don't think you can claim credit for the land value taxes as something that will reduce the harmful effects of speculation. It may increase them

31

in terms of the amount of land involved. It may decrease them in terms
of the macro-economic effect on land, but in the long run I think it is up
for grabs.

Matthew Edel: What if the rate is close to 100 percent?

Vickrey: If there is any margin left at all for the individual proprietor
as an incentive for his management of the land, speculation based on this
margin is possible.

Arlo Woolery: I might speak to what Bill was saying. I know the land
value increment tax in England was 80 percent, and the tax rate on land
values alone could be as high as 7.5 percent annually based on the increase in value established by the government. There the land value increment tax generated more revenues than the property tax. So the fact that
you have the kind of increases in value that produce the 8 percent
marginal rate would indicate to me that the tax was completely ineffec-
tive at holding the price down.

Hartojo Wignjowijoto: I wish to make a comment related to land
speculation and price expectation. Price expectation causing inflation
varies from region to region and state to state. What I am saying is that if
people are used to living with a double digit inflation rate, they will adjust their entrance to the land market accordingly. I think we should look
not so much at speculation, but at price expectation behavior of people.

Weld S. Carter: I had hoped that somebody else would tackle this
assignment. Since nobody has, I would like to question Bill Vickrey's
statement about speculation in land and his position that increased taxes
on land have no effect on speculation.

Take the case of the farmers in Iowa. There was an article in a recent
Forbes magazine about this. The farmers in Iowa, the young farmers
who have been speculating in land, have bought land at exorbitant
prices. Now the price of wheat and corn and things of that sort have
dropped and those guys are in trouble. They are in trouble at the banks if
they can't pay their interest or allotted sums on their mortgages; their
loans are going to have to be called and there are going to be tax sales.
Now those young men have been speculating in farmland.

Assume that their tax rate on land gets doubled. What is that going to
do to the market in land? What is that going to do to the mortages they
hold? What is that going to do to the banks that have invested in these
mortgages? I just don't think we have thought this thing through at all. I
would like to re-open this for further discussion.

Vickrey: What I was talking about is the long-term comparison of the
situation, let us say, a 6 percent tax on land where there has been a 2 percent tax on land as long as people remember. In this case I think we can

really say that if the tax is properly assessed, what you have done is simply increased the government equity in the land and decreased the equity of the owner.

If the tax is also capitalized, what this means to a person with $1000 to invest is that he can speculate just as much, only he buys more land with his $1000 than otherwise. He still undergoes more or less the same risks proportionately.

What I did not mention is what happens to the speculation that is now going on if we suddenly enact a change in the tax rate. Obviously, this is going to change things rather dramatically for some people. Again, there are two kinds of speculation. There is speculation in the natural economic forces and there is speculation in what the public officials do with respect to taxation. Obviously, if you have in the offing a possibility that there will be a shift to land value tax, there will be a lot of speculation on the effect of this action; there will be possibly more speculation rather than less.

Carter: You mean more farmers will be buying land on mortage?

Vickrey: No, I mean most of the more active people will be those who think they know what is going to happen to land values in the future. If you are threatening to increase the land tax, you will have, at least in the naive case, a reduction in the value of vacant lots and an increase in the value of buildings, or perhaps not in market value, but in true rental value.

If you look a little bit in the long run, it is not quite as clear what happens. After the tax has been removed from improvements and put on land, a speculator may not pick up the lot at lower value; he might be willing to pay more for it because he can put up his building on the assumption that there were going to be taxes on improvements, so he has not built as high as the speculator might have. So the gainers and losers may be quite different from the naive situation. You may get speculation in the sense that the person sees his taxes going up on the vacant lot but does not have the imagination to realize that a bigger building can now be put on it. So he sells the lot to the man who has the imagination to put up the bigger building. This is the kind of transaction that may take place.

Dick Netzer: Two things. First, I would like to join the colloquy between Roy Bahl and Matthew Edel on the question of site value taxation in developing countries. It seems to me there is a fairly simple explanation of why, in most developing countries I know anything about, some housing in the large cities is very luxurious and a tax on housing would be very progressive. The city, however, has other aims besides the taxation of housing. For example, it wants to encourage industrial investment. I think that is really a key thing. Again and again I have been involved in discussions of taxation of housing as a luxury tax, in Bogota and other places, but you have other things besides housing taxation to consider in favoring structures.

Second, I think many of us in North America tend to be perplexed by discussion of things such as a development land tax. This relates to the fundamental difference of land use controls here and in a good many other countries. In the United States, the control system says you can do anything you want with your land except what is specified as illegal. However, in Britain, as in Western Europe, the control system says you can only do those things that are explicitly permitted. In practice, this means that land on the urban fringe in the United States that is not in residential use can be readily converted to residential use. There may be some argument about density for residential development, but I think it is extremely rare to find outright prohibition.

Land tax is a strange animal. The only way it could make a change in value for us would be through a change in density with which land would be developed. Because of this, the reduction of the land-withholding effect of the land tax would be smaller in Europe than in Canada or the United States. It would be just a less important thing.

Vickrey: Actually, in many cases, you can do anything except build for residential use.

Netzer: But you don't say you can't build on it, period.

Vickrey: But you really can't build a residence on it because, for instance, you can't buy up the cemetery land.

Arthur P. Becker: Is this why there seems to be little private ownership of vacant land in Holland?

William Deyll: Yes.

Becker: Is it because the person who owns it can't use it for what he wants without being penalized?

Deyll: Well, we have plans determining how they can build. Homes or apartment complexes have to be built according to those plans. The ones who want to build have to build according to these plans. If you want to do something different, you have to go back to the agency who set up the plans.

In the past we have had a lot of speculation on vacant land, for example, just after the First World War. Municipalities and the national government tried to get away from that because there was an urgent need for home building. The municipalities tried to buy the land or acquire the ownership by loans.

Daniel M. Holland: Let me say something about developing countries (LDCs). Some of them at least have expressed the view that the simplicity of site value taxation makes it a desirable tax. They wanted to tax property but they lacked the resources. It was easier for them to get at land values and begin a meaningful attack on the problem that way.

Mason F. Gaffney: The reason so many recommendations are made along the site value taxation line by foreign visitors to LDC's is because there is so much land underutilized in these countries in comparison to the situation at home.

Richard W. Lindholm: The monopoly power provided by land ownership can be reduced by site value taxation while encouraging full development and avoiding government ownership and/or complete control over land use. These are rather important reasons why those interested in democratic development of LDC's recommend use of site value taxation.

II. LAND TAXATION
REVENUE POTENTIAL

Introduction

Shawna P. Grosskopf and Marvin B. Johnson have examined land value taxation and its relation to real estate values. The theories examined vary widely in their conclusions. They range from confiscation of land values to an increase in prices offered.

The impact of a land tax on land values is important because the authors want to learn if a land tax could be sufficiently productive to meet all local government costs. They conclude that cities can move with confidence toward use of only site (land) value taxation to finance local government.

Mary Teachout examines the assessment procedures and legal definition requirements for identification of only the unimproved value of land. The paper also examines in some detail relief procedures appropriate when land value only makes up the property tax base. Teachout generally concludes that nearly all of the valuation and hardship situations could be relieved and explained through administrative procedures plus a wide distribution of easily understood and accurate neighborhood land value maps.

Richard W. Lindholm and Roger G. Sturtevant have prepared an analysis of the changes that would occur in tax rates and land use decisions if a property tax using only land as its base were introduced into a medium-sized urban area. The urban area examined is that of

Eugene–Springfield in Western Oregon. The findings of the research are applied to a model developed by Grieson in his "The Economics of Property Taxes and Land Values: The Elasticity of Supply of Structures" (1974).

The data applied to the Grieson model conclude that substantial additional space for single family housing would become available if land tax replaced the existing property tax. Land value taxation is demonstrated to be an efficient growth control mechanism that can be helpful to planners in their efforts to develop a compact residential environment.

Ronald B. Welch emphasizes the point that the longer the introduction of land value taxation is delayed the greater the administrative difficulties. The problems of setting value on land in transition from being rural to urban are seen to be particularly difficult. In addition, serious difficulties are expected because owners of property have only a vague notion of the value of the land portion of a unit of property.

3 *Shawna P. Grosskopf and Marvin B. Johnson*

Land Value Tax Revenue Potentials: Methodology and Measurement

Economists have long recognized the advantages inherent to land value taxation. In *Progress and Poverty,* Henry George was able to invoke the endorsements of Ricardo, John Stuart Mill, and other "economists of standing" (1879, rpt. 1975, pp. 422–24). Economists of all postures have continued to be attracted by the efficiency and, to a lesser extent, the equity advantages of a land value tax over the more common real estate tax on land and building. However, some have doubted that a tax on land (or site) values alone would generate sufficient revenue. For example, in Hicks's view, the Georgian claim that a "land tax would be sufficient to finance all the services of the state . . . would certainly not be true anywhere today, in view of the much wider range of duties governments are now expected to undertake" (1961, p. 357). This opinion has led to the conclusion that the "site value tax must be rejected as an outright substitute for the traditional American tax" (Heilbrun 1969, p. 78). Our task is to address this question of revenue potential: Would substitution of a land value tax for the current property tax provide sufficient revenue to support local government?

The yield of a land value tax can be analyzed in three cases of increasing complexity and realism: (1) the partial equilibrium case, (2) the general equilibrium case, and (3) the dynamic case. In the partial equilibrium case, either land prices or ground rents (gross of any land taxes) are assumed to be unaffected by a switch to land value taxation. Possible adjustments in land prices caused by untaxing buildings can be analyzed in a general equilibrium framework. In both the partial and general equilibrium frameworks, the research question is simple: Can a land value tax generate the revenue presently required by local governments? In the dynamic case, the assumption that local government revenue requirements are fixed is relaxed and a new research question emerges: Can revenues collected solely from land keep pace with future increases in local government spending?

The purpose of this paper is to marshall and synthesize existing work on the revenue potential question, not to generate new or authoritative empirical answers. Relevant research is reviewed and synthesized using the taxonomy developed above. Emphasis is on existing measures of the revenue potential of land value taxes and, perhaps more important, the methodologies on which these measurements are based. Throughout the paper, a land or site value tax is defined as a tax on the capital value of land, i.e., as a tax on the value of the land including any value added by favorable location and by improvements attributable to public sector activities (such as the provision of roads and sewers, or water and electric services), but excluding structures. Finally, the paper focuses on urban governments in the United States.

The Partial Equilibrium Case

The most naive partial equilibrium approach simply dismisses the revenue potential question, yet provides the clearest introduction (and perhaps the best answer!) to that question. This optimistic argument can be summarized in a single sentence: A change in the local tax base changes the equal yield tax rate and changes the distribution of the tax burden among taxpayers, but it does *not* change the revenue-raising potential of local governments. After all, if a community has the capacity to raise the required tax revenue under the existing system of real estate taxation, it would retain that potential under a site value system. Changing the tax "handle" from land and buildings to land alone certainly would tend to redistribute the tax burden from building owners to land owners, but that phenomenon raises equity and efficiency — not revenue potential — questions. Of course, the exclusion of buildings reduces the size of the tax base and thus forces the nominal tax rate to rise. Therefore the only relevant research question concerning the revenue potential of a site value tax is simple: By how much must the tax rate increase if buildings are untaxed and local government revenues held constant?

With the help of one simple, controversial, and crucial assumption, the solution to that research question is easy to derive algebraically. Tax revenues under the two schemes can be indicated by

$$R = t_0 (L_0 + B_0)$$

and $$R = t_s (L_s),$$

where

R = required tax revenue (a constant in static analyses),
t_0 = required tax rate if both land and buildings are taxed,
t_s = necessary tax rate if only land (site) values are taxed,
L_0 = total land (market) values if both land and buildings are taxed,
L_s = total land (market) values if just land (site) values are taxed,
B_0 = total building values if both land and buildings are taxed.

The key assumption is that the change to site value taxation does not change the *market value* of land parcels in the aggregate: $L_0 = L_s$. In that case, the required equal yield site value tax rate can be shown to depend on the original tax rate and the proportion of the original total valuation in land *(P)*: i.e.,

$$t_s L_s = t_0 (L_0 + B_0)$$

and, since $L_s = L_0$ by assumption,

$$t_s = t_0 \frac{L_0 + B_0}{L_0}$$

or, letting $P = \dfrac{L_0}{L_0 + B_0}$,

$$t_s = t_0 / P.$$

The new and higher tax rate (t_s), when applied to all site values in the jurisdiction, provides the same tax revenue as before. The naive approach reveals no interesting questions or doubts about the revenue potential of a site value tax.

Adequacy of Land Values

Yet such doubts certainly exist. The cornerstone of these doubts is the fear that a site value tax would effectively "confiscate" private lands. Revenue potential pessimists point out that it is possible that local government revenue requirements approach, or even exceed, land rents. If site value taxes exceed gross land rents, net-of-tax land rents will be negative and economically rational private parties will no longer own land. According to the pessimists' argument, a site value tax can generate adequate revenue only if gross land rents exceed required tax revenues; if revenue requirements exceed gross rents, the state could confiscate all land and still not support the existing level of public services with the rent proceeds on the confiscated land.

Do local government revenue requirements exceed land rents? From the pessimists' perspective, this appears to be the crucial question for assessing the revenue potential of a site value tax and the relevant partial equilibrium empirical work has centered on this question. The conflicting evidence is reviewed here, although the true controversy between the optimists and the pessimists is shown to lead directly to general equilibrium analysis.

The most prominent proponent of the proposition that the required local government tax revenues exceed land rents is probably Heilbrun (1966, pp. 150–55). Heilbrun's pessimistic conclusion is based on an ingenious "sufficiency condition" for assuring that a switch to a site value tax will not result in the confiscation of land, and on a set of extraneous estimates for key parameters.

First, consider Heilbrun's sufficiency condition. If

N_0 = rent on land gross of real estate taxes on land,
L_0 = capital value of land after capitalization of the land component of the real estate tax, or the (properly) assessed value of land under the original real estate tax,
B_0 = capital value of buildings after capitalization or shifting of the building component of the original real estate tax or the (properly) asessed value of buildings under the original real estate tax,
i = rate of interest for capitalization of rent on land,

and R and t_0 are as before, then site value taxation is not confiscatory if $N_0 > R$. Heilbrun's argument runs as follows:

$$N_0 = L_0 (i + t_0)$$

and $$R = t_0 (L_0 + B_0).$$

Thus, $N_0 > R$ can be rewritten as

$$L_0 (i + t_0) > t_0 (L_0 + B_0)$$

which reduces to

$$iL_0 > t_0 B_0.$$

The above version of Heilbrun's sufficiency condition makes some intuitive sense: If the tax revenue foregone by untaxing buildings ($t_0 B_0$) can be made up out of existing land rents net of real estate taxes, then the required revenue certainly can be raised. Rearranging the terms yields a less intuitively pleasing, but more practical and common form of Heilbrun's sufficiency condition:[1]

$$i/t > B_0/L_0.$$

Determining the value of land (L_0), even assuming that land prices would be unchanged by a switch to site value taxation, is a monumental task well beyond the scope of this paper. Instead, we summarize estimates made by Goldsmith (1962, pp. 86–87; 1956), Manvel (1968, pp. 1–14), Kurnow (1960, pp. 341–48; 1961, pp. 155–68), and Gaffney (1970, pp. 157–212). Those estimates, along with the data and methodology on which they are based, are summarized in table 3.1. Goldsmith's pioneering efforts were based on United States Census data. His national wealth approach was followed by both Kurnow and Manvel, although the latter both had access to the then newly created *Census of Government* data. Manvel's estimates differ from Kurnow's in the adjustments for some of the biases in the *Census of Government* data. Gaffney estimated total U.S. land values by extrapolating from estimates he made for the city of Milwaukee in 1965 using a cadastral survey.

These estimates of land values have not been immune to criticism. Gaffney, certainly the most forceful proponent of the adequacy of land as a base for property taxation, offers the most critical survey of existing estimates (1970, pp. 167–82). He contends that Goldsmith underestimated land value because of his reliance on FHA loan data, which has three weaknesses: (1) it omits vacant lots and unsubdivided land, (2) it is restricted to lower middle class housing, which has a relatively low land/total valuation ratio, and (3) it neglects invisible assets such as minerals. Gaffney criticizes Kurnow for assuming that building values increase in step with construction costs (which are actually partially attributable to technological change) and thereby overestimating the value of buildings. Gaffney finds Manvel's estimates to be the least biased, although he faults them for not capturing the increase in farm and mineral values; he also suggests that a larger part of Manvel's estimates of the increase in real estate value should be attributed to an increase in the value of land. Gaffney argues that a reliable estimate of urban land value would involve a complete cadastral survey of all urban land; his results indicate that such a methodology, if applied to all land, would result in much higher land values than those estimated by Goldsmith, Kurnow, and Manvel.

---

1. Heilbrun 1966, p. 151. Heilbrun's derivation is repeated in full in the text so that the role of a crucial implicit assumption can be explored later.

Table 3.1 Estimates of U.S. land value

Author	Data	Method	Year	Estimate ($)
R. W. Goldsmith	Census, FHA Loan Data	Used FHA loan data for share of land in real estate. Omits vacant and undeveloped land. Used book value for corporate held lands.	1956	$ 207 billion
E. Kurnow	1957 Census of Governments	Used Census of Governments data to derive marginal valuation and state land ratio estimates to determine land value. Excludes Alaska and Hawaii. Does not correct for assessment bias of sales assessment ratios. (Excludes public utilities.)	1922 1930 1938 1956	94.8 billion 111.6 billion 94.2 billion 243.7 billion
A. Manvel	Census of Governments	Based on assessed values, adjusted by non-mapping techniques for undervaluation.	1956 1966	282 billion 523 billion
M. Gaffney	Tax Commissioner of Milwaukee	Cadastral map contouring technique.	1965	2,386 million (Milwaukee) 640 billion (U.S.)

While these estimates of total land values are interesting, they are of little use here even if the methodological feuds are ignored. Each of these estimates is, after all, over ten years old. Fortunately, estimates of land value per se are not required to work though either the optimist's or the pessimist's analyses of revenue potential. The key parameter is the proportion of total valuation in land (P). Specifically, if values for the appropriate interest rate for the capitalization of the rent on land (i) and the rate of real estate tax on the assessed value of land and buildings (t) are known or assumed, then the Heilbrun condition for revenue adequacy requires the ratio B_0/L_0 for completeness, or its equivalent, $(1-P)/P$. The principal reason for including the above four estimates of land value is to provide estimates of the necessary land/buildings ratios.

What percent of total valuation does land comprise? A wide assortment of answers can be found. Goldsmith and Kurnow find P nationally to be about 25 percent; Heilbrun excludes rural land and buildings from Goldsmith's data and estimates that land makes up only about 18.5 percent of urban land (1966, p. 152). Manvel finds land to be about 40 percent of total valuation. Gaffney claims that "land value today is at least half of real estate and probably more" and, at least in Milwaukee in 1965, "60-70 percent" (1970, p. 181). The key ratio of present building values to land values ranges from 4.4 (Goldsmith/Heilbrun) down through 2.9 (Goldsmith/Kurnow) and 1.5 (Manvel) to about .5 (Gaffney).

The gist of Heilbrun's argument against the revenue adequacy of a site value tax can now be stated. Heilbrun used $i = 6$ percent and calculated the ratio of property tax revenues to full market value of property (t) to be 1.5 percent in 1956–57; thus the (i/t) ratio was (.06/.015) or 4. Although it is greater than the B_0/L_0 calculated by Goldsmith for the entire nation, this (i/t) ratio is smaller than the 4.4 "non-farm" ratio. Although recognizing that some communities could raise adequate revenues under a site value tax, Heilbrun concluded that "unless we are prepared virtually to end private ownership of rights in land by taking almost its whole rent, it is no longer feasible to substitute a land tax for the real estate tax at the present level of yield" (1966, p. 150).

One argument against Heilbrun's pessimistic conclusion is that a "wrong" (excessively low) B_0/L_0 ratio was used. Another possible weakness is the reliance on nationwide aggregate data. In a recent article, Douglas (1978, pp. 217–23) deals with both of these objections by (1) using Manvel's (lower) B_0/L_0 ratios and (2) working with 15 localities. He used 1971 *Census of Government* data to calculate land's share of total valuation in each of the 15 localities. Douglas also manipulated Heilbrun's sufficiency condition to show the proportion of existing land rents that would be collected by a site value tax that raised the same amount of revenue as the present property tax (H):

$$H = \frac{t_0(L_0 + B_0)}{L_0\,(i + t_0)} = \frac{\text{property taxes}}{\text{gross land rents}},$$

which, in terms of the buildings/land ratio, works out to be

$$H = \frac{t_0\,(B_0/L_0 + 1)}{(i + t_0)}.$$

Values of H in excess of one imply that existing land rents are smaller than the required tax levy, or that the site value tax would be "confiscatory."

Douglas used local values for t and values of i of 4 percent and 6 percent to generate the results for 15 cities. His results, reproduced in table 3.2, seem to support Heilbrun's pessimistic conclusions. For $i = 4\%$, only 6 of the 15 cities have land rents in excess of real estate taxes. For $i = 6\%$, 13 of the 15 cities pass the sufficiency condition, but "at least ¾ of land's rental value must be taxed away in order to raise the required revenue for most of the localities shown" (1978, p. 220).

Table 3.2. Property taxes as a percent of land rents; selected localities

Locality	t (percent)	B_0/L_0	H ($i = 4$ percent)	H ($i = 6$ percent)
Honolulu, Hawaii	.9	1.81	.52	.37
Cook Co., Ill.	2.5	2.30	1.27	.97
Baltimore Co., Md.	3.4	2.09	1.42	1.12
Detroit, Mich.	2.4	2.44	1.29	.98
Hennepin Co., Minn.	2.1	2.03	1.04	.79
Ramsey Co., Minn.	1.9	2.28	1.06	.79
St. Louis Co., Mo.	2.0	1.92	.97	.73
New York City, N.Y.	1.9	2.28	1.06	.79
Cuyahoga Co., Ohio	2.0	2.15	1.05	.79
Franklin Co., Ohio	1.4	1.70	.70	.51
Oklahoma Co., Okla.	1.3	2.14	.77	.56
Philadelphia, Pa.	2.0	2.18	1.06	.80
Shelby Co., Tenn.	1.7	1.67	.80	.59
Harris Co., Tex.	1.5	2.00	.82	.60
Milwaukee, Wis.	4.1	2.38	1.71	1.37

Source: Douglas 1978, p. 218.

Douglas' results appear to be the best available estimates of the ratio of revenue requirements to land rent. However, even if Heilbrun's partial equilibrium framework is accepted, Douglas' results do not prove that a site value tax would fail to generate adequate revenue. A possible weakness is the reliance on Manvel's estimates of land's share of total valuation. As shown in table 3.3, the H ratio is extremely sensitive to the P and L parameters. If the buildings/land ratios of Gaffney are closest to the truth, then land rents exceed revenue requirements even if the average real estate tax rate is assumed to be 2 (or even 2.5) rather than the 1.5 used by Heilbrun.[2] If i is taken to be 6 or 8, "confiscation" occurs only if

2. A 2 percent real estate tax rate probably is a more reasonable approximation today. The average effective property tax rate for existing homes with FHA insured mortgages in the United States was 1.89 percent in 1975. Several states have average rates of 2.5 or more.
Source: Advisory Commission on Intergovernmental Relations, *Significant Features of*

Table 3.3. Percent of land rents required for local government revenues (*H*) for selected tax rates, interest rates and building/land ratios

Interest Rates (*i*)	Rates (*t*)	Buildings/Land Ratios (B_0/L_0)			
		4.4	2.9	1.5	.5
	1.5	1.47	1.06	.68	.41
i = 4 percent	2.0	1.80	1.30	.83	.50
	2.5	2.08	1.50	.96	.58
	1.5	1.08	.78	.50	.30
i = 6 percent	2.0	1.35	.98	.63	.38
	2.5	1.59	1.15	.74	.44
	1.5	.85	.62	.39	.24
i = 8 percent	2.0	1.08	.78	.50	.30
	2.5	1.29	.93	.60	.36

$$H = \frac{t(B_0/L_0 + 1)}{(i + t)}$$

$$\text{Land Share } P = \frac{1}{(B_0/L_0) + 1}$$

Thus,

P	B_0/L_0	
.19	4.4	Heilbrun/Goldsmith
.26	2.9	Goldsmith/Kurnow
.40	1.5	Manvel/Neuner, et al.
.66	.5	Gaffney

the most pessimistic estimates of the buildings/land ratio are used.

In sum, present local government revenue requirements are greater than existing land rents if land is a small share of total valuation, the rate of return on land is low, and/or property tax rates are high. Conversely, land rents exceed local government revenues if land's share of value is high, interest is high, or property tax rates are low. For reasonable combinations of *t, i,* and B_0/L_0, required revenues are a sizable hunk — but certainly not all — of existing land rents.

A Synthesis

But perhaps Heilbrun, Douglas, and the other pessimists are asking the wrong question. The tax base under a site value tax is *not* the value of

---

Fiscal Federalism 1976-77, vol. 2, *Revenue and Debt* (Washington D.C.: The commission, 1977), p. 107.

land under the present system of real estate taxation (L_0); the new tax base is land values under a site value tax scheme (L_s). The "naive" or optimistic approach asserts that land values would not change as a result of the tax switch. The pessimistic methodology makes the perhaps equally naive assertion that gross ground rents (G_0) will not change as a result of a major change in property taxation. Yet untaxing improvements will reduce the cost of building and maintaining structures, change the relative price of land and improvements, and presumably increase the demand for sites. Market forces should cause at least part of this increased demand to be translated into higher ground rents gross of taxes.[3] A cornerstone of Gaffney's definitive defense of the revenue potential of a site value tax is the assertion that *all* of the reduction in building taxes shows up in increased ground rents: "If the tax cost of buildings falls, land rent rises by the same amount, just as earnings on common stock would rise by the amount of any fall in interest on bonds" (1970, p. 188).

The dispute over ground rents under a site value tax scheme is the crux of the revenue potential controversy. The problem can be described most precisely with a minor modification to the model used by Heilbrun/ Douglas and Gaffney. As before, the original land value (L_0) is equal to the gross rent (G_0) discounted by the rate of return on land (i) and the real estate property tax rate (t_0):

$$L_0 = \frac{G_0}{i + t_0}.$$

But, in the more general case, gross ground rents under site value taxation (G_s) are equal to the original rents plus that fraction (α) of the building tax savings ($t_0 B_0$) that shows up as increased rents:

$$G_s = G_0 = \alpha(t_0 B_0).$$

Total land value under site value taxation (L_s) is simply ground rents discounted by i plus the site value tax rate (t_s):

$$L_s = \frac{G_s}{i + t_s} = \frac{G_0 + \alpha(t_0 B_0)}{i + t_s}.$$

---

3. Heilbrun recognizes the "important qualification" described here, but dismisses it by claiming that "it would, however, be imprudent . . . for any local government to bank on such an effect" (Heilbrun, 1966, p. 154). Douglas also mentions this possibility in passing (1978, p. 219).

Algebraic manipulation[4], along with the equal yield restriction $t_s L_s = t_0(L_0 + B_0)$, allows us to express L_s in terms of L_0, B_0, t_0, and α:

$$L_s = L_0 - \frac{(1 - \alpha)t_0 B_0}{i}.$$

Verbally, land values under site value taxation are equal to the original land values reduced by the discounted value of those real estate taxes on buildings which are not borne by landowners via reduced rents.[5]

Impact of Land Taxes on Land Values

Suddenly the naive model appears quite sensible. If Gaffney is right and $\alpha = 1$, then land values are unchanged by a switch to site value taxation. If tax savings *all* go into higher ground rents, then the revenue potential of a site value tax is equivalent to the revenue potential of a real estate tax. The new tax rate must be from 3.0 to 5.4 times the old tax rate (using $t_s = t_0/P$ and assuming P is between 19 and 66 percent), the tax burden is reshuffled among parcels (Harberger 1962), but private parties still own land — and still earn a return of i percent on their investment.

4. We start with two identities:

$$G_0 = (i + t_0)L_0,$$

$$G_s = (i + t_s)L_s - \alpha t_0 B_0.$$

Eliminating G_0,

$$(i + t_0)L_0 = (i + t_s)L_s - \alpha t_0 B_0,$$

and rearranging yields

$$i(L_0 - L_s) = t_s L_s - t_0 L_0 - \alpha t_0 B_0.$$

Since, for equal yield, $t_s = t_0(L_0 - B_0)$,

$$i(L_0 - L_s) = (1 - \alpha)t_0 B_0.$$

Thus

$$L_s = L_0 - \frac{(1 - \alpha)t_0 B_0}{i}.$$

5. All empirical work on the redistribution of tax burden among classes of property or individuals as a result of a switch to site value taxation implicitly assumes the naive or optimistic model. Examples of this work include Neuner, et al. (1974), Smith (1970), and Schaaf (1969).

Heilbrun, Douglas, and others who profess the site value tax to be confiscatory tell a different tale. They implicitly take $\alpha = 0$, so a site value tax causes net-of-tax rents to fall, property values to plummet, and new tax rates that need to be very high. In the extreme case, where present land rents are exceeded by revenues from the real estate tax, an infinite site value rate would not raise enough money because no one would own land.

So what is α? Gaffney says 1: all tax savings show up in increased rents, so land market values are unchanged. Heilbrun and Douglas say 0: all taxes on buildings now must be paid through unchanging ground rents, so land values plummet. An analysis of the question takes us into the realm of general equilibrium.

The General Equilibrium Case

The optimistic and pessimistic conclusions concerning the revenue potential of a site value tax were both based on restrictive assumptions: land values would not change or gross ground rents would not change. Both approaches involve partial equilibrium analysis of the revenue potential of a site value tax in the very short run. Alternatively, both approaches involve (extreme) assumptions about the long-run incidence of untaxing buildings. To analyze these long-run effects, and to gain further insight into the optimist/pessimist controversy, both restrictive assumptions must be relaxed thereby moving the analysis from a partial to a general equilibrium framework.

Begin by assuming that the economy is in equilibrium under the current property tax structure. Changing from a land-and-buildings tax base to a land base would be an exogenous disturbance to which the market for land, labor, buildings, and other capital will eventually adjust. After that adjustment, a new equilibrium—one with different equilibrium prices and quantities—will result. Classic comparative statistics should indicate if land prices and quantities will change, and in what direction. The relevance of such comparative statistics to the revenue potential question is obvious: we can determine whether the site value tax base (i.e., land prices) will fall (the pessimistic conclusion), remain constant (the optimistic partial equilibrium conclusion) or even rise. Much of the recent theoretical work in public finance has been dedicated to similar general equilibrium analyses of taxes (and expenditures), which indicate the final incidence of taxes and expenditures rather than their initial impact (McLure 1972, pp. 56–82). Such general equilibrium models have been used extensively to analyze the corporate income tax and also have contributed to what is dubbed "the new view" of the incidence of the property tax.

The Harberger model is an example of a simplified general equilibrium model that has been used extensively to analyze incidence. This approach is limited, however, by several of the model's assumptions. For example, it assumes that changes are all infinitely small and incidence is measured against a tax situation with no pre-existing distortions. Thus, this framework is not very helpful in analyzing a discrete change from a pre-existing non-neutral tax structure.

However, some insight into the general equilibrium effects of untaxing buildings can be gained by modifying the Harberger analysis (Schroeder and Sjoquist 1975, pp. 17–29). The general idea is to compare two equal yield tax systems, one in which land and capital are taxed, and one in which land alone is taxed. Our goal is to compare the change in land prices in the building and land property tax case to the change in land prices in the land tax case, holding revenue constant. Thus, we assume that "sufficient" revenue can be raised under a land tax in order to determine the effect of that tax on land and capital prices.

We can derive the general equilibrium effects on the price of land of untaxing buildings by using a simplified version of the Harberger model. In this model we assume that there are two goods; x and y, which are in turn produced via homogeneous production functions with two factors, land (L) and capital (K). Land is assumed to be fixed ($dL = 0$) and capital is mobile, but fixed in the aggregate ($dK_x = -dK_y$). Goods x and y are produced under perfectly competitive conditions.

The demand for x and y is specified as:

(1) $dx/x = -E_x \cdot (dP_x/P_x) + E_{xy} \cdot (dP_y/P_y),$

(2) $dy/y = -E_y \cdot (dP_y/P_y) + E_{xy} \cdot (dP_x/P_x),$

where the E refers to the respective own and cross price elasticities of demand. To further simplify the model, we make the following assumptions:

$$dP_K = 0 \quad \text{(therefore } K \text{ is numeraire)},$$
$$E_x, E_y = 1,$$
$$E_{xy} = 0,$$

and $P_x, P_y, P_K, P_L = 1.$

The production of x and y can be specified as:

(3) $dx/x = f_K \cdot \dfrac{dK_x}{K_x} + f_L \cdot \dfrac{dL_x}{L_x},$

(4) $dy/y = g_K \cdot \dfrac{dK_y}{K_y} + g_L \cdot \dfrac{dL_y}{L_y},$

where f and g represent output elasticities (which are assumed to sum to unity).

Substitution of factors in the production of x and y can be written as:

(5) $\dfrac{dK_x}{K_x} - \dfrac{dL_x}{L_x} = -s_x \cdot (dT_K - dP_L - dT_L),$

(6) $\dfrac{dK_y}{K_y} - \dfrac{dL_y}{L_y} = -s_y \cdot (dT_K - dP_L - dT_L),$

where s_x and s_y represent elasticities of substitution (assumed here to be unitary). Included in equations (5) and (6) is our representation of the current property tax. We assume that it is a uniform tax on immobile land and mobile capital in both sectors.

The pure land tax is represented by:

(5a) $\dfrac{dK'_x}{K_x} - \dfrac{dL'_x}{L_x} = -s_x \cdot (-dP'_L - dT'_L),$

(6a) $\dfrac{dK'_y}{K_y} - \dfrac{dL'_y}{L_y} = -s_y \cdot (-dP'_L - dT'_L).$

We also are imposing an equal yield condition:

(7) $T'_L P'_L L = T_L P_L L + T_K P_K K,$

which when totally differentiated and accounting for the assumptions made above, becomes

(8) $dT'_L \cdot L = dT_L \cdot L + dT_K \cdot K.$

The relationship between factor and product prices, assuming perfect competition, becomes

(9) $dP_x = f_L \cdot (dP_L + dT_L) + f_K \cdot (dP_K + dT_K),$

(10) $dP_y = g_L \cdot (dP_L + dT_L) + g_K \cdot (dP_K + dT_K),$

with the land tax version:

(9a) $dP'_x = f_L \cdot (dP'_L + dT'_L) + f_K \cdot (dP'_K),$

(10a) $dP'_y = g_L \cdot (dP'_L + dT'_L) + g_K \cdot (dP'_K).$

The simultaneous solution of equations 1–10 results in the following:

(11) $dP_L = [-E_x dT_L(f_K + f_L)]/[E_x f_L + s_x f_K],$

(12) $dP_x = f_K \cdot dT_K + f_L \cdot (dP_L + dT_L),$

(13) $dP_y = g_K \cdot dT_K + g_L \cdot (dP_L + dT_L),$

and for the equal yield land tax:

(11a) $dP_L' = -dT_L'(f_x + f_L),$

(12a) $dP_L' = 0,$

(13a) $dP_y' = 0.$

It remains to be seen whether $dP_L' \gtreqless dP_L$, i.e., whether a site value tax results in lower, equal, or higher land prices than an equal yield real estate tax in equilibrium. Simplifying equation (11) by accounting for our assumptions, we have:

(14) $dP_L = -dT_L,$

which we must then compare to $dP_L' = -dT_L'$. Given $dT_L > 0$, it is clear that both systems result in an absolute decrease in land prices. Recalling the equal yield condition and substituting $dP_L' = -dT_L$, we have:

(15) $-dP_L' \cdot L = dT_L \cdot L + dT_K \cdot K,$

which can be rewritten as:

(16) $dP_L' = -dT\left(\dfrac{L + K}{L}\right).$

Thus, whether $dP_L' \gtreqless dP_L$, it can be equivalently stated as:

(17) $-dT\left(\dfrac{L + K}{L}\right) \gtreqless -dT.$

Thus, if $\left(\dfrac{L + K}{L}\right)$ exceeds 1, then $|dP_L'| < |dP_L|$ and the fall in land prices

under a site value tax will be less than under a uniform land and building tax. This in turn implies that a switch from a property tax to an equal yield land tax will result in a *rise* in land prices.

Therefore, using an admittedly naive and restrictive general equilibrium model, one can analyze the long-run impact on land prices of substituting a uniform land tax for a uniform land and building tax. This does not, admittedly, predict whether the revenues from this land tax are sufficient. Rather, this result merely indicates that the adjustment to the tax changeover could result in a broader equilibrium tax base than predicted by the pessimistic partial equilibrium approach. In terms of the previous section, $\alpha > 0$ and perhaps $\alpha > 1$ (Shoven and Whalley 1977, pp. 211–24).

Several caveats are paramount at this point. We have not allowed for the dynamic, but rather only for the comparative static, impact of a land tax on land prices and thus the tax base. We have ignored the potential impact of increased land development on the urban fringe. Also, and perhaps for our purposes more important, we have ignored the fact that the current tax on land and buildings is *not* a uniform tax. It is well known that there are pronounced variations in effective tax rates both by class of property and by locality. As has been convincingly argued by Mieszkowski (1972) and Aaron (1975), these differentials will result in excise effects. The direction of the revenue effect of these excise effects on the equilibrium price of land and buildings is difficult to determine *a priori*. The usual assumption is that relatively high tax areas will have capital outflows, with the relatively immobile factors and local goods bearing the burden.

Thus, if rural areas had lower taxes under a tax on land and capital, they would ultimately have higher land prices and locally traded goods prices, since these are the relatively immobile factors in the system. Under a site value tax, however, the taxed factor would be relatively immobile and the important excise effects would be from *untaxing* buildings. Therefore, cities that had relatively *higher* taxes would realize an increase in land prices, with low tax cities realizing lower land price increases. Perhaps more important excise effects would be due to differences in urban/rural taxes on improvements. In this case, cities stand to realize relatively larger land price increases due to the excise effect of untaxing buildings.

There are other reasons for assuming that a change from the current system to a land tax system of property tax will not have the simple effect of reducing the price of land. As Feldstein (1977) has demonstrated, there are income and portfolio balance effects which could conceivably result in land price increases under a land tax.

In addition, the results of relying on the "new view" in determining general equilibrium effects on prices must be considered with due consideration of the assumptions involved. One implicit assumption with far-reaching implications is that of the independence of the savings rate and the rate of return. If consumers reduce their savings rate in response to lowered rates of returns, then equilibrium capital levels will be lower and the price of land will be lower. Also, the assumption that aggregate capital in the U.S. is fixed is probably incorrect. International capital flows must be considered. However, a shift away from improvement taxation could attract international capital, and have the ultimate effect of raising land prices. Thus, most of the potential biases are in favor of higher equilibrium land prices.

The ultimate answer to the general equilibrium issue is by nature empirical. Unfortunately, limited time and the problems inherent in accurately determining capital and land values do not allow us to derive an estimate of the impact of substituting a tax on land for an equal yield tax on land and buildings, although recent breakthroughs in estimating techniques and methodology now allow such estimation. Reliable data remain the critical bottleneck.

Computing General Equilibriums

Scarf (1973) is responsible for developing a method of computing general equilibrium solutions. His technique has been employed by several economists to analyze the general equilibrium effects of taxes. The property tax has been of particular interest, although to date no one (to our knowledge) has simulated a general equilibrium change from a mixed property tax base to a land property tax base. As extraneous evidence, we will summarize the results of attempts to analyze the current property tax system using the general equilibrium approach.

Arnott and MacKinnon (1977) analyze the effects of increasing the property tax rate uniformly in a closed system. Their model is innovative in that they do not assume that land is fixed, nor that the supply of buildings is perfectly elastic. Using a "vector-sandwich" estimating technique based on Scarf's algorithm, they compare a city with no property taxes to a city with a 25 percent property tax rate. They find that tenants bear a greater burden than landlords, but that the price of land does fall. Their analysis is limited, however, by the arbitrary values chosen for parameters of the utility and cost functions, and the fact that expenditures are ignored.

Courant (1977) has also used a general equilibrium approach to analyze the excise effects of heterogeneous local tax rates, relative to the effects of uniform tax rates. He restricts the analysis to a tax on capital and assumes that land and capital are fixed in the aggregate. Thus, he compares equal yield uniform and heterogeneous property tax rate systems. His general conclusion is that landlords' income falls under the uniform tax relative to the differential system. Again, public goods (expenditures) are excluded from the model. In contrast, Polinsky and Rubinfeld (1978) explicitly include local public services in their general equilibrium model to analyze the effects of an increase in the property tax. They find that if taxes are increased while service levels are held constant, land values will fall.

The most fruitful general equilibrium approach to estimating the effects of untaxing buildings and increasing land taxes would be to use the general method outlined by Shoven and Whalley (1977). They illustrate a method of estimating differential tax incidence, assuming equal yield tax alternatives. Unfortunately, this approach cannot capture the excise effects that would occur if buildings are untaxed and land is then taxed at a higher rate. To balance local budgets, which already are based on differential tax rates, equal yield land taxes would necessarily exhibit interurban differentials, although property class differences technically could be eliminated within jurisdictions. The shift from an excise type tax to a relatively uniform tax would, however, have its own excise effects as discussed by Courant (1977).

Expenditure Impacts

The revenue potential of a site value tax can be viewed in several time frames. Up to this point, we have considered the immediate effect and roughly determined that even using the most pessimistic approach and reasonable estimates of key parameters, land rents exceed revenue requirements. Thus, in a limited sense, revenue is sufficient in the short-run. After the changes in relative prices that the substitution in tax bases will cause, land values *could* rise. Thus, comparative statics suggest that the short-run value of land underestimates the base. Finally, we would like to know if land as a tax base can keep up with runaway local expenditures. That is, is the revenue elasticity of land as large as the elasticity of expenditures over time? Extremely little evidence is available on this critical issue. We will therefore summarize (1) trends in land prices and expenditures, (2) research on this issue, and (3) examples of the dynamics of the site value tax in practice.

Expenditure and Land Value Trends

There is no doubt that land prices, particularly urban and urban fringe land prices, have increased. There is also no doubt that local government expenditures have increased. As a rough indication of the relative rates of increase, some statistics are summarized in table 3.4. These figures should be viewed with great caution — as is well known, land value is probably undervalued (Gaffney 1970). In addition, these figures do not really capture the relationship between urban area expenditures and corresponding land prices, which are also considered *not* to be independent.[6] These figures merely give rough calculations of aggregate changes.

---

6. The literature on tax and expenditure capitalization is extensive. One example (which, by the way, finds *no* capitalization effects) is Wales and Wiens (1974). For a more recent example, which includes explicit measures of services (which are found to increase property values), see McDougall (1976).

Table 3.4. City government finances, 1960–1974

Year	Property Tax Revenue	Own Source Expenditure
1960	5,197	12,930
1965	6,537	17,146
1970	9,127	26,267
1971	10,041	29,364
1972	10,988	32,150
1973	11,879	34,323
1974	12,244	35,647

	Percent Change 1960–70	Average Per Year 1970–74
Total revenue	8.2	12.7
Property taxes	5.8	7.6
General expenditure	8.9	11.3

Source: U.S. Bureau of the Census, *City Government Finances*, annual.

These statistics indicate that city government expenditures from their own sources have increased over the 1960–74 period faster than property tax revenues. Total revenues, however, are roughly keeping pace, which indicates that city governments do not rely solely on the property tax to finance their operations. Thus, substitution of a land tax for the current property tax does not imply assumption of all local government financing. The increase in expenditures indicates, however, that to maintain roughly a one-third share of that total, property tax revenues *must* increase. We now turn to existing analysis of the ability of land tax revenues to maintain that pace.

Studies of Dynamic Land Tax Effects

A dynamic approach to analyzing the yield adequacy of a site value tax must take into consideration the dynamics of local urban expenditures relative to the tax base. The only analysis that explicitly analyzes the dynamic adequacy of land as a tax base is a study by Stone (1975). He uses a simple Ricardian model that includes expenditures and revenues. The dynamic element is brought into the model through the inclusion of population, which is assumed to be monotonically related to the labor supply.

Stone finds that, assuming a constant tax rate, zero income elasticity of expenditures, and unitary population elasticity of expenditures, revenues will be adequate only if capital increases at a given rate. This result is based on an extremely restrictive model. Land is assumed to be fixed, yet no allowance is made for the effect of a growing population on the real rent of fixed land; therefore, his results are likely to underestimate the change in the tax base. He excludes the land market in his model, which is important in developing a dynamic model of land tax adequacy.

One can modify the Stone model to include a land market. First, assume his basic four equation model:

$$E = A[N]^{\bullet}[y/n]^{\psi},$$

$$T = gR \qquad 0 \geq g \geq 1,$$

$$D = E - T,$$

$$Y = F[K,L,N],$$

where

E = expenditures,
N = population
Y = homogeneous consumption good,
D = deficit,
K = capital,
L = land,
R = real rent of land,
g = the tax rate.

Note that the public sector is basically independent of production and income if $\psi = 0$, which Stone assumes. Therefore, the public sector serves merely to reduce income. Stone also implicity assumes that $\partial R/\partial D = 0$, which is probably *not* true. Assuming perfect capitalization, one would expect $\partial R/\partial D < 0$. The land market can be represented simply as:

$$L_D = f(R,N,Y/N),$$

$$L_s = \overline{L_s},$$

$$L_D = \overline{L_s},$$

$$R = R(D,N,Y/N),$$

where L_D is the demand for land, and L_s is the supply of land, with the supply of land fixed at $\overline{L_s}$. Thus, we assume that the demand for land increases with population ($\partial L_D/\partial N > 0$) and is related inversely to land prices ($\partial L_D/\partial R < 0$). With supply fixed, the price of land R is demand determined. Land rent is assumed to be related to net government services as discussed above.

Assuming a balanced budget, $D = 0$, and $\Phi = \Psi = 1$, we have the following:

$$E = AY,$$
$$T = gR(N, Y/N),$$
$$Y = F[K, L, N],$$

substituting:

$$E = A[F[K, L, N]],$$
$$T = gR[N, Y/N].$$

Over time, growth in expenditures must equal growth in revenues to maintain the $D = 0$ condition. Differentiating the above functions with respect to time:

$$\frac{dE}{dt} = A \frac{dF}{dK} \frac{dK}{dt} + A \frac{dF}{dL} \frac{dL}{dt} + A \frac{dF}{dN} \frac{dN}{dt},$$

$$\frac{dT}{dt} = g \, dR/dN \, dN/dt + g \frac{dK}{d \, Y/N} \frac{d \, Y/N}{dt}.$$

Recall that land is fixed, therefore $dL/dt = 0$, and in equilibrium:

$$A \frac{dF}{dK} \frac{dK}{dt} + A \frac{dF}{dN} \frac{dN}{dt} = g \frac{dR}{dN} \frac{dN}{dt} + g \frac{dR}{d \, Y/N} \frac{d \, Y/N}{dt}.$$

Under the Stone formulation of expenditure growth assuming $\Psi = 0$, one would have:

$$A \, dN/dt = g \left(\frac{dR}{dN} \frac{dN}{dt} + \frac{dR}{d \, Y/N} \frac{d \, Y/N}{dt} \right).$$

If $A = 1$, and zero population growth is expected in urban areas (actually, current trends indicate negative population growth), then under the Stone expenditure model, a balanced budget is no problem. In fact, if capital grows, that is, if there is increasing Y/N, a surplus will result. If expenditures grow with income, the budget will be balanced if

$$\frac{dY}{dK} \frac{dK}{dt} = g \frac{dK}{d \, Y/N} \frac{d \, Y/N}{dt}.$$

Under the assumption that moderate capital accumulation occurs, that the demand for land is income elastic, population growth is zero, and that the marginal product of capital falls as it is added to fixed land and labor, revenue adequacy should be less difficult than in the original Stone formulation. His result is shown graphically in Figure 3.1.

As population increases (assuming K constant), rent (and potential revenue) increases, whereas per capita expenditures remain constant. Unfortunately, the model is unstable, in that population cannot meaningfully exceed N_2. By allowing capital to increase, the average and marginal products will shift out. Given Hicks's neutral progress and $\sigma = 1$, the relative shares of capital and labor should remain constant as population and capital increase. If per capita expenditures remain constant and land returns are demand determined (with population elasticity = 1), a dynamic balanced budget can easily be maintained. However, given identical population elasticities of revenues and expenditures (and a beginning balanced budget), nonzero income elasticities will determine the dynamic fiscal status. If the income elasticity of demand for land is less than one, a deficit will eventually result.

Note that this model is extremely oversimplified. There is a distinct bias in the results in that land revenues are expected to cover all expenditures, whereas our original contention is merely that land taxes should at least equal current property tax revenues. In a dynamic context, it is clear that intergovernmental revenues have grown as a percentage of total revenues. If that trend continues, land taxes would have to finance a smaller share of expenditures over time.

Examples of the Adequacy of Site Valuation Taxation in Practice

As our last piece of evidence concerning the yield adequacy of a site value tax, we appeal to practical examples of this type of taxation. There

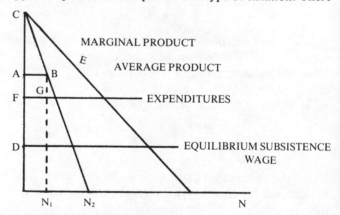

Figure 3.1. Dynamic Equilibrium in a Ricardian World

CAB = return to land (and maximum land tax revenue)
$ABDE$ = profits
$ODEN_1$ = wages
$OFGN_1$ = total expenditures

are many examples of countries that rely at least in part on land taxes. For the purpose at hand, we restrict the examples to those where urban areas rely on site value taxation (or taxation on unimproved land values) as their sole source of property tax. This does not presume that all local revenue is derived from the property tax. However, George Lent (1974) has conveniently summarized the developing countries that use an urban site value tax. His results are reproduced in table 3.5.

Table 3.5. Countries with site value taxation

Country	Description of Tax System
Barbados	The annual value system was replaced by a tax on site value by the Valuation Act, 1969; it was planned to be put into effect in 1972.
Republic of China	Tax on the unimproved value of land is based on self-assessment; a separate tax at higher rates is imposed on vacant and under-improved land. A highly graduated Land Value Increment Tax is also imposed on increases in value over a 10-year period, and at time of sale.
Greece	Municipalities with a population over 20,000 are authorized to levy an annual tax on the value of unimproved land within the town plan area. The tax is graduated with a person's total holdings.
Iraq	The urban land tax is based on the market value of unimproved land located within cities. In 1970 the rate was 5 percent. (There is also a real estate tax based on gross annual income derived from all real estate holdings.)
Jamaica	Jamaica converted to a site value tax by a law enacted January 18, 1957; the transition was interrupted in 1962, leaving a dual capital value and site value system in operation.
Kenya	All municipalities and most towns and county councils tax site values.
Tanzania	Urban council areas tax only unimproved values although they are authorized to tax improvement as well. Specified townships in district council areas levy house taxes, and Zanzibar employs a tax on net rental value.
Trinidad and Tobago	The Valuation of Land Act, 1969, provided for replacement of the annual value system by one based on modified site value; improvements are taxed only when they have a high ratio to land value. The new tax is expected to be implemented in 1974.

Source: G. E. Lent 1974, pp. 45–72.

It is reassuring that these are examples of site value taxation which are apparently viable. In most of these cases, however, other sources of revenue supplement the proceeds of the land tax. Also, as Woodruff and Ecker-Racz suggest in reference to Australia and New Zealand, "as a revenue producer, the land tax was never impressive" (1969). They attribute this problem to low rates and numerous exemptions. Exemptions were cited by the United Nations Secretariat (1975) as a major problem in maintaining revenue in developing countries. Holland also suggests that exemptions and low rates resulted in a land tax with low elasticity in Jamaica (1969).

It should also be stressed that the general equilibrium price changes discussed in the second section of this paper could be negligible if indeed the tax rates involved were low. Also, the efficiency effects usually cited in terms of encouraging land development could also be mitigated by low rates and exemptions. In Pittsburgh, a city that has a system in which land is taxed at twice the rate of buildings, R. L. Richman (1965) found little in the way of development effects, a condition which he attributed to differential tax rates and the assessment of land at its current rather than potential value.

The analysis here has ignored these issues in that the assumption was made that a site value tax would consist of a tax on the potential value of all land with no exemptions. This assumption, while extending the tax base, is probably not realistic. Implementation of site value taxes traditionally has included exemptions. Nevertheless, the existing evidence on site value taxation in practice indicates that this type of property tax is a viable source of revenue for urban areas.

Conclusion

The dynamic analysis of the revenue adequacy of site value taxation is positive on the whole. Trends in city expenditures cast some doubt on the ability of a site value tax to act as sole revenue source, but that is not the question at hand. As a substitute for the revenue provided by the existing property tax, there is a greater likelihood that revenues would be adequate. Theoretical evidence indicates that, given relatively fixed land (as is characteristic of older cities "locked in" by suburbs), land prices should increase at least as fast as expenditures. This does not take into consideration the possibility of rising expenditures due to deterioration of the "environment" in cities, i.e., the fact that needs may increase over time. However, a more rigorous analysis of the dynamic relationship of revenues and expenditures awaits a definitive statement of the way in which expenditures grow in cities. The last piece of evidence available on the long-run revenue capacity of site value taxation is empirical. Site value taxation has weathered the test of time in countries all over the world.

In the short run, site value taxation can indeed generate revenue equal to that of the current property tax in urban areas. In the longer run, however, untaxing buildings will cause a change in relative prices, which will in turn change the value of the tax base. Thus, by relaxing the partial equilibrium assumption that prices remain constant, *we show that land prices could well increase after adjustment to change.* Thus, our general equilibrium result is that the tax base could increase as a result of untaxing buildings and taxing land at a uniform rate. The dynamic issue of whether revenues from site value tax can keep pace with urban expenditures is difficult. Given a number of assumptions that are quite conservative, a site value tax can keep pace. Therefore, our revenue conclusion is that taxing land instead of land and buildings will not, in itself, cause cities to find themselves with financial difficulties. This conclusion is tentative, however, in that our analysis was limited by assuming the land tax would be administered properly (i.e., land would be assessed at potential value with no exemptions) and implemented at a uniform rate. Further research efforts are needed. Efforts in terms of current land value estimates based on cadastral maps, general equilibrium estimates following the approach used by Shoven and Whalley, and dynamic modeling which integrates a model of government expenditures, are all important in answering the question posed at the outset of this paper, whether site value taxation can finance local government activity.

References

Aaron, Henry. 1975. *Who Pays the Property Tax?* Washington, D.C.: The Brookings Institution.

Arnott, Richard J., and James G. MacKinnon. 1977. "The Effects of the Property Tax: A General Equilibrium Simulation." *Journal of Urban Economics* 4: 389–407.

Courant, Paul N. 1977. "A General Equilibrium Model of Heterogeneous Local Property Taxes." *Journal of Public Economics* 8: 313–27.

Douglas, Richard W. 1978. "Site Value Taxation and Manvel's Land Value Estimates." *The American Journal of Economics and Sociology* 37: 217–23.

Feldstein, Martin. 1977. "The Surprising Incidence of a Tax on Pure Rent: A New Answer to an Old Question." *Journal of Political Economy* 85: 349–60.

Gaffney, Mason. 1970. "Adequacy of Land as a Tax Base." In *The Assessment of Land Value,* ed. Daniel M. Holland, Madison: Univ. of Wisconsin Press.

George, Henry. 1879. Reprint 1975. *Progress and Poverty.* New York: Robert Schalkenbach Foundation.

Goldsmith, Raymond W. 1956. *Study of Saving in the U.S.,* vol. 3. Princeton: Princeton Univ. Press.

Goldsmith, Raymond W. 1962. *The National Wealth of the U.S. in the Postwar Period.* Princeton: Princeton Univ. Press.

Harberger, A. C. 1962. "The Incidence of the Corporate Income Tax." *Journal of Political Economy* 70: 215–40.

Heilbrun, James. 1966. *Real Estate Taxes and Urban Housing.* New York: Columbia Univ. Press.

Heilbrun, James. 1969. "Reforming the Real Estate Tax." In *Land and Building Taxes: Their Effect on Economic Development,* ed. Arthur P. Becker, Madison: Univ. of Wisconsin Press.

Hicks, Ursula. 1961. *Development from Below.* Oxford: Oxford Univ. Press.

Holland, Daniel M. 1969. "A Study of Land Taxation in Jamaica." In *Land and Building Taxes,* ed. Arthur P. Becker, Madison: Univ. of Wisconsin Press.

Kurnow, Ernest. 1960. "Land Value Trends in the U.S." *Land Economics* 36: 341–48.

Kurnow, Ernest, et al. 1961. *Theory and Measurement of Rent.* New York: Chilton Co.

Lent, G. E. 1974. "The Urban Property Tax in Developing Countries." *Finanzarchiv* 33: 45–72.

McLure, Charles E. 1972. "A Diagrammatic Exposition of the Harberger Model with One Immobile Factor." *Journal of Political Economy* 80: 56–82.

Manvel, Allen O. 1968. "Trends in the Value of Real Estate and Land." In *Three Land Research Studies,* no. 12: 1–14. Washington, D.C.: National Commission on Urban Problems.

McDougall, G. S. 1976. "Local Public Goods and Residential Property Value: Some Insights and Extensions." *National Tax Journal* 29: 436–37.

Mieszkowski, Peter M. 1972. "The Property Tax: An Excise Tax or a Profits Tax." *Journal of Public Economics* April: 73–97.

Neuner, Edward J., Dean O. Popp, and Frederick D. Seabold. 1974. "The Impact of a Transition to Site-Value Taxation on Various Classes of Property in San Diego." *Land Economics* 50:181–85.

Polinsky, Mitchell A., and Daniel L. Rubinfeld. 1978. "The Long-Run Effects of a Residential Tax and Local Public Services." *Journal of Urban Economics* 5: 241–62.

Richman, Raymond L. 1965. "The Theory and Practice of Site-Value Taxation in Pittsburgh." In *1964 Proceedings of the Fifty-Seventh Annual Conference on Taxation.* Harrisburg, Pa.: National Tax Association.

Scarf, H. E., and T. Hansen. 1973. *The Computation of Economic Equilibria.* New Haven: Yale Univ. Press.

Schaaf, A. H. 1969. "Effects of Property Taxation on Slums and Renewal: A Study of Land-Improvement Assessment Ratios." *Land Economics* 45:111–17.

Schroeder, Larry D., and David L. Sjoquist. 1975. *The Property Tax and Alternative Local Taxes.* New York: Praeger.

Shoven, J. B., and J. Whalley. 1977. "Equal Yield Tax Alternatives." *Journal of Public Economics* 8: 211–24.

Smith, Theodore. 1970. "Land Versus Real Property Taxation: A Case Study Comparison." *Land Economics* 46: 304–13.

Stone, Gerald W. 1975. "Public Spending, Land Taxes and Economic Growth: An Empirical Analysis of the Adequacy of Land as a Tax Base." *The American Journal of Economics and Sociology* 34: 111–26.

U.N. Secretariat. 1975. "Site-Value Taxation in Developing Countries." In *Readings in Taxation in Developing Countries* ed. Oldman and Brin, pp. 470–76. Baltimore: Johns Hopkins Press.

Wales, T. J., and E. G. Wiens. 1974. "Capitalization of Residential Property Taxes: An Empirical Study." *Review of Economics and Statistics* August: 329–33.

Woodruff, A. M., and L. L. Ecker-Racz. 1969. "Property Taxes and Land Use Patterns in Australia and New Zealand." In *Land and Building Taxes,* ed. Arthur P. Becker, Madison: Univ. of Wisconsin Press.

4 *Mary Miles Teachout*

Defining and Measuring Land Value — A Progress Report

In a paper presented at a previous TRED conference, Oliver Oldman and I set forth, for purposes of critical discussion and development, a proposal for the administration of a tax on land value in urban areas (Oldman and Teachout 1979). In that paper, we were primarily concerned with making equitable distinctions between taxable land and other forms and elements of real property, and also with developing a conceptual definition for "land value" as a tax base in urban environments.

The difficult task of identifying workable concepts of land and land value continues. Our own thinking on this problem has undergone considerable revision.[1] An article in preparation will elaborate on the conclusions we have reached following further analysis by ourselves and others of the problems of defining land value for purposes of taxing urban land without buildings.

Meanwhile, we are continuing our inquiry into the problems of defining and measuring land value by focusing on the procedures that would actually be used to establish land value assessments for a separate tax on land value. Our particular purpose here is to expand on an idea suggested only briefly in the previous paper. That is, when an assessment error is

---

1. Some developments of our research appear in print in Oldman and Teachout (1978a) and in summary form in the *International Center for Land Policy Studies Newsletter,* no. 5 (August 1978).

discovered or new information is brought to light during the appeal process, revisions should be made to assessments of all land parcels affected by the new information, whether the owners of those parcels appealed or not (Oldman and Teachout 1979, pp. 232–234). In the present paper, we have designed an appeals, review, and revision structure for implementing this concept. The result is a set of procedures quite different from those usually used for property tax appeals.

For purposes of this paper, we assume that "land value" has already been defined. We also assume assessment by mapping of land value information derived from market sources. That is, land value information gathered from market sources is recorded on a map and adjusted according to chosen techniques[2] so that adjacent, similar parcels of land have closely related values irrespective of the buildings that may currently be on them.

The assumption of close interrelationships of value among contiguous parcels of land is fundamental to our proposal. Its significance is best illustrated by example. Imagine two improved properties in an urban environment located on adjacent parcels of equal size. The site characteristics of the two parcels are identical; the geological conditions of the underlying land are the same and they both have the same relation to transportation facilities, traffic flow patterns, aesthetic conditions, and so forth. They are improved with buildings of quite different ages and types. The fair market value of one of the properties is $200,000, whereas the other has a fair market value of $500,000. Our assumption is that the *land* values of the two parcels are the same, despite the extreme difference in the improved values, because the characteristics that determine land value — the site characteristics — are identical.

We recognize that this assumption glosses over some difficult problems. It denies the possibility that the existence of an improvement on a parcel can or should have *any* effect on the land value of that parcel. Perhaps this assumption does not produce an equitable or socially desirable result, and should not be followed too strictly in the design of a separate tax on urban land value. For example, a government may not wish to tax the owner of the $200,000 property as heavily as the owner of the $500,000, even for purposes of a separate tax on land value, if the $200,000 property includes a well-maintained, functional building that could not be economically replaced.

2. Some of the available techniques are identified in Oldman and Teachout (1978b, pp. 184–85), and Oldman and Teachout (1979, pp. 225–28). See also Beach (1970), Jakarta (1973), Bahl (1979), and International Association of Assessing Officers (1978, pp. 198–210).

The relationship between land value and existing improvements, particularly improvements representing suboptimal uses, is complex. It presents some of the most difficult problems in the task of defining "land value" in urban environments, and will not be addressed here. For present purposes, it is sufficient to point out that the values of neighboring land parcels bear close and definable relationships to each other. Even if the land values of the parcels in the example are determined not to be identical according to the chosen definition of "land value," they are interdependent in a way that the improved values of the properties are not. There is an intuitive sense of this relationship that is reflected in the everyday question, "What is the value of land now in downtown (City X)?"

Because of the greater interdependence among land values than among improved values, we concluded that an appeals system for land value assessments ought to include a feature not generally found in systems for appealing improved value assessments. That is, when revisions are made to assessments following appeals, as many assessment revisions as necessary should be made to maintain an equitable pattern of assessed land values. Therefore, assessment appeals may result in revisions to assessments of some parcels whose owners did not appeal, as well as to assessments that were appealed. Furthermore, adjustments might lead to assessment increases as well as decreases.

For example, assume that our imaginary property Blackacre was originally assessed at $20,000, but on appeal the assessment is reduced to $15,000. Assume further that the several lots near Blackacre were assessed at approximately the same level as Blackacre because they were all determined to be of substantially equivalent value. When the assessment of Blackacre is changed on the map to $15,000, an assessment inequity is created if the assessments of the other parcels are allowed to remain at $20,000. Equity in asessment can only be achieved if the assessments of Blackacre and other contiguous parcels are reconciled.

Assume that the owner of Blackacre, in presenting his case on appeal, introduced reliable evidence demonstrating that, because of variations in site characteristics, other land parcels located in one part of the neighborhood also had a lower value than the map showed, whereas the values of parcels in another part were actually higher than mapped values. That is, the taxpayer's evidence showed that the mapped figure of $20,000, while a valid average for the neighborhood, was inaccurate because the assessor had failed to distinguish between site characteristics that made the values of some parcels higher and others lower than that figure.

Assuming the validity of the taxpayer's evidence, the implications of the appeal are not only that the appealed assessment should be changed but some other assessments should be changed as well. Some of the assessments should be reduced below $20,000 while others should be increased above that figure.

We determined that mechanisms for making such adjustments could be incorporated into a system for taxation of land value if the processes of appeal and revision become a function administered almost totally by the assessment agency with taxpayer participation, rather than by the courts. In addition, the land value mapping process would be continued throughout the course of assessment appeal proceedings. Accordingly, we propose for this system an administrative structure that differs in three respects from those currently used for improved property taxation in most American jurisdictions. First, the land value mapping process would be used not just as an assessment technique but as the foundation for review, appeal, and revision of assessments. Second, the assessment agency, in carrying out its responsibility to supervise the orderly administration of the tax, would expand its annual internal review procedures to include participation by taxpayers. Finally, taxpayers' rights to an appeal hearing would be exercisable only at the level of the assessment agency on issues of valuation fact. The power to appeal an assessment beyond this level would be severely restricted.

The practical operation of the proposal may be summarized as follows. Each year, after the land value map is initially drafted by assessors, but before it has been certified as final, the assessment agency administers a series of review and revision procedures. During this period, taxpayers would be notified of proposed assessments; they then have the opportunity to be heard in public hearings administered by the agency. Taxpayers would also have the legal right to an individual appeal hearing before an agency review board. Following these public and private hearings, the land value map would be reviewed by senior assessment officers and revised on the basis of the additional information presented at the hearings. Those taxpayers whose assessments were changed on the revised map as a result of appeals by others would have the right to a further private hearing before the assessments became final.

After this extensive annual administrative review and revision period, a final land value map would be certified for tax billing purposes. Following certification, there would be no further right to appeal on valuation questions. Judicial review would be restricted to questions of law and to cases of fraud, incompetence, or unauthorized action on the part of the assessment agency.

Further details of the proposal are set forth in the following pages. All of the steps described would probably not need to be repeated every year. Rather, each procedure is presented as it might be used during the first year or two of implementation of a separate tax on land value. Some steps necessary in the transition to this system could be eliminated or simplified later. In addition, not all of the procedures suggested here would be needed in every jurisdiction having a tax on land value. Some may be able to use simplified versions depending on the level of land values and the rate of tax.

Supervisory Review and Taxpayer Appeal

The period of supervisory review and taxpayer appeal would begin as soon as the proposed land value map is presented to the public, an event that should occur at a specified date each year. Once the system is installed, what takes place each year at that date is a presentation of changes proposed to the previous year's map.

Public Information Campaign

In recent years, assessors have increasingly advocated the use of public education efforts in order to increase taxpayer understanding of and support for assessments and to reduce the number of unfounded appeals. This approach may be particularly useful for a separate charge on land value based on a land value map because the process of land value mapping may not be familiar to taxpayers in most American jurisdictions.

Enlarged portions of the land value map should be displayed at neighborhood locations frequented by the public, such as government offices, libraries, post offices, and transit terminals. In addition, assessors should acquaint taxpayers with the proposed map through news releases and appearances on radio and television. Specifically, these media should be used to explain in general terms the basic outlines of the land value mapping process and to provide information about reading and understanding the land value map. Presentations would be particularly important during the first year a separate charge on land value goes into effect. In subsequent years the assessors should also use the media presentations to explain major changes made since the previous year's map and the reasons for such changes.

Notice to Taxpayers

At the time the proposed map is presented, personal notice should be provided to all landowners, by mail or otherwise, in order to inform them of their land value assessments as shown on the land value map. In each succeeding year, personal notice need only be given to owners of parcels on which the assessment is changed. Substitute forms of personal notice must be established in each jurisdiction with reference to jurisdictional law and the practice with respect to other forms of property taxation.

The notice should include information on the time and location of the public hearings dealing with the map. It should also inform the owner of his right to an individual private hearing on his land value assessment. Simple instructions should be included explaining how to make an appointment for such a hearing, and the kind of information that the taxpayer should be prepared to present in support of his objection. The notice should, of course, satisfy all due process of law requirements for notice within the jurisdiction.

Public Hearings

A public hearing should be held soon after public presentation of the map. The public should be allowed a period of time in which to become familiar with the map through inspection in public places and media presentations before the hearing is held. Nonetheless, the hearing should take place early in the review and revision period. If taxpayers have an opportunity to gain an understanding of the map early in the review period by attending a public hearing, the number of requests for private hearings may be minimized.

The public hearing serves three purposes. First, it gives the assessor an opportunity to explain the map to taxpayers in greater detail than is possible through brief introductions in the news media. An assessor should begin the hearing with a presentation in which he explains the methods used to assess land through land value mapping. He should describe the nature and sources of the data used in preparing the map, such as specific benchmark values, and explain how adjustments are made to obtain values for other parcels.

In cities, the public hearing could take place in a series of sessions, each one held in a different neighborhood. At such sessions, assessors should also describe any special problems or circumstances found within that district and how they affected the assessments on the map. Such sessions should focus primarily on the district in which the meeting is held, in order to aid taxpayers in their understanding of the map as it applies to their specific parcels. However, assessors should be prepared also to relate the assessments in that district to assessments in other parts of the taxing jurisdiction. Large jurisdictions may need a jurisdiction-wide hearing that focuses only on relationships of value levels among the districts making up the taxing jurisdiction.

The second purpose of the public hearing is to answer taxpayers' questions about the proposed map. This portion of the hearing provides taxpayers with an opportunity to obtain information that may help them determine whether their parcels have been assessed equitably and whether they should request a private hearing. By responding competently to questions at this stage, qualified assessors should be able to increase taxpayer understanding of assessments and thereby limit taxpayer appeals to cases involving special problems.

Some taxpayers may be able to obtain answers to specific questions. Others may have misunderstandings about the assessment map or process that can corrected at the hearing. Still others may derive from the public hearing sufficient confidence in the competence of the assessment agency to become satisfied that their assessments have been made in an objective and equitable manner. Conversely, taxpayers may become aware that their assessors are not doing their job competently. In either case, this second portion of the hearing, by promoting informal dialogue between taxpayer and assessor, allows the hearing to function as a forum for public education on questions of assessment processes and methods.

A third and major purpose of the public hearing is to offer an opportunity for taxpayers to voice their objections to the general contours of the map (as opposed to objections relating to specific parcels, which are addressed in private appeal hearings), and to offer information that the assessors might use in revising and improving the network of interrelated assessment values. For example, taxpayers in one section of a city may present evidence to show that land in their section is assessed at full value, whereas parcels in another district appear to have been assessed at a lower assessment–sales ratio. Owners of land in a given neighborhood may demonstrate together that their land parcels will not support multilevel building construction without extensive piling; thus their land value assessments should not have been interpolated from a benchmark parcel that will support highrise construction without additional investment.

This portion of the public hearing does not provide taxpayers with a right of appeal in the traditional sense. By current standards, it probably could not satisfy the legal requirements guaranteed by the due process clause of the United States Constitution, as well as many state constitutions. Rather, it is a hearing held as part of the assessment agency's internal process of supervisory review. Taxpayers are invited to present any information that might aid the assessing agency in revising and improving the map.

The public hearing can provide a more flexible hearing opportunity than is available at a taxpayer's appeal hearing on his individual property. Any person may speak at the public hearing; his remarks are not required to meet any legal standard of burden of proof, except they must be relevant to the question of land value assessment within the jurisdiction. It may be necessary to subject each speaker's remarks to a time limitation in order to ensure that the hearing proceeds constructively and efficiently. Any person also should be able to submit written presentations or evidence in place of (or in addition to) oral presentations, with no limitation that the material presented relate only to the value of his own property. In sum, the public hearing offers a flexible hearing for taxpayers, as well as a useful opportunity for assessors to gather additional value information for use in revising the map.

Private Appeal Hearings

Although some taxpayers may choose to present objections only at the public supervisory review hearing, every taxpayer is legally entitled to an individual appeal hearing before his land value assessment is finally determined. This legal right derives, in the United States, from the due process clause of the Constitution and from similar clauses in most state constitutions.[3] The appeals systems of many other countries offer similar rights of appeal (International Association of Assessing Officers, vol. 42, no. 11, 1976, p. 23–27).

After receiving a notice of assessment or assessment increase, a taxpayer should be allowed several days to consider whether or not to file an appeal. The deadline for filing an appeal, if possible, should not occur until after the public hearings have been held, so that taxpayers will have had the fullest possible opportunity to become informed about the basis of the assessment before deciding whether or not to appeal. Formal requirements should be few and simple. A taxpayer should be required only to submit a short form of notice of appeal and make an appointment for an appeal hearing.

The hearings may be conducted by panels of assessors or single hearing officers. They should be open to the public. The taxpayer need not be represented by counsel, present expert witnesses, or submit evidence in writing, but he may do all of these if he chooses. The hearing process should offer a meaningful opportunity for the smallest taxpayer with the least resources to be heard, yet it should also be able to accomodate the presentation of complex valuation evidence by experts.

All taxpayers should understand from the outset that this appeal hear-

---

3. For recognition of this right by the United States Supreme Court, see *Bull v. United States,* 295 U.S. 247 (1935), and *Hagar v. Reclamation District No. 108,* 111 U.S. 701 (1884).

ing is the *only* hearing to which they are entitled. Taxpayers should be informed of this limitation to their appeal rights on the original notice of assessment or assessment increase. Any evidence or information that they wish to present to the assessors on valuation must be presented at this time. There is no further opportunity until the following year, since there is no automatic right of appeal from the decision at this level.

A second important point is that all evidence that is presented at private hearings will receive exactly the same treatment as the information presented at public hearings. In other words, no preference is given to evidence presented at private hearings. All value information gathered during the review and revision period, whether from public hearings, private hearings, written submissions, or further data collection efforts on the part of the assessors, will be studied by senior officials of the assessment agency and used to revise the map to improve its accuracy and equity.

It is possible that no revisions will be necessary in certain years, despite numerous appeals. On the other hand, taxpayers may present evidence that warrants extensive revision to the proposed map. In any case, revisions may be made to the assessments of any parcels, whether or not the owners appealed or appeared at a public hearing. All decisions with respect to revisions are the responsibility of the chief assessor and should be made by him and his staff assessors according to their skill and judgement.

When the revisions are complete, the revised map is again presented to the public and should be available once more for inspection at public locations. It should be emphasized that this procedure means that all changes are made public, whether they are the result of private or public hearings. This represents a change from the prevailing practice in most American property tax jurisdictions, in which the results of assessment appeals are sent only to the appealing taxpayer and are usually not publicized, even though they are available to the public. The proposal provides the public with the opportunity to observe the results of appeals as a whole and judge their impact on relative tax burdens.

Taxpayers who made formal appeals should be given personal notice as to whether their assessments were changed or not. Personal notice of assessment change should also be given to all taxpayers whose assessments were changed as a result of the revisions, even though they themselves may not have filed individual appeals. Such notice should inform them that they are entitled to a hearing on the new assessment of their property; this notice also should tell them how their right of appeal may be exercised.

This further right of appeal is reserved for those taxpayers who did not appeal their original assessment and whose assessments are nonetheless changed by the revisions. It is necessary to grant them this extra opportunity for appeal in order to protect fully their legal right to a hearing before their assessments become final. Appeal rights are limited to this group only at this stage in order to prevent the process of appeal–revision–appeal from continuing indefinitely.

Further Rounds of Public and Private Hearings

A final public hearing is held after the revised map has been presented to the public. The assessors should open the hearing with brief explanations of the important changes made during the revision process and the reasons for these changes. Taxpayers should have an opportunity at the hearing to ask questions about these revisions. Once again, the final hearing may be held in several sessions in different regions of a large jurisdiction. However, if the revisions are minor only a single meeting may be necessary.

The second round of private appeal hearings are also held to hear the appeals of those taxpayers who did not appeal previously but whose assessments were changed on the revised map. The hearing opportunity of these taxpayers should be identical to that provided taxpayers during the first round of individual appeals.

After the final round of public and private hearings, the assessor should make any revisions necessary to the assessments of those taxpayers who appealed during the second round of appeals, but not to any other parcels. When appeal results are mapped and are sent to those who appealed during the second and final round of appeals, the land value map is complete. It is then certified by the assessor as the official assessment map for the tax year, and it is ready to be used for tax billing. No further appeals may be heard on issues of valuation accuracy.

In the first year of implementation of a land value tax and land value asssessment map, both rounds of public and private hearings would be necessary. Even a third round may be desirable during the initial year, if data adduced from the second round of private hearings make further changes appropriate in the first map to be certified as final. In later years, after the process is understood and the accuracy of the map has been refined to the extent that the map needs only annual updating, only a single round of public and private hearings may be necessary each year.

Special Hearings

Occasionally there are developments within a taxing jurisdiction that have an unusual impact on land values. Examples might be the location of a new major transportation facility such as an airport or a transit system, or the loss from the jurisdiction of a key employer or center of economic activity, such as a large factory or a military base. Under these circumstances, significant shifts in land value patterns may occur in a relatively short period of time. The assessor may need to gather a great deal of land value information in order to make the extensive revisions to the map that this kind of unusual development requires.

The assessor should have, therefore, the statutory authority to convene special hearings if he, in the exercise of his discretion, deems additional hearings to be desirable for accurate revision of the map. These special hearings would be in the nature of the public hearings that are part of the supervisory review process. The difference is that they need not be called only during the annual revision period, but could be held earlier in the year to aid assessors in updating assessments as part of the process of preparing the annual proposed draft. In the usual tax year in which there were no significant unusual developments affecting land value, the assessor would not need to convene special hearings.

Judicial Review

A basic feature of our proposal is the omission of judicial review of questions of fact in determining land values. The reason is the usual one of judicial deference to administrative expertise. That is, the findings of specific valuation facts often requires the skill of an assessor who has been trained in specialized techniques of land valuation and land value mapping. A great deal of technical knowledge and experienced judgement may be required for mapping land values, especially in urban areas, in order to establish a carefully balanced network of interdependent land value asssessments.

Although judges should not be in a position of interfering with assessors' uses of technical valuation methods or upsetting a coordinated set of interdependent assessment values, the judicial function of interpretation of the law need not be abandoned with respect to legal standards of valuation. Thus, judicial review is available for questions of valuation law, as well as for fraud, incompetence, and unauthorized action on the part of the assessment agency. Although the proposal to limit the availability of judicial review is an integral part of our framework for a land value tax, it presents a difficult legal problem. It is seldom easy to distinguish questions of valuation fact from questions of valuation law. Disgruntled taxpayers will always seek to characterize their objection to an assessment as an issue of valuation law in order to obtain judicial review. What criteria should be used to determine whether a particular appeal presents a reviewable question of law or a non-reviewable question of fact? This is a problem that we have, for the moment, reserved for further study.

Another issue that we have reserved is the design of procedures and standards for providing relief in hardship cases. Although the desired market effects of land value taxation are promoted most efficiently if no exemptions from the land value charge are allowed, such a tax is apt to fall harshly on elderly or low-income homeowners or marginal business owners whose properties are located in neighborhoods that become subject to new development pressures. If the land value charge coexists with other forms of property taxation and is levied at a relatively low rate, no hardship provisions may be necessary.

If, however, the land value charge were to be the primary form of property taxation in a jurisdiction, some mechanisms for providing partial relief in specified situations might be desirable on the basis of equity. The Taxation Relief Board used in Jamaica may provide a useful model, but this issue would need to be analyzed in relation to the specific land value charge contemplated and its relationship to other forms of property taxation in the jurisdiction.

Conclusion

The scheme of asessment and appeal procedures described above does not provide a complete answer to the question of how "land value" should be defined. For example, it does not solve the problem of assessing a parcel of land that has on it a building of substantial value that does not reflect the current highest and best use of that parcel, or of establishing the proper relation between that land value assessment and the assessment of a contiguous vacant parcel with identical characteristics. These problems still need to be resolved.

Nonetheless, through the exercise of designing a set of procedures whereby assessment values for urban land would be measured, we can begin to flesh out a conception of what "land value" might mean as a tax base for urban environments. One characteristic of land value assessments is that they will have been derived from market information and will have been determined with reference to land values of contiguous parcels. They will have a definable relationship to the assessments of neighboring parcels.

A second characteristic of a land value tax system based on these procedures is that taxpayers will have, through the land value map, a mechanism by which they can judge whether their land value assessments are equitable in relation to those of their neighbors. Taxpayers might be able to keep track of market values of their improved properties so that they are able to judge the fairness of their improved value assessments in relation to assessments of like properties. However, they are not as apt to have access to enough information on underlying land values to determine if their own land parcel, whether improved or not, has been assessed fairly in relation to other land parcels. The land value map provides this information in visual form so that it can be readily understood. Ultimately, it may be the assurance of equity provided by procedural mechanisms such as this that will make the concept of a separate tax on urban land value acceptable to the taxpaying public.

References

American Institute of Real Estate Appraisers. 1973. *The Appraisal of Real Estate.* Chicago: The institute.

Back, Kenneth. 1970. "Land Value Taxation in Light of Current Assessment Theory and Practice." In *The Assessment of Land Value,* ed. Daniel M. Holland. Madison: Univ. of Wisconsin Press.

Bahl, Roy W. 1979. "The Practice of Urban Property Taxation in Less Developed Countries." In *The Taxation of Urban Property in Less Developed Countries,* ed. Roy W. Bahl. Madison: Univ. of Wisconsin Press.

Bird, Richard M. 1960. "A National Tax on the Unimproved Value of Land: The Australian Experience, 1910–1952." *National Tax Journal* 13: 386–92.

Bonbright, James C. 1937. *The Valuation of Property.* New York: McGraw-Hill.

Copes, John M. 1970. "Reckoning with Imperfections in the Land Market." In *The Assessment of Land Value,* ed. Daniel M. Holland. Madison: Univ. of Wisconsin Press.

Downing, Paul B. 1970. "Estimating Residential Land Value by Multivariate Analysis." In *The Assessment of Land Value,* ed. Daniel M. Holland. Madison: Univ. of Wisconsin Press.

Finkelstein, Philip, and George Kerchner. 1977. "A Study of Full Value Land Taxation in the Huntington Town Portion of the Half Hollow Hills School District." Mimeographed. New York: Center for Local Tax Research.

Gaffney, Mason. 1970. "Adequacy of Land as a Tax Base." In *The Assessment of Land Value,* ed. Daniel M. Holland. Madison: Univ. of Wisconsin Press.

Gaffney, Mason. 1975. "The Many Faces of Site-Value Taxation." In *Proceedings of the 27th Tax Conference of the Canadian Tax Foundation.* Toronto: Canadian Tax Foundation.

Groves, Harold. 1949. "Impressions of Property Taxation." *Land Economics* 25: 22–27.

Gwartney, Ted. 1970. "A Computerized Assessment Program." In *The Assessment of Land Value,* ed. Daniel M. Holland. Madison: Univ. of Wisconsin Press.

Hall, Bartil. 1978. "Real Estate Assessment Procedures in Sweden." *International Assessor* 44, no. 8: 9–12.

Hicks, Ursula K. 1970. "Can Land Be Assessed for Purposes of Site Value Taxation?" In *The Assessment of Land Value*, ed. Daniel M. Holland. Madison: Univ. of Wisconsin Press.

Holland, Daniel M. 1966. "The Taxation of Unimproved Value in Jamaica." In *Proceedings, Fifty-Eighth Annual Conference on Taxation*, Harrisburg, Pa.: National Tax Association.

Holland, Daniel M. 1970. "Introduction." In *The Assessment of Land Value*, ed. Daniel M. Holland. Madison: Univ. of Wisconsin Press.

International Association of Assessing Officers. 1976. "Overview of the Property Tax in Europe." *International Assessor* 42, no. ll: 23–27.

International Association of Assessing Officers. 1977. *Property Assessment Valuation*. United States: The association.

International Association of Assessing Officers. 1978. *Improving Real Property Assessment*. United States: The association.

Jakarta (City of). 1973. *Jakarta Real Estate Tax Project, Implementation Report*. Jakarta: The city.

Mitchell, R. Else. 1967. *Report of the Royal Commission of Inquiry into Rating, Valuation and Local Government Finance*. New South Wales, Australia: Government of New South Wales.

Oldman, Oliver, and Mary Miles Teachout. 1978a. "Land Valuation Under a Separate Tax on Land." In *1977 Proceedings of the Seventieth Annual Conference on Taxation*. Columbus Ohio: National Tax Association-Tax Institute of America.

Oldman, Oliver, and Mary Miles Teachout. 1978b. "Valuation and Appeals Under a Separate Tax on Land." Paper prepared for International Center for Land Policy Studies. Mimeographed. Cambridge: Harvard Law School International Tax Program.

Oldman, Oliver, and Mary Miles Teachout. 1979. "Some Administrative Aspects of Site Value Taxation: Defining 'Land' and 'Value'; Designing a Review Process." In *The Taxation of Urban Property in Less Developed Countries*, ed. Roy W. Bahl. Madison: Univ. of Wisconsin Press.

Peterson, George. 1978. "Differential Taxation of Land and Improvement Values." Paper prepared for the District of Columbia Tax Revision Commission. Mimeographed. Washington, D. C.

Rybeck, Walter. 1979. "The Only Alternative to the Property Tax – A Better Property Tax." *Assessment Digest* 1, no. 2: 2–5.

Vickrey, William S. 1970. "Defining Land Value for Taxation Purposes." In *The Assessment of Land Value*, ed. Daniel M. Holland. Madison: Univ. of Wisconsin Press.

Williams, Ellis. 1974. "Site Value Taxation." *National Tax Journal* 27: 29–44.

Woodruff, A. M., and L. L. Ecker-Racz. 1969. "Property Taxes and Land-Use Patterns in Australia and New Zealand." In *Land and Building Taxes: Their Effect on Economic Development*, ed. Arthur P. Becker. Madison: Univ. of Wisconsin Press.

5 Richard W. Lindholm and Roger G. Sturtevant

American Land Tax Roots: Plus Experimentation in Oregon

The year 1979 is the one hundredth birthday of Henry George's *Progress and Poverty*. The economic positions of this book, written by a Californian newspaperman, are based largely on the economics of David Ricardo and Adam Smith — the eighteenth-century founding fathers of modern capitalism. The basic premise of Ricardo and Smith is that since the supply of land cannot be increased, high land prices do not encourage production expansion. Land absorbs funds without increasing production efficiency. George, however, went beyond this purely economic position. He envisaged the land tax as the way to eliminate poverty. He was sharply challenged in this position by the leading British economist of the period, Alfred Marshall. Marshall asked George to prove that poverty would disappear if a major land tax were introduced. George, of course, could not. Nevertheless, Marshall became a supporter of the land tax as a desirable approach to municipal finance, even if it would not eliminate poverty (Marshall 1920, rpt. 1936, pp. 794–804).

Land value taxation (LVT) has roots extending into the social philosophies of all civilizations. The early church fathers, imbued with ancient Hebrew traditions, took the position that land was given to the rich and poor in common (Neilson 1933, p. 90).

Use of LVT in the U.S.

The move of the thirteen colonies toward independence from Great Britain brought the abolition of the law and custom of entail and right of primogeniture. The democratizing of land ownership was an important portion of the American Revolution. Another democratizing impact made its appearance in the sources of revenues of the states. The economic conservatism of the U.S. Constitution shows itself in the limitations placed on the tax role of land. In the states themselves, the poll tax was replaced with a land tax, and Ely, in his 1888 book, reported that by 1796, all of the fifteen states except Delaware had a land tax. Four of the fifteen also had a general property tax (Ely 1888).

It is of interest to note that the first federal direct tax, i. e., other than excise, provided for a progressive tax rate on land and improvements. The tax, enacted by Congress on July 14, 1798, was limited to real estate used for residential purposes. Congress was reluctant to tax productive activity; in the area of taxation, they wished to remain on the consumer side of the economic coin. The U.S. Constitution (Sec. 9, Par. 4) limits the federal government to a property tax that is an equal per capita levy.

U.S. Land Policy and Progress and Poverty

The passage of the Homestead Act in 1862 finally settled "land policy" for the major United States political groups. The "solution" did not last long. The great depression of 1873 to 1877 revived agitation centered on land control. Prior to the 1870s, not many American economists had accepted David Ricardo's law of economic rent that was included in his *Political Economy* (1817). This situation was changed by the observed economic pressures of the 1870s. Into this dynamic political and social environment, Henry George published his book *Progress and Poverty* (1879, rpt. 1929). American economists were pushed into consideration of land problems by the immense influence of the "book." Tariff and currency problems no longer occupied the center of the American economic stage. Land use and ownership problems came to dominate economic policy considerations.

Progress and Poverty was read widely throughout the English-reading world and was later translated into many languages, including Chinese. Cheap paper editions outsold the most popular novels of the day. Some two million copies of this 568-page book were published, and Henry George moved from California to New York, where he was nearly elected mayor.

The concept of land taxation, differing from the taxation of other wealth, had found favor immediately following the American Revolution. In 1879, one hundred years after the Revolution, the idea enjoyed a substantial revival in the United States. Social reform, through collecting in taxes a substantial portion of the economic rent of land, was advocated as a way of taxing without raising prices and reducing the monopoly power of landowners.[1] Today, after another hundred years, the problem of monopoly power through the control of land has re-entered the arena of political economy. Again, economist tariff and currency discussions are being replaced by fundamental analyses, such as resource availability, monopoly, and economic rent (surplus).

Democracy and LVT in Oregon

Concern in Oregon over economic rent from control of land and the use of LVT to finance government services, while stimulating greater efficiency in land development, is entwined with the promotion and adoption of what is often called the "Oregon political system." This "political power to the people" program was to be carried out through the initiative, the referral, and the recall (Thompson 1929). Once the people acquired political power, they would vote in LVT. Economic power to the people was to be from political power to the use of LVT. The backers of the program were frequently called the "single taxers," deliberately by the concept's enemies and through ignorance by many others (Gilbert 1916, pp. 25–52). Actually, Henry George never envisioned LVT as constituting the sole source of government revenues; neither had he endorsed it to be collected at a rate so high that land would lose its value.

The leader of the LVT advocates in Oregon was William Somon U'Ren (1859–1949)(Woodward 1915, pp. 112, 119). He was also the leader in bringing about the initiative, the referral, and the recall. In his *Report of the Single Tax Conference* (1910, pp. 21–22), U'Ren pointed out that he saw the initiative and referral procedure included in a complete concept of LVT.

A politically influenced tax package developed by Governor McCall in 1973 provided lower property taxes for households, somewhat higher real estate taxes for businesses, and substantially higher property taxes in certain areas on forest, range, and farm lands, and, in addition, on vacant urban areas. This impact was to be brought about by including all income-producing real estate into a statewide base that was to bear a

---

1. Owners of land had to explain why returns from land ownership varied even though the quantity of investment on the land was the same. Monopoly turned out to be the source of economic rent. David Ricardo, *Essay on the Influences of the Low Price of Corn on the Profits of Stock* (1815), *passim*.

uniform tax rate. These funds, plus additional state funds, would support 10 percent of the costs of providing an average level of schooling. The approach, which had been approved by the Oregon legislature, under House Bill 2004, Regular Session, in March 1973 was rejected by the voters. It attracted only two out of five votes. The sharp rejection was attributed to the breadth and complications of the legislation. There was something bad, as well as good, for everybody. The concept of a simple and single rate LVT had become buried in political complexities.

The farmer in 1973, as in the days of U'Ren, turned out to be an active opponent of LVT. It was generally agreed the lower land prices expected from LVT would make it easier for a young farmer to gain control of enough land for an efficient farm unit. However, the stabler land prices also reduced the capital gains expectations of the older farmers; the older farmers, in Oregon as elsewhere, provide most of the farmer leadership.

Several bills have been introduced in the Oregon legislature providing for city and county choice and a statewide modified LVT.[2] The statewide tax would be applicable to all taxable land at a uniform rate. All the funds collected were to be dedicated to the finance of education. None of these bills were reported out of committee.

Current LVT Developments

The current LVT expansion and discussion is a portion of urban land planning, energy conservation, and a reduction of the taxes based on the capital values of the necessity shelter. In Pennsylvania, recent legislation has permitted local governments to increase the portion of the property tax rate resting on land (the graded property tax). The resultant growth of LVT in Pittsburgh and a statewide increase in total property taxes are being pointed to as a reversal of the California "Proposition 13" trend. Property taxes as a land tax are apparently more attractive than property taxes that also include personal property and structures in the tax base.

The information available to political leaders and voters on, for example, the distribution of land ownership, the effect of land tax rates on land use decisions, the attractiveness of LVT to new industries, and the expansion of old industries, remains scarce. However, a number of studies similar to the Eugene, Oregon, study summarized below have been completed (Schroeder and Sjoquist 1975, p. 8). They are only partial analyses and can answer only a few of the basic questions being asked as LVT becomes a viable policy alternative in the area of municipal finance.

2. House Bill 1769 Regular Session 1969, House Bill 1726 Regular Session 1971, and Senate Joint Resolution 48, Regular Session 1977.

A Hypothetical Application of Land Value Taxation to Eugene, Oregon, and Its Effects on Urban Growth

The general property tax is no longer identified as the most unpopular tax in the United States (Sturtevant 1979, p. 7), but it continues to provide more revenues to local governments than any other source. A compilation of U.S. Bureau of the Census material indicates 84.5 percent of all tax collected at the local level is attributable to the property tax (Netzer 1966). The use of the property tax is widespread as a fiscal tool. The concern herein, however, is with the property tax and its relationship to developer decision-making and resultant urban development patterns. It has become apparent that numerous unintended consequences have emerged. Among these consequences is the rather recent concern with the allocative effects prompted by the property tax levied on both the value of land and the improvements. Evidence has been accumulating which suggests that the property tax in its present form encourages certain forms of urban sprawl (Gaffney 1973b, pp. 115–51).

The conventional property tax is a dissuasion to both the quality and quantity of new construction and to the proper maintenance of existing structures (Grieson 1974b, pp. 139–40). The intensity of development within urban land markets and the highest and best use of parcels is restricted by the property tax as an allocative side effect (Shoup 1978, pp. 105–32). The withholding of vacant land from urban markets in expectation of future windfall profits caused largely by the provision of public improvements has prompted sprawling "leapfrog" development patterns to persist. A United Nations publication has noted that vacant land has been increasing faster in market value than any other type of land (Manuel 1973, p. 35). Speculators are quickly attracted to this potential for "unearned" profit. A further inducement to exploit socially created land values is due to a preferential property tax treatment of land over improvements. Preferential tax treatment of capital gains provides an additional vehicle to avoid taxes on any increment of land value. The pursuit of "unearned increments" as a hedge against inflation promotes speculation in vacant land. The resultant high prices force development to locate in areas beyond the urban area periphery (Gaffney 1973a, pp. 17–34).

Oregon's growth management program, designed to reduce sprawling urban development, adopted Senate Bill 100, more commonly designated the 1973 Land Use Act. Under the act's goals, guidelines have been developed for orderly and rational growth, preservation of agricultural lands, low cost housing, efficient transportation, urban infilling, increased densities, and designated urban service boundaries.

The city of Eugene, Oregon, has received national recognition through the work of the Lane Council of Governments and the local application of this legislation (Oregon Land Conservation and Development Commission 1974). The city continues to use the conventional property tax on land and building value, but in addition it has pushed up assessments on vacant land more rapidly than on improvements. Growth controls also have been introduced, which attempt to contain development and increase urban capital-to-land ratios. A recent study of this dichotomous relationship between the property tax and urban growth in Eugene is summarized below; this study lends empirical support to the use of land value taxation as an effective land use planning instrument, as well as a fiscal tool providing tax relief to homeowners.

Grieson Model Applied to Eugene

The model used is an adoption of an economic analysis developed some years ago by Ronald Grieson (1974a). In applying the model to Eugene, it is important to keep the limitations of the model, as well as its usefulness, firmly in mind. In an actual application for policy purposes, a detailed land use investigation is needed, as well as community input. In addition, alternative taxation approaches need to be evaluated. It is, of course, quite possible that the efficiencies in land use may be politically unworkable. However, general voter support may be forthcoming. Lindholm, for example, found that "the property taxes collected on single family residences for the entire Eugene–Springfield metropolitan area would decline by 24 percent from current levels if existing property taxes were replaced with LVT raising the same quantity of revenues (1978, p. 23).

The city of Eugene includes 19,498 single family residences, with a total single family residential land value of $118,494,000. Improvement value for the same group totals $427,986,000. Assessments are at 100 percent of market value (Lane Council of Governments 1976). From these figures the average value of single family residential land, building, and property value can be determined: average single family residential land value = $6,077; average single family residential building value = $21,950; and average single family residential property value = $28,027. Employing a 10 percent discount rate and a 3 percent average property tax (Lindholm 1978, pp. 23–24), an application of the Grieson model can be made to derive the "price effects" of the alternative tax.

Given an average effective tax factor of .33 percent, i.e., 3 percent tax rate at 100 percent of assessed market value divided by the 10 percent discount rate, and the elasticity of supply of structures for single family Eugene residences,

$$n_s = \frac{1}{2} \frac{\text{value of improvements}}{\text{value of land}} = .5 \frac{\$21,950}{6,077} = 1.8,$$

the following elasticities are derived:
(a) elasticity of quantity of structures supplied:

$$n_{Qt} = \frac{-1}{1/n_s + 1} = \frac{-1}{1/1.8 + 1} = .64;$$

(b) elasticity of land value:

$$n_{Vt} = 2n_{Qt} = 2(-.64) = 1.28;$$

(c) elasticity of property values:

$$n_{Pt} = \frac{n_{Qt}}{n_s} = \frac{-.64}{1.8} = .36;$$

and (d) elasticity of price of structures:

$$n_{Bt} = n_D(n_{Qt}) = -1(-.64) = .64.$$

Applying the removal of the effective tax factor, i.e., $1.33 - 0.33 = 1.0$ or 25 percent reduction, to the elasticities above yields representative allocative values for the city of Eugene without the conventional property tax's burden on investment:
(1) Quantity of structures per given land area:

$$n_{Qt} \text{ (tax factor)} = .64 (.25) = .16;$$

(2) Land values per given land area:

$$n_{Vt} \text{ (tax factor)} = 1.28 (.25) = .32;$$

(3) Property values per given land area:

$$n_{Pt} \text{ (tax factor)} = .36 (.25) = .09;$$

and (4) Price of structures per given land area:

$$n_{Bt} \text{ (tax factor)} = .64 (.25) = .16.$$

Table 5.1 summarizes the allocative effects of a land value tax replacing a conventional 3 percent property tax for Eugene. The two top horizontal lines show the present property tax and a switch to land value taxation *from* that basis as it exists today. Note the higher rate of land tax necessary to cover revenues. The 10.9 percent rate has been estimated by Lindholm as the uniform rate on land value necessary throughout the city

Table 5.1. A comparison of the effects of a 3 percent conventional property tax with a land value tax applied at equal revenues for the city of Eugene, Oregon

Type Tax	Rate (Percent)	Land Use	Average Lot Size	Number of Lots	Number of Structures	Average Lot Value	Average Property Value	Average Structure Price	Total Land Consumed	Total Land Conserved	Number of Added Structures	Average Consumer Tax Burden	Average Homeowner Tax Burden	Average Total Tax per Dwelling Unit
Conventional (Land and Buildings)	3.0	Single Family Homes	10,000[a]	19,498	19,498	6077	28,027	21,950	4,476 acres	0	0	538	302	840
Land Value Tax- Recent Changeover	10.9[a]	Single Family Homes	10,000	19,498	19,498	6077	28,027	21,950	4,476 acres	0	0	0	662	662
Land Value Tax- Structures Constant (equilibrium)	8.25	Single Family Homes	8,620[c]	19,498	19,498	6915	29,442	18,438	3,858 acres	618 acres	0	0	571	571[d]
Land Value Tax- Land Area Constant (equilibrium)	8.25	Single Family Homes	8,620	22,618	22,618[e]	6915[f]	29,442	18,438	4,476 acres	0	3,120	0	571	571
Land Value Tax- Lot Size Constant (equilibrium)	6.9	Single & Multi- Family Homes	10,000	19,498	22,618	8022	30,549	18,438	4,476 acres	0	3,120	0	571	571

Note: Totals may not necessarily sum due to derivation procedure

[a]Actual average single family lot in Eugene is 10,370 sq. ft. Lane Council of Governments, Inventory of Existing Land Use, Housing Characteristics and Historic Resources, Feb. 8, 1978.

[a]A 10.9 percent land value tax has been estimated by Lindholm (1978) to replace current nonequilibrium revenues.

[c]If single family housing is demanded without substitutes, e.g., duplexes, then increased capital intensity will be found in smaller lot sizes.

[e]Increased capital intensity diminishes infrastructure costs in equilibrium which reduces amount of tax necessary to finance urban area (estimate only).

[d]If quantity of structures demanded is not held constant, then the 618 acres of conserved land (13.8 percent) can be used for compact expansion of 3,120 additional single family homes.

[f]Equilibrium land values are derived from the Grieson model which does not include the capitalization of taxes.

of Eugene to cover the revenue lost by "untaxing" improvement values (Lindholm 1978, pp. 23–24). As growth occurs, however, developers will decrease the amount of land input for single family residences or supply higher density substitutes if market demand allows it. The assumption has been made that duplexes and townhouses will not act as substitutes for single family home consumers. This assumption is not critical and can be relaxed. Capital intensity in this case would grow through higher density multiple family dwellings providing similar land conservation and price effects.

Lines three and four of table 5.1 display the capital intensity effects through a 13.8 percent decrease in land consumed for single family residences.[3] The total savings in land would amount to 618 acres that is being used currently for residential purposes under the influence of the conventional property tax. The data on these two lines is compiled for comparison as if Eugene had historically developed having a land-only tax for local government revenue finance. Note that the total tax per dwelling unit is only $571 in line three. This results from the calculation that the total land consumed by single family residential use is decreased by about 13.8 percent compared to the area pre-empted by the same number of single family stuctures under the current property tax.

Infrastructure costs will be lowered by the decrease in r^2 as distance varies with land area used while the tax costs of education will remain constant. Note also that in line four, the total quantity of structures has been allowed to increase to the point at which land consumed just meets the equivalent number of acreage consumed by current residential use. A total of 3,120 single family homes has been added to housing stock without any increase over present consumption of land. Total tax burden per lot remains constant, given the added population and the use of smaller lot sizes. Costs may rise somewhat because newcomers will be somewhat further away from service mains. The savings with a compact growth form is substantial (Real Estate Research Corporation 1974).

Land Use Shifts

The value increases for land, property, and capital intensity, and the decrease in price of structures are derived through the model in aggregate form for a given area of land. In this case the total value for the given 4476 acres of single family residential land (see table 5.1) increases by 32 percent. When structures are held constant, total land area must be reduced by the amount of land conserved (13.8 percent or 618 acres) and the value of land on a per lot basis must be calculated excluding this

3. A 13.8 percent decrease in the consumption of land is equal to a 16 percent increase in capital intensity for a given number of structures.

amount, i.e.: total land value + 32 percent land value increase − 13.8 percent total land value (area) decrease ÷ 19,498 structures = $6,915 per lot at 8,620 sq. ft. The price of structures is found to decrease with increased capital intensity. This decrease compensates for increasing land values.

Whether increased capital intensity is a function of smaller lot sizes or higher density construction, i.e., duplexes and townhouses, the price will decrease per unit of land by 16 percent. Property values increase uniformly for the 4,476 acres of land currently in single family use by 9 percent in equilibrium.[4] If structures are held constant, then only 3,858 acres of land will be consumed, given equilibrium conditions and an original imposition of land value taxation. Equilibrium property values in this case must equal present total property value + a uniform 9 percent increase per care for 4,476 acres − value of conserved land ÷ 19,498 structures = $29,442 in property value per 8,620 sq. ft. lot. Given total land (4,476 acres) as a constant, 3,120 additional structures or a 16 percent increase will be available for new urban growth. If new growth is included, the divisor above will be 22,618 and the value of land conserved 0. At 3.4 persons per structure, the urban area presently occupied by single family residences would be capable of housing 10,608 additional residents if land value taxation had been the original property tax.

Conclusion

It can be seen that the model developed provides data that can be useful to planners and administrators as they attempt to implement goals development. It is apparent that within the constraints of the model, a land value tax would be an efficient growth control mechanism to assist planners in attaining a compact residential environment within the urban service boundary. For the city of Eugene, Oregon, it appears that the magnitude of the compact growth effects would constitute a 16 percent increase in the capital intensity of single family housing for a given land area. Whether this would be achieved by the market through smaller lot sizes or a substitution of demand with greater building densities requires further study of local market conditions. Summarily, it appears that land value taxation has an effective relationship of a great enough magnitude to warrant its use. Care must be taken in manipulating the tax rates so that growth control variables are affected sufficiently while needed revenue capacities are being met.

4. This is a per-acre calculation and must be modified for given changes in lot sizes. The capitalization of tax burdens is not quantified in Grieson's method and may offset the increased land and property values substantially.

References

Ely, Robert T. 1888. *Taxation in American States and Cities.* New York: Vanguard Press.

Gaffney, Mason. 1973a. "Land Rent, Taxation and Public Policy: Taxation and the Function of Urban Land Rent." *American Journal of Economics and Sociology* 32: 17–34.

Gaffney, Mason. 1973b. "Tax Reform to Release Land." In *Modernizing Urban Land Policy,* ed. Marion Clawson. Baltimore: Johns Hopkins Univ. Press.

George, Henry. 1879. Reprint 1929. *Progress and Poverty.* New York: Vanguard Press.

Gilbert, James H. 1916. "Single Tax Movement in Oregon." *Political Science Quarterly* March 25–52.

Grieson, Ronald. 1974a. "The Economics of Property Taxes and Land Value: The Elasticity of the Supply of Structures." *Journal of Urban Economics* 1, no. 4, October: 367–381.

Grieson, Ronald. 1974b. *Urban Economics: Readings and Analysis.* Boston: Little Brown.

Lane Council of Governments. 1976. *Lane County Geographic Base File.* Eugene, Oregon: Metro Cap Tape.

Lindholm, Richard W. 1978. "Tax Liabilities of Single Family Residences in the Eugene–Springfield Metropolitan Area Under Current Property Tax and Land Value Taxation." Unpublished paper. University of Oregon.

Manuel, Allan D. 1973. "Trends in the Valuation of Real Estate and Land." In *Urban Land Policies and Land Use Control Measures, vol. VI Northern America.* New York: United Nations.

Marshall, Alfred. 1920. Reprint 1936. *Principles of Economics.* 8th ed. London: Macmillan.

Neilson, Francis. 1933. *The Eleventh Commandment.* New York: Viking Press.

Netzer, Dick. 1966. *Economics of the Property Tax.* Washington, D.C.: The Brookings Institution.

Oregon Land Conservation and Development Commission. 1974. *Statewide Planning Goals and Guidelines.* Salem, Oregon.

Real Estate Research Corporation. 1974. *The Costs of Sprawl.* Washington, D.C.: U.S. Government Printing Office.

Schroeder, Larry D., and Daniel L. Sjoquist. 1975. *The Property Tax and Alternative Local Taxes.* New York: Praeger.

Shoup, Donald C. 1978. "The Effect of Property Taxes on the Capital Intensity of Urban Land Development." In *Metropolitan Financing and Growth Management Policies,* ed. George Break. Madison. Univ. of Wisconsin Press.

Sturtevant, Roger G. 1979. "An Evaluation of Land Value Taxation as an Effective Instrument to Encourage Compact Urban Growth." Mimeographed. Department of Urban and Regional Planning, University of Oregon.

Thompson, Cecil T. 1929. "The Origin of Direct Legislation in Oregon." M.A. thesis, University of Oregon.

Willcox, Walter R. B. 1938. *The Curse of Modern Taxation.* New York: Fortuny's.
Woodward, R. C. 1915. "William Simon U'Ren in an Age of Protest." M.A. thesis, University of Oregon.

6 *Ronald B. Welch*

Land Value Taxation: Administrative Feasibility — Retrospect and Prospect

I have been puzzling over the Program Cochairman's choice of a subject for my remarks. Eleven years ago Professor Lynn asked me to speak at a TRED conference, and he gave me this topic: "Property Taxation: Policy Potential and Probabilities." Now I am to talk about the administration of land value taxation—"retrospect and prospect." In emphasizing the future in both instances, does Professor Lynn think I have an exceptionally clear crystal ball? Or does he think that the role of the soothsayer is especially suited to one who is old enough to make predictions without fear that they will expire before he does?

Administration of LVT in Retrospect

Land value taxation looks more attractive to me in retrospect than in prospect, whether I view it from a policy standpoint or from an administrative standpoint. In a manner similar to a reformed drunk whose advocacy of abstinence delights the WCTU, I delighted my friends who championed LVT a decade or so ago when I remarked extemporaneously (but with no subsequent regrets) that future generations would probably wish our own generation had followed the advice of Henry George, just as we might well wish that George's contemporaries had done so. The longer the delay, the more difficult it becomes to reap the benefits of cap-

95

turing rent surpluses because vested interests in these surpluses grow more valuable day by day. Furthermore, the owners of most of these surpluses have plausible claims to indemnification because they have acquired them to some extent out of earned incomes. In addition, the longer the delay, the more difficult it becomes to separate the "original and indestructible powers of the soil" from the improvements made by a succession of owners who have drained, irrigated, leveled, excavated, contoured, fertilized, and otherwise altered the land.[1]

Approaches

From an administrative standpoint, retrospect is not as clearly superior to prospect but is nevertheless a rather pleasant view.

Summation Appraisals

Until quite recently, summation appraisals were widely employed by private appraisers and almost exclusively by the assessors of large jurisdictions. A summation appraisal, as economists well know, is an appraisal made by adding an improvement value to a land value, each value having been derived without specific reference to the other or to the total value of the improved property. It may surprise some younger members of the profession to learn that summation appraisals were widely employed by private appraisers a generation or two ago. This is a surmise on my part based on the fact that Frederick M. Babcock published a book in 1924 titled *The Appraisal of Real Estate* (not to be confused with his 1932 book, *The Valuation of Real Estate,* in which he extolled the income approach to value, the very antithesis of the summation approach), advocating much the same urban land valuation methods that property tax assessors in some of our larger cities had been using for years.[2]

What these assessors had been doing, according to an early writer, was originated by William A. Somers in St. Paul, Minnesota, in 1896 (Boyle 1908, pp. 132–33). Center lots in each block front were appraised by a committee of citizens (not all of Somers' disciples used committees), and the values of other lots were computed from these center-lot, or "street," values by using depth formulas, corner influence rules, and so on (Somers 1901). Buildings were assessed separately after fieldmen had filled

1. Anyone who is unimpressed by the theoretical desirability and administrative impossibility of making this separation should read William Vickrey's brilliant analysis, Holland (1970).

2. I last saw this book 38 years ago and no longer have access to it. It is possible but improbable that my memory of its contents is somewhat biased.

out forms containing spaces for recording 50 facts, and were valued "at so much per square foot of ground covered" (Boyle 1908, p. 133). I have found no rural counterpart to this so-called "scientific" method of valuing urban real property. One may surmise, however, that the best assessors assigned farm land to different productivity classes and valued them at prices per acre that reflected productivity and distance to markets.

Summation appraisals had fallen from favor among private appraisers by the late 1930s. Many assessors belatedly followed suit, but summation appraisals still predominate on assessment rolls *(International Assessor* 1976, p. 14). In the absence of changes in real property tax bases, however, it seems quite likely that they eventually will be supplanted in preponderance by unit appraisals. The legal requirement that land and improvement values be stated separately on the assessment rolls seems to have strong survival powers, but allocations of unit values satisfy this requirement just as well as summation appraisals do. The accuracy of these allocations is of little significance as long as both land and improvement values are taxed at the same rate and in the same proportion to market value.

Vacant land appraisals, fractional land appraisals, and allocations of unit values would be considerably easier if there were numerous vacant land sales. These appraisals would still be difficult, however, because each land parcel is unique in location and often in its combination of other value-influencing attributes. This uniqueness, when added to the infrequency of vacant land sales and ground rentals in many areas, makes land appraising one of the more difficult tasks an assessor faces.[3]

There are ways to lessen one of these sources of difficulty. Vacant land sales and ground rentals can be supplemented with credible allocations of improved property values that are well authenticated by sales or rentals. The best such allocations come (1) from sales of properties whose improvements are to be razed by their purchasers at relatively slight net costs and (2) from sales or rentals of properties with recently constructed improvements that have suffered none of the ravages of time and are believed to be well suited to their sites.

Vacant Land Valuation

In some cases these allocations of improved property values are even more credible evidence of land values than vacant land sales prices. Vacant land sales prices may be suspect for at least two reasons. First, if such

3. Like Donald Beach (Holland 1970, p. 91), I take exception to the belief of some LVT advocates that land valuation as a whole is easier than building valuation as a whole.

a sale occurs in an area largely improved with buildings that are old but not old enough to be ready for demolition, the price of the vacant lot is likely to be well below what appear to be reasonable allocations of sales prices or capitalized rentals of improved properties in the area. Who wants to improve a vacant lot which is surrounded by decadent improvements? (But, then, who knows how to allocate the sales price or capitalized rental of an improved property when the improvement is substantially depreciated?)

A second problem with vacant land sales is the difficulty of analyzing some sales prices. I would be the last one to renounce the use of sales prices to estimate market values. But they cannot be used blindly without jeopardizing the validity of the value conclusions. When part of the consideration in the sale contract is discharged by means other than cash or something readily convertible at face value into cash (e.g., when the seller loans the buyer part of the purchase price at less than a market rate of interest), the nominal price is not necessarily the "cash equivalent." Moreover, when the purchaser acquires less than an unencumbered fee simple estate, e.g., when the buyer assumes a mortgage (the face value of which is not necessarily the amount to be added to the price paid for the encumbered fee), the purchase price is not the full market value the assessor is usually seeking. Finally, when the purchaser is paying the seller for improvements not yet constructed—a golf course or a clubhouse, for example—the price includes property not yet in existence and hence not taxable. Vacant land sales, I suspect, are proportionately more often subject to these ailments than improved property sales.

Nonvacant Land Valuation

When vacant land values are inferred from allocations of perfectly derived unit values of improved properties, they are suspect for another reason. In theory the allocation is simple enough: just deduct from a unit value the depreciated replacement cost of the improvements. In practice, we are confronted by the inexorable fact that accrued depreciation defies accurate measurement, especially when, as is so often the case, it contains obsolescence as well as physical depreciation. It is for this reason, of course, that residually derived land values are generally considered highly reliable only when the improvements are totally depreciated or not depreciated at all.

Up to this point I have been concerned with the paucity of bare land sales prices and their proxies and with the quality of sales prices as evidence of bare land values. The other closely related obstacle the land appraiser faces is the uniqueness of each land parcel. Because of its uniqueness, a perfectly derived land value is clearly applicable only to the parcel for which it was derived; it is not necessarily transferable to any other parcel. What are the best ways of making the comparisons by which to derive a value for an unsold (and unrented) parcel from the value of a recently sold (or rented) parcel?

The conventional approach often requires two or three steps. First, the sale price will usually need to be time-adjusted to the price that would probably have been negotiated as of the assessment date. Next, if the recently sold lot is not of standard size, shape, topography, and so on, the sale price will need to be rectified by use of a depth table, a width table, a shape rule, a corner influence rule, an alley influence rule, and so on, until an assumed sale price of a standard lot has been derived. Finally, the standard lot value must be transferred to nearby nonstandard lots by using the same tables and rules in reverse. How much confidence one can place in these tables and rules is questionable. At any rate, they are probably better than the nonstandardized, undisciplined lump-sum or piecemeal adjustments used by the skeptics — especially if the rules have been tested locally against the market rather than, as is too often the case, merely copied from practices in some other assessment jurisdiction.

However, a standard lot value is seldom good for more than a few block fronts (and sometimes not even for all of one front or for two facing fronts). One must resort to interpolation and even to that much more dangerous art, extrapolation, to fill the gaps between and beyond the lots whose values are firmly pinned on sales or rentals.

Agricultural Land Valuation

Valuation of agricultural land has a different set of problems. Aside from trees, vines, dairy barns, and poultry sheds, improvements contribute relatively little to the value of most farms. Therefore, sales prices and capitalized rentals can be allocated between land and improvements with little danger of materially distorting land values. When the land in a recently sold or rented farm is fairly homogeneous, a credible value per acre can be derived easily. This value then can be transferred to other farmland of like quality that is similarly located relative to markets and the amenities that make farming an attractive way of life.

Difficulties arise, however, when the farm that serves as a benchmark contains nonhomogeneous land. Now the farm's value must be allocated not only between land and improvements but among land areas of different quality. In much of California, and probably in all of the other agriculturally oriented states, there are soil surveys and productivity indexes that can be used to delineate areas of a nonhomogeneous farm and allocate values among the areas.

Interpolation between benchmark farm values would not be an

especially difficult process, except that farms which are seemingly alike in all respects aside from size have rather different values per acre. As a matter of elementary logic one would expect a farm that was too small to constitute a viable economic unit to have a lower price per acre than a larger farm. What seems to defy logic is the discovery by rural appraisers that large farms sell for less per acre than medium-sized farms, other things equal, even though the large farms can be divided at virtually no cost into medium-sized ones.

With three or more important variables affecting farm values — productivity, location relative to markets and amenities, and size — and no conventional rules for dealing with all of these variables, farms would seem to be a natural subject for appraisal by multiple regression analysis (MRA). It is inconceivable to me that no assessor has successfully employed this method of appraising rural land, yet I know of no such assessor. Perhaps the widespread abandonment of market value as the standard on which to tax farmland has discouraged extension of MRA to this kind of property.

Difficult as it is to appraise urban land and farmland, those parts of an assessor's responsibilities can be discharged with relative ease as compared with the appraisal of transitional land. Here the problem is mainly the prediction of timing. How soon will commercial farmland be converted into subsistence farms or rural homesites? When will rural acreage be subdivided, and how long will it take to market the subdivision lots? How rapidly will the area's population grow, and in which direction from the central city will it spread? Will the planning and zoning authorities hasten or delay the transition in a particular area? The questions are highly relevant to value, and their answers are highly elusive.

Land Valuation in Prospect

The spectacular success with which multiple regression analysis has been applied to the appraisal of residential properties has encouraged LVT advocates and has spawned a multitude of studies by academicians and property assessment contractors of its applicability to land valuation. Before taking a look at this prospect, however, let me pause briefly to mention two other less esoteric prospects.

The British Columbia Assessment Authority has designed computer programs with which to implement the conventional urban land value process. They were described by George L. Hamilton, one of the Authority's area assessors, at a colloquium that the Lincoln Institute sponsored in 1979. These programs permit the assessor to initiate or change the value ascribed to a standard lot on a block front and let the computer derive the values of all lots for which this standard is used. They also permit the assessor to initiate or choose a depth table, a width table, and other adjustments of the standard lot specifications. The system is designed to assure greater speed, accuracy, and economy in the application of conventional land assessment practices.

The second prospect I want to mention before turning to MRA has been used in the District of Columbia for about 20 years. It was described by Kenneth Back, the District's Director of Finance and Revenue, in an excellent paper prepared for the 1969 TRED conference (Holland 1970), and by its inventor, John Rackham, at the Lincoln Institute colloquium. The part of the program that is most significant for this paper is a method of dividing the value of an improved property between the land and the improvements. Having no means of testing it, I am not prepared to advocate it; I would commend it to the attention of those with research facilities.[4]

Multiple Regression Analysis

We come at last to MRA. The "exciting future" which I predicted for this appraisal method when I discussed it in 1967 has indeed been realized. But its success thus far has been largely if not entirely confined to improved residential properties. Applications to other property have been, for the most part, academic exploratory exercises. What are the prospects for application to land valuation problems?

I do not pretend to be in close touch with the assessment world any longer, and it has been many years since I was close to academia. My observations must be judged with these limitations in mind.

Paul Downing's paper at the 1969 TRED conference and the papers presented at the Lincoln Institute's recent colloquium on land valuation do not reveal a large measure of progress in the application of MRA to land valuation. Professor Downing concluded that "The predictive power of this technique is much less than was hoped for" but that "it provides a useful starting point for land value assessments" (Holland 1970,

---

4. The procedure employs two equations:

$$(1) \quad \frac{\text{Total value of property at age } n}{\text{Replacement cost new of bldg. at age } n} - \frac{\text{Land ratio at age } 0}{\text{Bldg ratio at age } 0} = \text{Bldg percent good at age } n$$

$$(2) \quad \text{Land ratio at age } n = \frac{\text{Land ratio at age } 0}{\text{Bldg ratio at age } 0 \times \text{Bldg percent good at age } n - \text{Land ratio at age } n}$$

"Age" refers to age of improvements. "Land ratio" means the ratio of land value to total value, and "Bldg ratio" means the ratio of building value to total value. These ratios at age 0 (zero) are derived from sales of newly improved lots; they presumably vary from one area to another.

p. 123). David Jensen, the Calspan representative at the Lincoln Institute's colloquium, reported inconclusive results from an experiment in a small bedroom community near Boston, Massachusetts, with models that "represented the sales data reasonably well [but] failed to perform up to expectations when applied to unsold parcels of particularly improved land." Cynthia Ray, of Barton-Aschman Associates, concluded at the colloquium with the finding that "computer-generated estimates more closely approximated market values than the existing assessments . . . [but] the current assessments were the most uniform" and that "a refined modeling effort for vacant land [should] be pursued." Robert Soma, Assessor of Washoe County, Nevada, reported on successful use of MRA to appraise a largely vacant subdivision in the Lake Tahoe area. However, the program used was the one developed for improved residential properties, and it is my impression that Soma does not intend to develop regression models tailored to land valuation objectives. The most upbeat conclusion at the Lincoln Institute's colloquium was that of Jack Lessinger; this University of Washington researcher, using research tools that seem promising, is pursuing goals that will culminate with an offer to assessors and others to cooperate in implementation of his method under actual field conditions.

Two problems confront the user of MRA when deriving land values. One is the scarity of established land values with which to construct and test regression models and implement those that pass the test. The other is the scarcity of appropriate independent variables to regress against those values.

The first of these problems is common to conventional land appraisal methods and MRA, so it has already been discussed. It was pointed out in earlier passages that actual sales and rentals of unimproved land can be supplemented with sales and rentals of properties with improvements that are either undepreciated or fully depreciated. Even with this supplementation, I think that MRA enthusiasts will often be hampered by inadequate data.

The second problem arises largely from the importance of location as a land value determinant and the difficulty of quantifying location. Quantification of location by measuring the distance or travel time from an urban site to the central business district (CBD) may have been sufficient at one time, but it is no longer enough. Accessibility to employment centers, shopping centers, amusement centers, and elsewhere is as important as accessibility to the CBD, and none of these amenities is as easily identified as the CBD. Several of the other land value determinants, such as view and the neighborhood value trend, are subjective. Some useful variables, such as income level and ethnic composition, are measurable only at decennial intervals, since the U.S. Census is the only credible source. Only such mundane and comparatively unimportant considerations as width, depth, area, shape, corner or inside location, and availability of utilities are indisputable, objective, and current.

Most of the problem of location variables, MRA enthusiasts hope, can be eliminated or reduced to insignificant proportions by dividing the assessment district into a multitude of neighborhoods. But with each subdivision of the assessment district, the problem of the small number of land value observations becomes more acute. The smaller the neighborhoods, the less the variation in land characteristics and the less the need for MRA.

Conclusion

While land and improvements are equally taxed, MRA will be used widely to derive unit values of residential properties and to a lesser extent to derive unit values of other property use types. Most of the MRA programs will provide for allocation of unit values between land and improvements, but few honest assessors will claim that these allocations are highly accurate. Should exemption of improvements or lesser degrees of differential taxation be adopted, MRA will be used less extensively, and conventional land valuation methods will regain some of their former popularity. The imperfections of these older appraisal methods, and of MRA-developed values where they are prepared, will be tolerated because owners of most improved properties have only a vague notion of the land portions of unit values and almost no evidence with which to fortify whatever notions they have.[5]

The loss of value evidence is a sobering thought. Development of assessment ratio findings by state equalization agencies (and by the Bureau of the Census) will come to a halt. Without such findings, the deterioration of assessment levels will be encouraged and taxpayers will be deprived of their best protection against *relative* overassessment (Welch 1977, pp. 139–45). So it is essential, in my judgment, that adoption of LVT be associated with (1) repeal of all laws that make interjurisdictional equalization of assessments necessary or desirable and (2) enactment of laws that will assure substantial improvements in the competence of assessment personnel and the quality of their product.

5. Back (Holland 1970) has expressed the opinion that conversion of the property tax to LVT would increase appeals. Perhaps it would in the first year or two (as would a reassessment where LVT is not in use); I would expect it to have the opposite effect after a short transition period.

References

Boyle, James E. 1908. "Methods of Assessment as Applied to Different Classes of Subjects." In *Proceedings of the First (1907) National Conference on State and Local Taxation,* New York: Macmillan.

Holland, Daniel, ed. 1970. *The Assessment of Land Values,* Madison: Univ. of Wisconsin Press.

International Association of Assessing Officers. 1976. "Empirical Data on the Three Approaches to Value," *International Assessor,* 42, no. 4:14.

Somers, William A. 1901. *Valuation of Real Estate for Purposes of Taxation.* St. Paul, Minn.

Welch, Ronald B. 1977. "Use of State Ratio Findings in the Local Equalization Process." In *Proceedings of the Sixty-Eighth (1976) Annual Conference on Taxation.* Columbus, Ohio: National Tax Association – Tax Institute of America.

Comment Centered on Land Valuation

Arthur D. Lynn, Jr.: There was one discussion in Mary Teachout's paper where I sensed as an academic observer that those people who tend to deal with reality had a slight difference of opinion.

Ronald B. Welch: I would like to add something to what I said this morning to prove I have two arms. Teachout pointed out afterwards in our discussion that there is a difference, perhaps a material difference, between a review of a land value tax base and a general property tax value review. The land value tax base is established with the use of street values, land value maps, and so on, and that perhaps the room for maneuver isn't as great with the land tax base as it is with the general tax base. I admitted that I was thinking in terms of the general property tax, but it needs some better thinking than I had brought to it at the spur of the moment.

Lynn: Are there any further comments on this?

Mary Teachout: I think another reason is that under our proposal the assessors would be subject to a high level of public exposure on the work they were doing. The land value map is going to be posted in every bus stop and post office; there is going to be an incentive within the assessment departmnent to be accountable to the public. The assessment decisions they reached will be something that they must live with. Having them posted in each and every bus stop assures that.

Another matter is, as Ken Back pointed out, if you have an outside assessment agency, it may be very hard to find local personnel who can act as hearing officers. Not many will have the requisite knowledge and expertise on assessing matters.

William S. Vickrey: An outside review agency?

Teachout: Right, an outside review agency may be needed.

Lynn: Other comments?

Vickrey: In a sense, the technique of publishing the maps and the values would be available also with the general property tax, where you have more or less identical houses, such as in many suburban communities. There you may have two lots cheek by jowl similar in every respect but with quite different buildings on them; and land value produces an immediate and almost glaring opportunity for objection to improper assessment. However, if the assessments are equal and proper, but different on the houses, it is not easy for the taxpayer to protest or to realize that he should protest.

Teachout: It is much easier for the taxpayer to figure out the amount he should pay in the case of land valuations only.

H. Clyde Reeves: I think indeed anybody considering this problem gets two-handed very readily because there are advantages and disadvantages to either side. In making a choice, I think it is well to bear in mind that traditionally and historically the independent review agency operated in a simplistic way. It was a committee that reviewed the property and co-exercised a kind of overseerage. They were appointed because they were nice people. They had good sense. They were good businessmen. They were not tax professionals in any sense of the word.

Now there is a tendency, I think, in this country, even at the state level, to appoint those same kind of people to independent review agencies and the problem is not that simplistic. I would say that the principal thing to do if you are going to have an indepentent review agency, is to try to establish safeguards to professionalize it, so that it can confront the problem where the problem is.

Teachout: Are you talking about establishing professional qualifications?

Reeves: Yes.

Vickrey: I was wondering in the earlier presentation this morning, what does your ceiling really amount to?

Teachout: What we have actually done with the site value concept is to try to use it as a legal definition for taxable land value for assessment purposes. We thought from a legal point of view we couldn't define it accurately enough i.e., we couldn't achieve an acceptable level of legal definition for site value.

I think the same problem would exist if you put 70 percent site value as a ceiling, because you are taking a percentage of what we can't define for legal purposes. So what happens is that we use current market value and the legal standard for taxable value, but we use the site value concept basically as a tool in constructing the assessment. We are imposing a ceiling only to the extent that the value of buidling improvements and value of submineral rights are excluded from taxable value.

Then we go further in the law to say that the value of subsurface mineral rights and the existence of mineral improvements are specifically excluded from land value. However, our legal definitions for taxable value would not purport to include all the things that our site value includes, meaning permanent improvements to the land.

Vickrey: It is a little reminiscent of the old fable about the farmer who made a pact with the devil. The devil could have everything below the ground and the farmer took everything above the ground. The farmer planted corn. The next year the devil took everything above the ground and the farmer had everything below. So the farmer planted potatoes.

Your definition includes some of this type of thinking. Everything that goes above the ground is building or structure and everything that goes below is land.

Teachout: That is the way it seems. I don't think we want to come out that way necessarily. At the moment, our definition for site value is concerned with the value of the land for land use purposes rather than the value of the land to the owner. Value of the land to the owner may include mineral rights which he can process to his benefit, in addition to the surface use of the land.

Matthew Edel: Rather than talking about site value, it might be simpler to say that if the current improvements have a negative value to the land, they get excluded.

Teachout: You would suggest excluding those demolition costs from taxable value?

Edel: Yes.

Teachout: We really haven't looked carefully at that problem. That is one of the next steps that we must examine, but I do not think our tentative solution lies in that direction.

Edel: I can see conflicts both ways on that.

Vickrey: In line with your exemptions, you might, say, assess at the net value of the property after deducting the demolition costs; then after the house is demolished you would exempt for ten years the improvements that result from demolishing the building.

Teachout: I think that is a possibility. This is one of the reasons we have attempted to move to a site value concept that is not specific but can vary from one jurisdiction to another.

C. Lowell Harriss: The study is obviously quite interesting; I would certainly like to give my moral support to further research. As a practical matter I would also suggest that if you have only limited resources, they might better be directed into the excise tax aspect of the problem. This seems more desirable because any future change in the United States will not likely be a change on a national scale but rather within particular communities or on a statewide basis. Therefore, methodology for examining potential effects in limited areas might be more generally useful than the broader nationwide aggregate action.

I would like to go back to Mary Teachout's presentation to underscore the desirability of establishing procedures for public education and information. I know that there are people here who know a good deal more about the need for this than I do. However, my general impression from Taiwan, where there is public participation in the land value assessment, is that the public over the years has gotten an education. The interested parties know what is involved so that they can participate, if not happily, at least to allay fears to their own satisfaction. My general impression in the United States is that we have become so accustomed to poor valuation that getting our mind straightened out on full value of property would take quite a bit of education. Yet I think it could be done if we spend a little time on it, rather than on whatever else we spend our time.

You probably know that at one time New York City published tax maps; you could buy the map of your part of town for 25 cents. However, that was abandoned in the 1930s, I believe.

Philip Finkelstein: The excuse Mayor LaGuardia gave was that they were saving paper for the war effort.

Welch: I had some concern about the appeal procedure that Mary spoke about. I got the impression that an assessment and an appeal were both handled by the same agency. I would be the first to admit that having separate agencies doesn't produce good results, but I think it is preferable to having the same agency handle both procedures. To have the assessors handle the appeals is dangerous for the assessing agency, and I don't think it is desirable for the taxpayer.

On the latter point, the taxpayer who has an independent agency to which to appeal thinks he has an appeal even though he might not. I think the public relations aspects are sufficiently great to justify a separate appeals agency. From the standpoint of the assessing agency, I think it is destructive to morale to have the heads of the assessment agency overruling their technical staff, since the supervisors frequently are not technically qualified. On the other hand, a staff could survive an outside agency doing it. Their response would be "Well, they didn't know what they were doing, but that is the way it goes."

Teachout: I appreciate those comments. I think the particular structure of the public appeals is something we must examine more carefully. This very situation has been a problem in many areas where we have an agency administering and hearing appeals on the same matters. One of the things that we have to develop in the future is a different type of agency, in order to find the best possible workable model for separating out the people who do technical work in the first place, and people who hear the appeals and make decisions on them.

My own question is as follows: Do you feel the alternative of having taxpayers appeal directly to the courts is preferable?

Welch: No, I agree with your concept there. That is, unless you want to define courts in a somewhat different manner. Under your procedure you have a specialized court. It is called a court, but in this context it is really equivalent to an administrative agency. I think the specialized court can handle the appeal satisfactorily, or at least as well as any other government agency. But I don't think the general courts are qualified to operate in this field, and I would particularly dislike having the New York system imposed upon other states. Pennsylvania is another one that has the same sort of system as New York State. I think the results of those experiences speak for themselves.

Vickrey: Of course the moment you call it an open court you tend to cause the courts to be formal.

Welch: The best example of tax courts is in Oregon, and I don't think the courts there have suffered the fate of being too formal. But it is a possibility.

Reeves: I want to make one point here. When you have an appeal to a court or board, and you have a decision appeal procedure, the agency as well as the taxpayer should have the right to appeal.

Kenneth C. Back: I have been through both sides of this issue, i.e., the assessment and appeals function in the department, but we have now gone to an outside appeal agency. Unfortunately, they have done a poor job in my opinion. We do not have the right to appeal their decision to the courts, so we must do something about that. I also agree that you get a much better job done if the appeal is not heard by the individual assessor who made the assessment; however, the appeal still should be heard in the office of the assessor.

What you encounter with an outside agency is that they are not staffed and therefore become basically political appointments. Conscientious as they might try to be, the agencies are not prepared to do a job on an appeal on a large valuation of millions of dollars. They have no appraisal staff.

I would like to go back and comment on what I think Mary Teachout was saying. By the way, I don't understand why market value isn't enough for assessing purposes and why you worry about it. Once the system is established and you went through the pains and tortures of getting your first land values set, you are ready for the main job — assessing properties. The main job on land valuation will be the easiest part of the assessor's job, if he knows how to go about it.

I can assure you that people in towns know the value on a bulding separate from the land if you talk to them. You have to know the right people, those who know what the values are, and you must separate them because they will talk about each other when they are separated. Land values can be found; that has been my experience in the District of Columbia.

What bothers me in these discussions is some idea on land use comes out from the concept of site value, but I don't know what that is. Vickrey has been trying to tell me for years. I think it is too late now for you to teach me.

Dick Netzer: Vickrey, you once worked in New York City and I live there now. New York is now a single tax city. All future new investments in buildings are tax exempt. Somebody might speculate on what that is going to do.

Vickrey: Is this assured or just unofficial?

Netzer: No, there is no new construction that isn't included.

Finkelstein: This is the expectation.

Netzer: Yes, 90 percent of tax is abated the first year.

Vickrey: How long does the abatement continue?

Finkelstein: In ten years, the structure is supposed to be fully on the tax rolls.

Netzer: And if it is housing?

Vickrey: Only if it is middle income housing.

Netzer: No, I believe it applies to anything new.

Weld S. Carter: That is a complete abatement. It is not just for other improvements.

Netzer: Basically, what you start with is a freeze of existing taxes, then the taxes on the further investment are abated. It is in the direction of single tax.

Vickrey: Well, it saved New York.

Richard W. Lindholm: Becker, do you have any comment on how you think Proposition 13 is going to work out in California?

Arthur P. Becker: In connection with the question of inflation, it seems to me there ought to be a drastic increase in realty values in California as a result of reducing the property tax from $14 billion down to $7 billion. Although this might increase the income tax collections by $1.5 to $2 billion, there still is a net gain to property owners of about $5 billion. If you capitalize that at 10 percent you have a $50 billion sudden increase in realty values, or at least the possibility of values going that high. That amount, plus all the foreign money coming in, will create all kinds of special situations that will add to the inflation.

Roy W. Bahl: I don't know anything about Proposition 13, but when you were talking about that, it seemed to me that the expenditure base of local government would decline. The decline in expenditures and government benefits available would work in the other direction and property values would decline.

Becker: I am not sure that expenditures are going to drop rapidly in California. We need several more years.

Vickrey: Well, if you couple Proposition 13 limits on local revenues together with state funds that are running out, this certainly means fewer employees and fewer services.

Bahl: Which could be capitalized.

Becker: Well, service charges are being established here and there. That would offset it a little bit, I suppose. The income tax has been slashed, what is it, by $1 billion, so people will have a little extra money to spend on other things, maybe buy services from private individuals, i.e., use private sector garbage firms.

Vickrey: They will have another confrontation on local regulation of generalized service charges.

Reeves: The assessed value of property when sold would be increased; therefore it would pay more taxes than if it wasn't sold. This occurs if you have increased property values by virtue of Proposition 13. All the more reason for adding the land value tax.

Karl Falk: Speculating now not in land but in ideas, if some of the provisions that H. Clyde Reeves has talked about in Proposition 13 stick, I wonder to what extent ownership of property may change? You might find a lot of people leasing in order to avoid the new higher assessment and the new higher tax.

Welch: The legislature understood the leasing possibilities and therefore passed a law that, I think, treats a lease of ten years or more as a sale and invokes the new value. I am not sure that it will hold up in court and I am not quite certain about the number of years, but shorter term leases certainly could be employed.

Another thing that is going to happen in all probability is an owner sells a property that is decreasing in value rather than rising; then the new owner can take advantage of the new value that comes from the sale. All kinds of crazy things may happen.

I would like to ask about the incidence of taxation. In the event of a sale, the Property tax will rise rather considerably in many instances, at least after a few more years, but we already have a 1975 base so there is considerable capital gain that can be realized by sale. Will the higher tax to which the new buyer is subject be capitalized in the form of a lower purchase price or not? I think the experts in incidence will come up with an immediate answer.

Netzer: This is a perfect case in which it has to be capitalized. You are dealing with a marginal situation, truly marginal transaction at the margin. Of course it will be capitalized. The sale price will still be higher than it would have been before Proposition 13, because of the other part of it which is the tax limit. Nothing is going to vitiate that benefit.

Welch: I would like to have your immediate response to another point. Suppose there had been no reduction in the tax rate, but only the requirement that the tax or the value remain constant until a sale occurs. Under those circumstances would the higher price that the buyer would pay then be fully or substantially fully capitalized?

Netzer: We're talking about a case in which nothing else has happened except that the system is altered, so that (1) if you didn't sell the property, you had a freeze in valuation and (2) if you sold the property, it was valued at the market rate. If this was the only differentiation, then present owners would get all the windfall gains or losses associated with the change.

Vickrey: I think you have to examine the motives behind the buyer and the seller. If you are thinking of sellers who are selling in one location because their family is growing or declining and they want a larger or smaller house in another location, then the tax freeze is going to inhibit strongly their desire to place their property on the market. Therefore, the supply of properties for sale is going to go down. I think you start with that.

What does it do on the demand side? Well, there are also properties, of course, that go on the market because the owner dies or they are moving out of the jurisdiction entirely for some good reason. Unless they are going to convert the sale into a lease to get around the restrictions the legislature placed on them, they are going to have to sell anyway. I don't really see that it changes things all that much.

You still have people who want to buy property. To the extent that property values are rising, the fact that they can have assessments frozen at whatever level they buy in at means that it is more important for them to get a lower price, since that will reduce their taxes. If they take that into account, they probably won't buy. On the whole, I think the buyers are likely to be more eager to buy because of the tax freeze.

Vickrey: If people are moving, this demand will shift, and there will be further transactions but at the same price.

Netzer: As far as single family houses are concerned, the largest number of transactions are the ones involving people moving from one house to another in the same general area, upgrading the family composition, something of that sort. In those transactions you have fewer of them, but nothing else will change.

Daniel M. Holland: Do I hear three possible answers developing? I think I did. The answers seemed to be that the price may go up, the price may go down, and the higher value may be borne by the owner, and it may be borne by the buyer.

Vickrey: We have the three-handed economist.

Holland: We also have to remind ourselves that the meaning of inflation is comparative rather than absolute. When you ask about the effect of the land inflation on tax, you also have to ask: Comparable to what? Comparable to another tax which is widely available, such as the income tax for example, or to some other revenue source. I believe the effect of inflation has been much less decimating to the income tax than to the property tax.

Alan R. Prest: That is because the property tax is not progressive.

Vickrey: On the other hand, if you do the accounting rigorously, inflation produces an income tax base that is a real net income plus a percentage of net worth. For some purposes that is a better tax base than the traditional income base.

Holland: Yes, for the purposes of abstract values such as equity and others, but not for the retention of the original intent of the legislated tax and rates.

If you do the accounting correctly, many people on net balance will have no spurious capital gains but real capital gains and the debt burden will have declined, so on net balance you will be better off. The implication of spurious capital gains is an inaccurate assessment of many situations.

Vickrey: If someone borrows to invest in stocks that show a capital gain and then he is excused from paying the tax on the capital gains on the grounds that it is spurious gain in terms of inflation, he probably won't be denied the deduction for the interest that he paid in order to carry these securities.

Prest: That is really saying you can't index the income tax without changing many other basic provisions in the tax law.

Vickrey: Exactly.

Holland: At least to our satisfaction, but Congress seems to be happy.

Vickrey: Anything that produces a correction also creates new opportunities to reduce taxes. Every loophole is subject to leverage. That is, it is one thing to say you will index capital gains if you have in mind a person whose assets are purely in capital assets without liabilities. The problem is that the moment you allow him to do this with his assets, he will borrow in order to take advantage of this and you will have the phenomenon of a person who borrows to carry tax-exempt bonds.

Lindholm: Well, the IRS has a provision regarding that.

Vickrey: Yes. I wonder if anybody knows how long it has been since that provision was actually invoked.

Lindholm: I don't know, but it is the law.

Netzer: It is invoked if you put it down on the return.

Prest: How many do put it on the return?

Holland: Evidently no one here.

Welch: One of the effects of inflation in the property tax field, as I am sure you are aware, is the shifting away from tax rate restriction to restriction on the levy. I think you are going to see a large number of such shifts. A major reason California has Proposition 13 is that they had a dual limitation. They had a tax rate limit and a levy limit, and you could take the larger of the two. With inflation the tax rate limit becomes much less oppressive as a budget limitation than does the levy limitation. I think California will soon have only a levy limitation. Even though California has a tax rate limitation, I think it is going to be wiped out, in effect, by a supplementary levy limit. It will be eliminated by something more restrictive than the one percent rate limit and it will be applied to all levels of government.

Edel: I am trying to relate some of this up-to-date practical discussion to the things Henry George had in mind. We should remember that even before George, one of the major arguments for the land tax was that it would discourage speculation, and that land speculation was seen as a major cause for depressions. Current land speculation, may the land price increases by two-tiered, many tiered, or affecting all levels, is in fact interrupting the more normal economic relationships. This effect exists in the capital sector and market sector in terms of supplying one of the major consumer goods to the work force, that is, housing. The evidence is not in yet whether inflation will reduce housing. I think, however, that this possibility has to be kept well in mind. It is not just the question of the effect of inflation on the ease or difficulty of collecting taxes, it is how inflation is affecting the functioning of the economy.

Vickrey: I am no longer convinced I want site values. Operationally what I want is assessment independent of what the man does with the property; that can be a figure that is produced by some complicated formula that includes, say, distance from the CBD, or accessibility, and so on. You mix this together into one formula and, since there is nothing in the formula that relates to how the property is actually being used, you have the property value that you are seeking in the site value tax.

If I want to get 100 percent, or nearly that, of the site value rents for public purposes, then I must have a formula that tracts site values quite closely. However, as long as I am only taking 50 percent of the site rental value for public purposes, the problems of setting value are negligible. The closer you get to the ideal, the greater the difficulty.

Mason F. Gaffney: I must have been wool gathering. I heard you say we had to abandon intercounty equalization, but I didn't catch the reason why.

Welch: Because we don't have any acceptable tests for assessment level anymore. Sales are not meaningful. Capitalizing income is not meaningful. The best you can do is have a state agency to second guess the assessment, and I don't think that is worth much. Nobody knows what the valuation is, so why second guess?

Gaffney: I missed the reason why sales are no longer meaningful.

Welch: Because you don't have enough of them to do you any good. You have a few, but some of these are suspect in themselves. You may have a few good sales of totally depreciated or totally unappreciated property, but not enough to provide you with a land assessment level to use, in my judgement.

Gaffney: Well, the first reason you gave why the sales weren't valid was because the property might have a lease and it seems to me that is more likely to be a case with improved land than vacant land.

Welch: That is true, but you do have these cases, which have been quite common in California recently, where a person subdivides property and he has a planned unit development. He agrees to put in a golf course, a clubhouse, and so on, and the price includes these future property ownership benefits. Value is not just in the property you are buying, and at least for a time you are going to have to adjust for that. I am sure there are many other illustrations.

Gaffney: Back to your original point where you say there are not enough sales. You must have in mind a small county; if, for example, you are comparing Los Angeles and San Bernardino County, you would have a lot of sales.

Welch: Of course, sales are always a poor test of the proper assessment level because they are not randomly distributed over your universe. However, when you are confined to bare land sales, I think you become even less representative of the assessment role. Again, I have no data with which to support my assertion.

Gaffney: Thank you.

Finkelstein: I tried to understand the objection to the use of sales data. If sales data are not reliable, the paucity of them is not a defect.

Prest: Would you get along without anything?

Finkelstein: That is the point.

Welch: Exactly. I am sure I made that clear in my statement. I am the last one to renounce the use of sales, since they are the test of value, but unfortunately in this instance we have fewer of them than we want. We don't have them distributed randomly over the universe we want — I am going back to assessment levels for a moment — but I think we have a real problem; we have to recognize that we are going to have a less equalized property tax base if we are using land value rather than total property value. I don't think that is included in my remarks. However, that is not a reason why we can't move to a site value tax, because there are a good many pluses in site value taxation.

Harriss: There is no virtue in repeating what was said, except that other people won't remember it was said before. Yet, it has always seemed to me that the higher the tax rate applicable to land or site value, that is, to the absolute rate, the greater the need for quality assessment. Therefore, the strains on the assessment process will be greater. This I think is one of the real problems of a shift to site value taxation. There will be larger disputes over the value of land as a portion of the value of the total property.

One of the points involved, on which Back can speak, is the use for income tax purposes of property tax values. The owner is interested in making the relative value of buildings high so depreciation costs can be larger.

Vickrey: I always come back to land value tax in the first place. I raised the question that perhaps what we don't want is not literally land value tax, but a tax that is independent to the use of the property. If you are willing to take that definition of the objective, then it is of no consequence that multiple regression analysis doesn't reproduce market value. It seems to me that we may be after the wrong solution. It is wrong to judge the quality of an assessment system by how closely it tracts market value. It is more important that it provides a secure and certain system for raising revenues independent of what the taxpayer does with the property.

Now you do have questions of equity. All right, well, this again comes to the point of transition. We are at the point where we are going to have a transition from what we have to something else. In this transition there will be inequities in terms of upsetting what people have come to regard as legitimate expectations. However, I see no reason that the inequities of transition of land value tax should be any greater than the transition to any other kind of arbitrary assessment that is independent of what the taxpayer does with the property.

In the long run, of course, if you have a set of prospective future tax payments that are well defined, this gets capitalized into values and the question of equity gradually washes out no matter how arbitrary or how capricious the assessment seems to be, as long as they are fixed and certain.

Becker: What about the inefficiency? When you have inefficiency, they won't wash out.

Vickrey: As long as there is no end abuse, you get efficiency. In two properties, if it is known for all time that one property costs $1,000 in taxation and the other costs $500 tax per year, and they are identical properties, you won't get inefficient use.

Lindholm: The market value of the identical property carrying the $1,000 tax would be lower than the $500 tax property. The difference in value given to identical properties is not important in the case of land because a reproduction cost or a depreciated value does not exist. There is, however, the point that the land with the higher tax can be more readily purchased by the less wealthy person because the capital cost would be less. The higher tax acts the same as the cost of additional borrowed funds that the less wealthy person may not be able to command.

Carter: Well, we have a very imperfect assessment situation at the present time; however, we have gotten along with that for a long time and it is theoretically based on market values. It seems to me that one consideration is the effect on the market for land if you institute a system of land value tax, in which the tax is removed from improvements. Would that improve the market process? Would there be more of a market for land or would there be less? Anything that would improve the market process should improve the assessment process. Even though we have had an imperfect assessment process, it has been viable; any improvements upon it should certainly result in a more viable system. If we institute a land value tax, we also lessen the complications of the assessment process by getting rid of the major job that the assessor now has to do. The system that results is a vastly improved and more accurate assessment procedure.

Gaffney: I would like to return to your comment on values of land in slum areas, Welch, although you didn't use that word. I forget how you described it, a rundown area. When we did our Milwaukee land value map, we got extremely low values for sales of vacant land in slum areas, but true to our principles we spread those around and put low values under the buildings throughout that area. I gather from what you say, however, that the common process is not to do that. I assume from this

position of yours that the sale of vacant land is somehow not a true in-
dicator of the worth of the land under a house in a slum area.

Welch: I don't know what the common practice is on that. It would be
difficult to make an allocation on land out of the total value of the property. Back knows more about this than I do, although he doesn't have
too many vacant lots to worry about.

Back: Yes, there are not very many vacant lots in Washington, D.C.
My experience mostly has been with urban built-up areas. Here we
work with a group of people, including realtors, builders, and contractors. I can assure you that those people can tell you what every acre of
land is worth in the city today and what they would pay for it if it were on
the market. This is generally the way we go about collecting our land
values. Certainly in doing the overall appraisal job I feel that most
assessors devote less time to land than to buildings.

One point Welch made is the aim of going to property unit valuation.
Assessors are getting away from separate assessments of land and improvements and are looking only at the total. Under current tax procedure there actually is no reason to take them apart. The only reason it
is done now in Washington, D.C., is that the law requires it. When you
begin to use unit value or Multiple Regression Analysis (MRA) or any
approach in which you get total valuation, you don't need to break it
down into land and improvements. At least in my city, you can't appeal
only one; you must appeal the total.

What we are seeing now is that assessors are increasingly avoiding the
traditional land value approach that you and I grew up with.

Welch: I agree that is the case, but I think if we put the tax solely on
land, we have to go back to land value maps, similar to those used in the
1930s. Current assessors are getting away from them because they are using MRA and are not concerned about the land value portion, only the
total value.

Netzer: I am struck by how radical this whole notion of Welch's
remark on equilization and Vickrey's doomsday book concept are. We
really live now with a property tax and a valuation system that does more
than allot a portion of the tax burden within a given jurisdiction.

In the rest of the nation the task assigned to the evaluation system is
not as simple as it is in the District of Columbia. All that is required there
is an apportioning of the tax burden amongst taxpayers in a way that
forms some generally accepted notions of personal equities and
minimizes efficiency losses in land use decisions. To meet these needs
there are a number of approaches, including Vickrey's approach, that are
feasible, but they come up with a set of numbers that can be used only
for the apportionment of taxes within that jurisdiction and no other purpose. They actually mean nothing for any other purpose.

This approach not only makes me uncomfortable professionally but it would have a major impact on the institutions of local and state government finance. In most states the valuation system is used as a measure for other purposes, i.e., tax limits, debt limits, and the like. In a real sense the approach makes a change over to site value taxation even more radical than many of us have believed. It makes sense to accept this radical solution but we should recognize just how much of a disturbance we are causing.

Holland: Why one base? Why not several bases each for a definite purpose?

Netzer: I agree, this is possible but you must realize you are talking about quite a broad range of institutional changes. If there are limitations on local taxes imposed by the state, you must determine a new way to do it because you will have numbers that are not commensurable from one place to another. You must find another system. The same would be true of debt limitations for the allocation of state aid money.

Vickrey: You would have comparable figures if you had the same MRA formula statewide.

Edel: That is incredible.

Vickrey: To carry forward in a sense what we are both saying, I think equalization has had its day. At one time the property tax was the best economic data available for various purposes including the assessment of state property taxes. But we have other sources of data now, and there is no reason that we should stick to this obsolete method of operation when we have all these other data sources available.

Becker: It disturbs me about Vickrey's point. It seems to me the tax on land ought to have some connection with the economic rent from land. You are completely at sea if this is not true.

Vickrey: Well, of course, but why do you want the value to be related to the economic rent of land?

Becker: I think there is some merit in taxing economic surplus.

Vickrey: You are clever enough to convince me about that, but you can't convince most tax people.

Netzer: I think the question is improperly put. The issue is not that you are not taxing economic rents of land but rather that you are taxing the economic rents of land under a system in which the tax rate is varied.

Netzer: As long as it is less than 100 percent.

Vickrey: As long as it is capitalized.

Welch: That brings up the transition problem.

Vickrey: We are going to have a transition problem anyway. Is some other transition system going to be more arbitrary?

Lindholm: The income tax has largely abandoned realistic economic definition of annual incomes, and therefore it has reduced this source of useful economic data. Is this the situation to be expected also in property tax administrative data?

Back: Well, I think that land can be assessed separately from buildings with a reasonable degree of accuracy. However, it would require a much greater effort and degree of accuracy in land value determination than is practiced today in most jurisdictions of which I have knowledge. I can appreciate Break's position that it would be more difficult to explain land valuation alone to the taxpayer than it is to explain a total property valuation. How many people who own homes know what the land is worth under their homes? Very few, I would guess, since vacant land sales are not readily available to the average property owner. Accordingly it would seem that the best approach to informing the property owner would be to make land valuation maps available to the public, which show the pattern of land valuation by size of lot and other peculiar characteristics for comparative purposes.

Traditionally, vacant land has been underassessed more than any other type of property. This happens because with vacant land you don't really know what is its highest and best use until it is actually committed to be developed. Someone may be working on an assembly of land parcels and at the moment the land is cheap. Suddenly it blossoms and the land is worth ten times what you assessed it for and you look terrible. So you have problems with vacant land value determination.

Most of us know how to make a land residual computation to develop land values of improved properties. While this can be done, it takes more effort than most assessors now put into it, because a high degree of accuracy doesn't mean that much to them. The taxpayer is not going to argue too much with you about the allocation between land and improvements as long as the total value is acceptable, but he might and perhaps would argue if the tax is applied only to land. Of course, the commercial property owner always wants the allocation to be high for structures in order to support large depreciation costs.

Falk: I have a comment relative to what Prest mentioned this morning. From our own savings and loans experience with appraisers, not assessors, we are finding it harder and harder to appraise. I agree absolutely with Ken Back when he says you can find people who know the worth of every piece of property in town or out in the country. Our appraisers do what they have to do with the clipboard and tape measure, and then we ask them to step across the street and take a good look at the property to develop a general evaluation. If the estimate is still in the ballpark we start adding an increase factor of about one percent a month to account for inflation.

If you don't stay somewhere near current market values, it is going to be tougher and tougher to account for the inflation, especially in areas of rapid growth and sometimes where one part of the city is growing more rapidly than others. Not only is there a time element involved but I still think it is not impossible to establish value. I still feel that a good place to base it is somewhere approaching the market value.

I also want to toss in the thought that perhaps inflation and rapidly changing values are scaring us off – making us believe that any kind of an accurate assessment is impossible, land or structure. Would you respond to this observation?

Welch: I would like to respond by saying I hope I didn't give anybody the impression that the market value is not a good basis or sales is a good basis to estimate market value. I just say they are not invaluable and I say the sale of an improved property gives you only a minor clue as to the value of the land portion of the improved property.

Arlo Woolery: To what extent are foreign investors, particularly those from West Germany and Japan, giving us a two-tier price structure for land in the United States, in that they are trading with a strong currency and a different attitude towards land. They are minority purchasers at the moment, but, to the point, do they contribute to higher prices being quoted to the buyer?

Falk: We have had some in our area, and they have been ready to pay inflated prices for farmland. In Southern California we also have people who sold their citrus groves to developers. These farmers came north and they didn't know what land was worth. They have just ruined the market completely. I think you are putting your finger on a very good thought – we are beginning to get a two-tiered market in real estate as well as in land value.

Finkelstein: An urban prospective would give a slightly different cast. There is no special two-tiered effect as a result of the foreign investments, but rather the foreign investments seem to be concentrated on the higher ranges of the market, that is, the most valuable and the most desirable properties. What is happening is that the gap between the most desirable parts of New York and the rest of the city is widening in prices, in values, and so forth, so that prices in midtown and downtown Manhattan have gone through anybody's roof. The rest of the city has not quite caught up and is probably falling behind, and I have a strong suspicion that the same is happening in other cities as well.

Prest: Roughly the same kind of thing is going on in England. St. John's Woods which is usually thought of as a prosperous area and also a Jewish area, now has signs for sale in Arabic.

Hartojo Wignjowijoto: Not only German and Japanese buyers but also OPEC residents are buying real estate for cash. The Americans, on the other hand, purchase on the installment plan. The news tells of large real estate purchases for cash by OPEC nationals. This is an important topic to examine in relation to the declining dollar value and land prices. These people are using a lower valued dollar.

Carter: Isn't this a beneficial thing, Woolery, in terms of imbalance of trade figures? Isn't this our own money coming back and being spent in this country.

Woolery: I was thinking in terms of the tax administration. We talk about land value but to what extent is the assessor being misled or the public observer being fooled by what may be a two-tier market. Are we really using the correct yardstick when we make some of these comparisons?

Netzer: The other side really is that since heavy demand by foreign purchasers in some section of the market is the ingredient for rapid value increases, then the long-standing political difficulties in more adequately taxing land values should be less rather than more.

Woolery: I agree with that, but Proposition 13 runs counter to this because it increases the incentive to buy and hold.

Netzer: I think anybody could write a scenario on Proposition 13 if you had those actors in it. If you had those Los Angeles assessors and so forth, you could do that.

Reeves: I don't agree we are developing two tiers of land values. My perspective on foreign versus domestic is limited, but I do live in a community where OPEC, East Germans, and Japanese have all in the last few years made substantial investments, but, the highest bids by far on blue grass property are made with Texas money. So I question whether it is foreign-oriented. I don't question that there is a difference in the pure use of land as a tax haven, and its use as an escape from the losses of inflation.

Lindholm: Well, McGuire, you are our only international economist.

Carl W. McGuire: I wonder how large this is. This flow of funds doesn't show up as being sizeable in the balance of international indebtedness or through the balance of payments in a particular year. It must be having an effect in particular areas, but overall I wonder if it is changing the situation appreciably.

Reeves: The fact is, we don't know right now. I just gave Woolery the Yale report dated June 12, which is the latest and best statement made on the subject. All it says is that we don't know.

Lindholm: People from Europe, OPEC, and Japan find our land prices to be cheap, and the ownership protection to be good. These foreign owners will also be able to benefit in some cases from tax treaties that basically make capital gains exempt of U.S. income taxes. If the dollar strengthens as land prices increase, these foreign owners will experience a double gain.

III. IMPACT OF THE USE OF LAND AS A TAX BASE

Introduction

George F. Break looks at Henry George's strong belief in the economic desirability of a tax on land and the problems that must be overcome if the economic benefits of land taxation are to be realized in a modern urban setting. Doubt, based on a recent article, is expressed as to the incidence of a pure land tax. In addition, Break questions the desirability of the community rather than the participants in the market place benefiting from increases in land value.

Alan R. Prest describes the current situation in the taxation of land in Great Britain. British practice is based on the seventeenth century local property tax and the 1976 Development Land Tax. In addition, town planning and speculative land ownership developed into the 1947 Town and Country Planning Act. As a result, much of land development gains became community income. There is much confusion in Great Britain relative to tax treatment of gains from land ownership. Both site value tax and land value increment taxation are supported without any clear understanding of the difference in the two approaches.

The theme of Professor Gaffney's discussion is that many economists, in writing for over two centuries about taxing land rents, have in the process indirectly shaped or warped major elements of economic doctrine.

According to Professor Gaffney the strong opponents of taxing land rent are John B. Clark, Philip Wicksteed, Vilfredo Pareto, Frank

Knight, Henry Carey, Wilford King, Karl Marx, Charles Spahr, Ragner Frisch, Richard Ely, Alvin Johnson, Francis Edgeworth, and Edwin Cannan. He sees as some strong supporters of taxing land rent Leon Walras, John R. Commons, François Quesnay, Knut Wicksell, Ralph Turvey, Richard Lindholm, Lowell Harriss, Harold Hotelling, Colin Clark, Dick Netzer, William Vickrey, and Adam Smith. Many more economists take their stands at various intermediate stations.

The debates have ranged well beyond the explicit issue of taxing land rents. They shape the very core of economic theory and policy: marginal productivity and distribution; the meaning of capital and its supply elasticity; the nature of property; earned and unearned income and wealth; the forms of collective ownership; the social function of land-ownership; the meaning of rent and economic surplus; the incidence of taxes and benefits from public spending; the nature of land value; optimal timing of development; optimal settlement patterns and densities; tax cuts, investment incentives, and macro-economic policy; marginal-cost pricing; concentration of wealth and economic power; fixed versus variable costs; optimal scale and proportions; location theory; capital theory; replacement theory; economic development; institutional economics; public choice; and so on. Economists addressing the issue of taxing land not only contributed to these topics, they originated or revolutionized some of them in the very process of supporting their respective positions.

It is fascinating to see stereotypes fall away and surprising to see new light fall on the goals and juxtapositions of well-known economists. Georgians and Keynesians, so often at odds, share a common interest in cutting taxes on capital. Chicago school economists, generally defenders of property, support the taxation of capital. Frank Knight joins Karl Marx in treating capital as "eternal," like land. The most explicit anti-George polemicists, Francis Walker, E. R. A. Seligman, and Alfred Marshall, are actually rather close to George in substance, if not in style.

Professor Gaffney points out that George's more effective opponents, J. B. Clark, Vilfredo Pareto, and Frank Knight, attack indirectly by rewriting economic theory. John R. Commons, the "institutionalist," favors land taxation because it lets the market make unbiased decisions; Commons, the "liberal," is a pioneer advocate of accelerated depreciation. Leon Walras, the detached theoretical technician, is an impassioned land taxer. Knut Wicksell, Keynes' godfather, comes out for radical land taxation in an early essay on, of all things, "Public Choice." Colin Clark, the tax limitation pioneer, favors a progressive Federal land tax calculated to redistribute local land rents nationally. The business of destereotyping often results in new insights, as Professor Gaffney demonstrates.

Arlo Woolery examines the manner in which the citizens of the Fairhope, Alabama, land tax colony have managed their affairs. The enclave of 350 acres, called the Fairhope Single Tax Corporation, was established in 1894 and currently has 110 members. The rapid increase in land values and rents, due mostly to oil development prospects, have caused lessees to bring court action to prevent the Corporation from absorbing the economic rent in higher rent payments. The placing of an appropriate value on Colony (corporation) lands has always been a problem.

Mathew Edel looks at the differences and similarities in the economic and social reform movements stimulated by George and Marx. *Progress and Poverty* was published only a few years after Marx's *Capital*. For a short period of time, ending in an 1886 blowup, a political coalition existed in the United States of the single taxers and the socialists.

George's concept of the setting of wage levels used the frontier and its no-rent land labor productivity. Marx, on the other hand, set the basic wage level at the subsistence minima. Both, however, were believers in a labor theory of value. To George, however, capital increased in value on its own and was not taken from the production of labor. This approach permitted George to avoid the basic conflict between labor and capital that was fundamental to Marx.

The similarities in the concepts of George and Marx explain why the two groups have cooperated on occasion, for example, in early urban land policy. The differences have resulted in sharp disputes and the disruption of understandings.

George F. Break

Henry George and Tax Reform — 100 Years Later

In this year of grass-roots tax rebellion — I carefully avoid using the word "reform" — it is particularly appropriate to examine the work of that great 19th century tax guru, Henry George, messiah of a vigorous subculture that is alive and well and invariably adept at infusing its theology into any tax discussion. As was Proposition 13, Henry George's crowning work, *Progress and Poverty,* was born in California, and although I do not wish to push the comparison too far, they share fundamental elements that give them, despite the century that separates them, an unmistakable kinship — notably the passionate intensity and simplistic reasoning that constitute their very warp and woof.

Henry George and Adam Smith's Canons of Taxation

To a modern tax economist more interested in the pragmatic than the philosophical (or theological) aspects of George's reasoning, one of the most interesting sections of *Progress and Poverty* is the one which immediately follows the revelation in Book VIII of his "simple yet sovereign remedy" for curing society's ills by abolishing "all taxation save that upon land values" (1879, rpt. 1960, p. 406). Acknowledging that the infallibility of his prescription may not at once be apparent to all his readers, George proceeds to "try the remedy . . . by the accepted canons of taxation" (1879, rpt. 1960, p. 407). Although anyone familiar with the classic "maxims" of Adam Smith will recognize the source of these "accepted canons," George treats them as though they were as universally conceived as the laws delivered to Moses on Mt. Sinai. The number, general format, and some of the phraseology are patently Smith's, but no direct mention of that source is made until late in the chapter. At that point, George launches boldly into battle with Smith's definition of tax equity without acknowledging the extent of his debt to the great Scot; at last and at least, however, he there quotes his source instead of merely paraphrasing him without credit.

Despite such borrowings, George's treatment of the subject is entirely his own. He is a new and different Moses receiving a revised edition of the law. He makes free with the original version, preserving its essential framework but shifting points about, adding, and deleting. Though still four in number, his commandments have a strikingly new order and emphasis. In this version the first is last and the last first.

Smith's monumental equity — or "equality" — maxim has been dropped to fourth place and fundamentally altered. In its stead at the top of the list is a succinct paraphrase of Smith's double-barrelled Maxim Number 4, entitled "economy of collection" but actually encompassing the far broader concept of economic efficiency. George has elevated Smith's point about neutrality to separate status, emphasized its importance for economic growth, and made it the first "condition" for a good tax:

1. That it bear as lightly as possible upon production — so as least to check the increase of the general fund from which taxes must be paid and the community maintained (1878, rpt. 1960, p. 408).

The opening part of Smith's fourth maxim then becomes George's second canon, its wording so similar as to be an uncomfortably close echo:

2. That it be easily and cheaply collected, and fall as directly as may be upon the ultimate payers — so as to take from the people as little as possible in addition to what it yields the government (1879, rpt. 1960, p. 408).

George's third canon is Smith's "certainty" rule (Maxim Number 2), tightened in phrasing and deftly summarized:

3. That it be certain — so as to give the least opportunity for tyranny or corruption on the part of officials, and the least temptation to lawbreaking and evasion on the part of the taxpayers (1879, rpt. 1960, p. 408).

The fourth of George's canons is vaguely worded, deliberately sidestepping Smith's clear and ringing phrases defining "equality" as the principle of taxing people "in proportion to their respective abilities":

4. "That it bear equally — so as to give no citizen an advantage or put any at a disadvantage, as compared with others " (1879, rpt. 1960, p. 408).

Here the revisionist Moses marches to a totally different drummer, as anyone who has followed his logic through the book will find no surprise. "Equality" for George is not measured quantitatively but qualitatively. The needs of the taxpayer and the source of his money make some incomes more equal than others. This will be discussed in detail later.

In discussing the application of his four canons to the world, George shows himself to be more priest than pragmatist, or as Alfred Marshall put it, "by nature a poet, not a scientific thinker" (1883, rpt. 1969, p. 186). Reading George's words today, one is struck by his perceptive insights into human nature and the pathos of the human condition — a view as relevant today, in many respects, as a century ago. At the same time one is discouraged by the consistency of his tunnel vision, especially the narrowness of his purview, the facile nature of many of his arguments, and his bold use of assertion in lieu of evidence or deductive proof. As was Hamlet's gravedigger, George is uncommonly "absolute."

George deals only with the substitution effects of different taxes which he has labelled as bad — those on manufacturers, commerce, capital, and improvements — while ignoring the income effects. Judged solely on that basis, these taxes are seen to discourage economic activity and hence do not measure up to the first canon. In contrast, the same logic finds that land taxation has no substitution effects but instead only a special kind of income effect; therefore it either leaves economic activity unaffected or may actually encourage it, since it is based on potential rather than actual income and thus induces "highest and best use."

This reasoning, while persuasive to many, is specious. It results in incomplete analysis of both categories of tax. In fact it can be demonstrated that most or all existing taxes, including the land tax, have both substitution and income effects. Any tax on potential rather than actual income or output has zero substitution effects. In such cases the marginal rate of tax is zero. There is nothing unique about land as a tax base in this respect. Any tax on potential values, furthermore, is subject to an important additional hazard, namely, its vulnerability not only to administrative error but to the very demons named by George in his third canon — tyranny and corruption.

Administration

If George's analysis of Canon Number 1 raises serious questions, his treatment of Canon Number 2 is little better. Once again, and more explicitly, he rests his case for the land tax confidently on the assumption that the value of land "can be readily ascertained." Take that for granted, and it can be clearly seen that "A tax on land values can, of all taxes, be most easily and cheaply collected" (1879, rpt. 1960, p. 414). Pull that rug out from under him, however, and the point becomes shaky indeed. The basis for George's confidence in his position was clearly indicated in a lecture he gave at Oxford in 1884, an occasion which brought him into direct confrontation with Alfred Marshall. The report in the *Oxford Journal,* fascinatingly entitled, "Mr. Henry George at Oxford, Disorderly Meeting," summarized his remarks:

In the United States, although their system of taxation was, in some respects, worse than ours, in others it was better, so that system would enable him to explain what he meant. Their local taxes were by the assessment on the value of all property; once every year all property was assessed, or supposed to be assessed. The value of land was assessed separately, then the value of buildings and other things. What he proposed was simply that they should levy their taxes on the value of land, and exempt all buildings and improvements (Marshall 1883, rpt. 1969, p. 220).

Only that and nothing more. Anyone who has wrestled with an assessment problem in today's urbanized world, where property values are changing rapidly, can only shake the head and wish things could be so simple. Where parcels of land cannot readily be compared because they are not uniformly adaptable to given purposes, not equally convenient to build upon, or for other reasons not similarly desirable, their values (even current, let alone potential) are by no means easy to assess accurately. In addition, where little vacant land exists, even lots of similar size offer serious problems of valuation since market data do not make the critical separation between the price of the land and the price of the improvements. Even for recent sales this breakdown is largely "guesstimation," and determining "highest and best use" values for land in areas where few if any vacant land sales have taken place for years means placing quite abstract figures on all parcels. "Cleared" land cannot be compared to "vacant" land; a vast array of variables must be introduced into each computation. In such a process accuracy can be achieved only at great cost and trouble, or as many assessors point out, reliance must be placed on expert opinion. (See Chapter 4.)

Incidence

George makes another assumption in Canon Number 2 which looks
less safe today than it once did. That one concerns the incidence of the
land tax, which (with the backing of classical economic theory) he takes
to "fall as directly as may be upon the ultimate payers." It has generally
been accepted, since Ricardo drove the point home, that a tax on the site
value of land cannot be shifted but is simply capitalized into lower land
values. Everyone has known that — that is, until recently. In an article
aptly titled "The Surprising Incidence of a Tax on Pure Rent: A New
Answer to an Old Question," Martin Feldstein rather persuasively shoots
down even that deep-rooted bit of conventional wisdom (1977, pp.
349–60). This act of iconoclasm will probably not erode the faith of true
believers, but it seriously challenges one of the cardinal assumptions that
have made the land tax appealing to many thoughtful adherents.

Feldstein argues that a tax on pure rent is indeed shifted, both in the
short run and in the long run. The short-run result comes from the
manuevering of investors to balance their portfolios in the near term,
when the reproducible capital shock is in effect fixed. As investors weigh
different assets on the basis of their relative current yields and risk
characteristics, they find that a reduction in the price of land (as a result
of imposing a land tax) will unbalance their portfolio holdings and thus
make land a more attractive investment. The resultant surge of the
market toward land and out of produced capital mitigates the tax-
induced drop in land prices and shifts some of the tax to other asset
owners. (See Chapter 3.)

In the long run, of course, the capital stock is not fixed. People accumulate savings to finance their retirement consumption and to leave
bequests. Long-term savers will react to the drop in their wealth caused
by the tax-induced fall in land values by saving more in the form of produced capital. This build-up of capital will raise the gross rental value of
land and lower the rate of interest, thus pushing up land prices and
shifting part of the land tax to owners of produced capital. Feldstein is
still pursuing the implications of his "new answer," but his logic should
remind us of the danger of over-relying on abstract foundations as the
basis for anything so pragmatic as a tax system.

Certainty

Aside from its application to a land tax, George's "certainty" canon
sets forth simply and clearly what any citizen expects from a tax system.
In explaining his principle he strikes chords that should resonate in any

modern reader: "Taxes which lack the element of certainty tell most fearfully upon morals. Our revenue laws as a body might well be entitled, 'Acts to promote the corruption of public officials, to suppress honesty and encourage fraud, to set a premium upon perjury and the subornation of perjury, and to divorce the idea of law from the idea of justice'" (1879, rpt. 1960, p. 417). If this eloquent denunciation seems somehow to adumbrate the reaction which turned Proposition 13 into a national movement, it may also contain a warning that ought to be heeded concerning an even bigger issue, namely, the income tax.

Although many people cling confidently to the notion that the income tax is the fairest and most incorruptible of our taxes, there are rumblings in the distance that may foretell a rising tide of disillusionment with it. There is evidence that income tax evasion may not only be growing by leaps and bounds but also moving out of the shady fringes of our society and becoming a popular household sport. Cheating the government is apparently being regarded more as a virtue than as a vice by many citizens. This growing problem of the "subterranean economy" is fascinatingly described in a recent article by Peter M. Gutmann (1978, pp. 9–14).

Reading *Progress and Poverty* today, one can be caught up easily in George's persuasive eloquence. Like Keats listening to the nightingale, a reader finds himself carried away by the entrancing music of George's seductive and reassuring words — until, that is, the real world intrudes and brings him down with a thud. Just as the spell is broken for Keats by mention of the word "forlorn," George's soaring thought ends for the reader with a jarring return to the practical: "Were all taxes placed upon land values, irrespective of improvements, the scheme of taxation would be so simple and clear, and public attention would be so directed to it, that the valuation of taxation could and would be made with the same certainty that a real estate agent can determine the price a seller can get for a lot" (1879, rpt. 1960, p. 418). So it still comes down to that; the touchstone of value is inescapably the market price. Without the marketplace, price lacks certainty; without comparable sales, certainty in valuation is more hope than reality. The disappearance of vacant land, parking lots, or completely depreciated structures from a tax jurisdiction means the introduction of increasingly arbitrary variables.

It is in the discussion of his fourth canon that George applies his whole philosophy of value most directly to the tax issue. Ironically, in doing this he is brought into head-to-head combat with the very man whose exposition of tax principles he has been echoing — Adam Smith. His pure labor theory of value will not permit him to accept Smith's concept of taxation according to ability to pay and benefits received from government. Yet "equality" and/or "equity" are principles that neither can nor should be ignored. George is obliged to take the Scot to task for failing to see that "equality" in this matter refers not to how much a person earns but how the income is earned and how much it is needed. A taxpayer with a large family, George argues, needs more than a taxpayer with a small family; charging them the same tax would be an injustice. Furthermore, all income should not be considered equally taxable, since "Nature gives to labor; and to labor alone" (1879, rpt. 1960, p. 419). What one earns by his exertion is not comparable to the rent from land, which is Nature's gift to all mankind. Rising land values are windfalls provided by Nature, and they rightfully belong to the community.

One hundred years after George wrote this book it is appropriate to note that a tax system constructed on the basis of his concept of values has the potential of consolidating power in the hands of those who act for the "community." The more the tax base is taken out of the economic arena, i.e., the marketplace, and made a matter of political decision-making, i.e., how land is zoned and what it "ought to be" worth, the less objective, certain, and efficient the tax process is likely to be.

Alternative Tax Bases

However, the very existence of meetings that discuss the thinking of Henry George indicates that he offered the world something more than rhetoric. I should like to close with a few random thoughts triggered by George's eloquent and appealing equity arguments. He reminds us that a tax system must take other elements than market value into consideration. Indeed, one might argue that one reason our income tax has been less unpopular than the property tax is that it does make more concession to such inter-personal differences as size of family and use of resources. What one especially objects to in George is the simplistic nature of his economic arguments. If he were living today in our inflationary economy he might well be less concerned about the "monopolistic" character of land ownership and more concerned about the plight of individuals trying to keep up with the serious erosion of their assets by inflation, especially as they near retirement age. In today's world land is one of the few relatively inflation-proof investments available to the ordinary person. If people are seriously frustrated by the government's failure to keep the price level stable, as all the polls suggest they are, there is likely to be little appeal today to a special tax on land values or on land value increments.

One thing that ought to be kept clearly in mind about George is that he was writing about an undeveloped economy. The booming GNP and multi-billion dollar budgets of today's California were far in the future when George was formulating his ideas. The tax equity issues are very different for developed and undeveloped economies, and one needs only to look south of our border for an example of the latter.

This distinction was enunciated clearly nearly a century ago by no less an authority than Alfred Marshall, who (a year before his spirited debate with George at Oxford) delivered three lectures on *Progress and Poverty* while still at University College, Bristol. It is interesting that Marshall found George's work sufficiently challenging to devote so much attention to it, since it was ignored by most economists of the day. Marshall clearly was touched by George's concern for humanity, while also offended by his lack of historical perspective. Marshall wrestled with the question of land rights and weighed the justice of George's claim that land should be nationalized:

Is it possible to undo a wrong done in distant ages, so that the punishment will fall on the right persons? If the original landholders had no good right to their title-deeds, are not an immense number of the present landholders the descendants of working men and others who have bought the title-deeds with the sweat of their brow? (1883, rpt. 1969, pp. 200–1).

Such considerations suggest for general tax policy purposes that a tax on land value increments would be more equitable than a land tax, except in undeveloped economies, where the effects of the two approaches would be similar.

Conclusion

Henry George's lasting attraction a century after his *magnum opus* was written must tell us something about the universality of his theme, if not about the perfect efficacy of his "sovereign remedy." In cases where land needed for production is neglected by heedless owners who lack either interest or incentive to develop it, the land tax could well provide an efficacious prod. It might also be a useful policy tool in the development of those new, ambiguously owned acres under the sea, where great new wealth in the form of mineral resources remains to be developed. If formulation of an international agreement is hampered, in part at least, by the lack of a general philosophical framework, future conferences could do far worse than to develop a manifesto from the theoretical base provided by Henry George.

References

Feldstein, Martin. 1977. "The Surprising Incidence of a Tax on Pure Rent: A New Answer to an Old Question." *Journal of Political Economy* 85, no. 2: 349–60.

George, Henry. 1879. Reprint 1960. *Progress and Poverty.* New York: Robert Schalkenbach Foundation.

Gutmann, Peter M. 1978. "Off the Books." *Across the Board* 15, no. 8: 9–14.

Marshall, Alfred. 1883. Reprint 1969. "Three Lectures on Progress and Poverty by Alfred Marshall." *Journal of Law and Economics* 12: 181–226.

8 *Alan R. Prest*

United Kingdom Land Taxation in Perspective

There are two main ways in which land is taxed in the United Kingdom, as well as a number of subsidiary ones. The main ways consist of the old local property tax dating from 1601 (at least) and the new Development Land Tax dating from 1976. In addition, a number of titles are applied currently to taxes that rest on land value, for example, betterment charges, income tax, capital gains tax, stamp duties, and value added tax; in the future, there also is the potential for a wealth tax.

Local Property Tax (Rates)

I recently have set out the features of the United Kingdom rating system in some detail (Prest 1978). This paper will be a precis of that discussion. The amount of tax payable in any one year is a function of two variables: the rateable value of the property and the rate in the British pound. The rateable value is in principle equal to the annual rental acceptable to both landlord and tenant assuming that the latter pays for repairs. It therefore embraces both land and buildings and is concerned solely with current, as distinct from potential, usage of a site. Rateable values are supposed to be reappraised every five years (and ad hoc if, say, major improvements are made to a property) but in England, if not Scotland, this principle has been honored more in the breach than the observance during the postwar period. Whereas rateable values are determined in principle on a uniform national basis, the rate in the pound is fixed each year by the individual local authority according to the amount of revenue it needs to raise, given its expenditure commitments and other sources of finance (principally central government grants nowadays).[1] So, if the rateable value of a property is, say, £400 and the rate in the pound in a given year is 75p (or 75 percent), then the tax liability for that year would be £300, and £320 if the poundage were 80p.

Various features of the rating system have to be appreciated. First, it applies to commercial, industrial, and domestic property; machinery is included, as well as industrial buildings. At the same time there are many concessions and exemptions, e.g., agricultural land is totally exempt, buildings of charities are 50 percent exempt, and there is substantial alleviation in respect of domestic property. The major features that distinguish the British system sharply from those found in other countries are that (1) it is explicitly a tax on annual rather than capital values and (2) it is a tax on occupiers rather than owners, with the consequence that traditionally no tax was payable if a building was unoccupied, though this practice has been modified somewhat in recent years.

Many criticisms have been levelled at the tax over the years, e.g., that it was a deterrent to property development, that it bore harshly on lower income groups, and so on. However, its supporters have argued that the tax has many advantages, such as predictability of yield and ease of administration, which made it extremely suitable as a base for local finance. The most recent of many occasions on which these arguments have boiled over was during a major review of local authority finances by a Committee headed by Sir Frank Layfield (Local Government Finance 1976). After a good deal of evidence for and against the present form of the tax, the Layfield Committee argued strongly for retaining it in much the same form as at present except for two important changes: (1) assessment of domestic property in England and Wales on the basis of capital values, on the grounds that there was no longer sufficient worthwhile evidence to determine annual values and (2) rescindment of the exemption of farmland, on the grounds that the exemption was an anachronism. Not entirely surprisingly, the government subsequently indicated (Local Government Finance 1977) that it favored the first but not the second of these recommendations.

---

1. Of the total local government revenue of some £15b, each year 30 to 35 percent comes from rates, about 15 percent from property income (including rents of publicly owned housing) and the rest from grants.

Development Land Tax

In sharp contrast to rates, Development Land Tax (DLT) is a completely new tax, initiated on August 1, 1976. It is closely related to a sister Act, the Community Land Act of 1975, which effectively provided for the ultimate nationalization, or at any rate municipalization, of development rights in land. The DLT itself can be thought of as a set of interim provisions that will prevail until the ambitions of the Community Land Act are fully realized. However, not even the most fervent supporters of the legislation envisage that the millenium will arrive quickly, so it is worthwhile to examine this "temporary" phase in some detail. The temporary phase may be short-lived for an entirely different reason; if the Conservative Opposition is returned to power, the entire legislation may be repealed.

The essence of DLT is that it is a very special capital gains tax. It is levied on the difference between the value of land after the granting of planning permission for change of use or redevelopment and something resembling the current use value (to be defined more precisely below). It should be noted that the tax is mainly on increases in value associated with *changes* of land use category; insofar as land values increase while remaining in a particular use category, the capital gains tax (CGT) generally applies, but not the DLT. The DLT has a single 60 percent rate; the first £50,000 of development value became exempt as of June 12, 1979.[2]

DLT differs from the usual run of capital gains taxation in being tied, at least in part, to accruals rather than realization of gains, because the tax has to be paid at the commencement of material development or on realization (whether by lease or sale), whichever takes place first. It also differs in not making any allowance for the possibility of losses, presumably on the grounds that they would be extremely rare. It is not surprising that, like most capital gains in most countries, there is no indexing for inflation.

The interaction with other taxes is carefully established in the legislation; essentially their base excludes the amount on which DLT is levied. Thus, if a builder makes a gain of £500,000 on land for which permission for building development is given, he pays DLT on this sum; however, this £500,000 is *excluded* from his trading profits for income tax or corporation tax purposes. Nor, as we saw earlier, is it subject to CGT.

Without going into the details of an extremely complex piece of legislation, a few more points are sufficiently important to warrant mention. It

2. See *Economist,* June 16, 1979, p. 75.

was stated earlier that the basis for the calculation of tax was roughly current use value. In fact, there is a choice of three bases;[3] the taxpayer can choose that which is most to his advantage, i.e., the highest of the three. Various categories of landholders are exempt (in whole or in part) from the tax, for example, small owner-occupiers, charities (in part), and nonresidents; the same applies to land devoted to certain uses, for example, agricultural or forestry usage. There is no constructive realization on the occasion of a bequest or a gift; the recipient simply takes over the donor's base value. Arguments about hardship occasioned by payment of tax before realization have been countered by provisions for payment by installments. In addition, when land is acquired net of tax by a local authority, there is a provision for splitting the net profits from disposal in the ratio of 40:30:30 (changed in November 1978 to 30:50:20) between central government, the local authority concerned, and all other local authorities.

To date, the record of the tax is not overly impressive. In the financial year 1977/78, only £6.6 million was collected in revenue, while costs of public administration amounted to about 25 percent of the total, which is a high proportion by any standard. In fact, it appeared that the productivity of the staff engaged in assessing and collecting the tax was such that each staff member was only managing to make one assessment every two months, i.e., a total of six per annum. Nor has the land-purchasing record of the local authorities in England and Scotland under the Community Land Act been of a scintillating character. In England, for instance, local authorities were only able to make some 150 acres of land available for development in the first 2½ years of operations. Whether this was because of or despite the large number (135 in all over three years) of officially issued instructions, advice, and orders under the Act[4] is a matter for conjecture. At the same time it should be observed that the Welsh part of the scheme was working much more effectively in the sense of purchasing and releasing land for development. So the conclusion can be drawn that if one wants to implement land acquisition policies of this sort, a special statutory land authority, as is found in Wales, is likely to be more effective than the standard local authority organization that has the responsibility for implementation in England and Scotland.

Before leaving DLT, it would be useful to take a glance at the later stage envisaged in the 1975 legislation. The plan was for local authorities to

---

3. *Either* 110 percent of current use value at date of disposal plus expenditure on improvements *or* acquisition cost plus cost of improvements and increase in current use value since acquisition *or* 110 percent of acquisition cost plus cost of improvements.

4. See *The Times* (London), November 7, 1978.

buy all land that is on the point of development on the basis of current use values. In other words, none of the development gain would accrue to the private sector, and the tax as such would disappear. Therefore it would be more correct to depict the situation as one in which public sector powers will be able to abolish private sector gains rather than to levy a tax at a rate of 100 percent. In other words, we cross the boundary from purely tax measures on development gains to their direct acquisition by the public sector.

Other Land Related Taxes

There are many other taxes impinging on land in the United Kingdom today, but none of them is nearly as important as rates and DLT. Therefore, a mere summary will suffice.

Capital Gains Tax

The normal capital gains tax (maximum rate 30 percent) applies to land gains other than those taxed under DLT.

Stamp Duties

These are essentially a tax at 2 percent of sales values on transactions in various capital assets, including land.

Income Tax and Corporation Tax

These apply to land rents; there is no tax on the land rental component of imputed income from owner-occupied property.

Capital Transfer Tax

The normal progressive schedule is applied to transfers of land by gift or bequest.

Value Added Tax

Land transactions are exempt.

Betterment Charges ("special assessments")

Charges have been levied for many years on landowners specifically benefitting from improvements executed by local authorities, e.g., drainage provision. It could be argued that these charges are not taxes in the strict sense but it is better to include them to provide a comprehensive picture.

Wealth Tax

If a wealth tax is enacted, as seems highly probable if a Labor Government is re-elected in 1979, land holdings will certainly be chargeable under it.

Antecedents of the Current Position

A full account of the evolution of the present arrangements would require much more space than a single article, so all that can be done here is to paint with the broadest of brushes. Even so, everything which does not relate to the development of the local property tax and the national development land tax must be omitted.

Roots can be envisioned at three different levels; academic thinking, popular movements, and government enquiry and action. Taking *academic thinking* first, there is a long tradition of argument in favor of urban land taxation. Confining oneself to the United Kingdom only, the line of argument can be traced through many of the famous economists of the past from Adam Smith onwards. We can give some flavor of this history by referring to the writings of J. S. Mill and A. C. Pigou.

Mill (1848, rpt. 1969, pp. 818–21) essentially took the view that land rent justifiably could have been taxed from the time of Adam and Eve onwards. Nevertheless, he was acutely conscious of two limitations on any attempt to tax away the whole of current rent payments to landlords. First, he recognized that rents might include payments for landlords' improvements and therefore not fully correspond to the notion of a true surplus. Second, whatever undeserved surpluses might have accrued to landowners in the past, the present generation may well have bought land at prices based on the expectation that current and expected returns would not be subject to any special tax. In other words, a special land rent tax would impose a capital loss on a largely different set of people from those who had over the generations enjoyed capital gains from land rentals. So Mill's proposal was to exempt the present value of land from any impost, but instead to tax new future increments in value, unless it could be shown that these were the fruits of individual effort, enterprise, and so on. In other words, Mill advocated a capital gains tax on certain land value increments after a given date.

Pigou's views (1947, chaps. XIV and XVI), paralleling those of Marshall (1926, 1920), were somewhat different. Pigou clearly distinguished between what he called taxes on public value of land (i.e., that element of land value which cannot be attributed to individual initiative, enterprise, and so on) and taxes on unexpected windfalls. In the former case, he argued that there was a strong case for heavy taxation on efficiency grounds, a case more or less parallel to that for taxing monopoly revenue. At the same time, he was hesitant about the equity aspects. However, he did take the view that unforeseen gains, or windfalls, should be taxed heavily, the analogy there being wartime excess profits taxation. He did not fail to see the point that some gains do not fall neatly into either the anticipated or the unanticipated box, and he therefore spent some time on the interaction between the two tax bases. The upshot is that Pigou, unlike Mill, can be claimed as academic authority for both a tax on land values and a tax on unanticipated increments in land values, though it should be added that he had no great expectations of raising vast sums of revenue by either means. Such is the sort of legacy that was left by nineteenth and early twentieth century academic discussion of land taxation.

When we turn to *popular movements,* there are two, or perhaps three, major ones to be distinguished. Henry George made a great impact on England, as elsewhere, and the 25 years or so before World War I saw a great deal of discussion, both verbally and orally, of the propositions that land values are socially and geologically created, that landowners have no right to them, and that taking away rents from landlords would amount to depriving robbers of what they should never have had, rather than an unwarranted expropriation of property rights. There is still support today in the United Kingdom for site value taxation (e.g., the views of the Liberal Party) which stems back to the popular movement sparked off by Henry George and his immediate followers. However, it cannot be said to be a major force in the way that it was before 1914.

The other popular movement in the United Kingdom is the long tradition in Labor Party circles, stemming from the early Fabians, that the appropriate way of dealing with unearned increments was to be found in land nationalization. This is a battle cry susceptible of many different meanings; it may be questioned whether some of those who have chanted it for so long have ever distinguished clearly between these meanings or even understood that there were any distinctions to be made. The concept can in fact mean anything from state ownership of all land interests (whether freehold, long leasehold, or even short leasehold) to the vestment in the state of future land development rights — and perhaps not all such rights and perhaps even then only on the basis of compensation. If land nationalization is taken to mean the transfer of development rights to the public sector, it is obviously much nearer to Henry George's position than if it implies, say, major State acquisition of freehold and long leasehold interests in land. Even so, it would not be identical in mechanics or effects.

Whatever the variety of meanings sheltering under the land nationalization umbrella, there can be no doubt that it has been a powerful
influence politically. This has been especially so in the context of the
town planning movement, which could be considered a third major
popular force from some viewpoints. Attempts to regulate the layout of
towns encountered many problems before World War II, most especially
in trying to tie in development charges and compensation payments to
the system of granting (or refusing) permission for development. What
actually happened in the 1940s was a fusion of land nationalization and
town planning arguments, culminating in the 1947 Town and Country
Planning Act, which effectively nationalized development rights and tied
in the whole process of compensation and betterment to that of planning
legislation.

This brings us in turn to roots at the *government* level. There has in
fact been a vast amount of such activity over the years. There have been
many official commissions and committees that have discussed site value
taxation or land increment taxation or both, ranging from the Royal
Commission on the Housing of the Working Classes in 1885, to the well-
known Uthwatt Committee Report of 1942, to the Layfield Committee of
Enquiry into Local Finance of 1976. Various governments have issued
White Papers stating their views on the arrangement of land taxes, e.g.,
in 1944, 1965, 1974, and 1977. Many bills have been introduced into
Parliament over the years, some being privately promoted (such as a
London County bill in 1938 to introduce site value rating) and others
officially sponsored. Legislation has resulted on a number of different occasions, but it has also been repealed soon afterwards, e.g., legislation of
1910 repealed in 1920, 1931 in 1934, 1947 in 1953, 1967 in 1971, and so on.
Over the years, there have been major divisions of opinion between the
political parties about the appropriate method of levying land taxation.,
There is little reason to expect that the most recent legislation to reach the
Statute book, the Development Land Act of 1976, will become settled
land tax policy.

Points at Issue

The motivations of people advocating heavy land taxation or extensive
state intervention in land policy will be mentioned first; this will be
followed by an examination of some of the emotional forces which have
come to the surface. Finally some of the confusions of thought in this
whole area will be outlined.

One powerful *motivation* has been the equity argument in one shape or
another. Some 70 to 80 years ago the cry for special land taxation was

well grounded in the comparison between the splendid houses and grounds of the aristocracy at that time and the slum-dwelling conditions of many of the working population — witness the famous Lloyd George statement that dukes cost more than battleships to maintain and did not even have any scrap value. In more modern times the emphasis has shifted to the large profits said to have been made by "speculators" in urban development and redevelopment. So the plea for taxation of unearned increments in one form or another was backed by an appeal to distributional arguments, though usually in general terms and without any supporting statistical evidence on the probable effects on the distribution of income or wealth.

Another theme, although a much less powerful one, was that of efficiency arguments for site value taxation, either in terms of income effects generating fuller usage of partly utilized land or the substitution effects of encouraging building and improvements as a result of the replacement of a general property tax by a site value tax. However, these standard arguments by academic economists have never had much impact at political levels. Although town planning has often had an aesthetic aspect, supporting arguments have also frequently been made for it on efficiency grounds by appealing to externality and merit wants principles.

Others used nationalization of land as the supreme objective — sometimes without thinking what the phrase meant or even realizing that it might have different meanings. One example of a recent set of proposals is found in Brocklebank et al. (1974), which calls for the compulsory conversion of all freeholds and leaseholds extending for periods in excess of 99 years into 99-year leases from the Crown. By this means all land would eventually revert to the Crown and would then be leased at an appropriate rental, thus permitting the abolition of the rating system. The justification for these proposals was:

It would in our view be better to concentrate exclusively on the nationalisation of land (at the expense of proposals to nationalise bits of industry) on the grounds that this is *the greatest* source of power and undeserved gains, of ill-directed enterprise and undesirable social pressures; as well as being a source of hardship for the victims of land speculation" (Brocklebank et al. 1974, pp. 14–15; italics in original).

There are innumerable examples of *emotional* overtones to discussion in this field, the above quotation being one example. Sometimes the case for heavy taxation is based on the proposition that land gains may be sudden and individually large.[5] Taxes on windfalls can be supported easily; as such, however, that is no justification for singling out land windfalls from other windfalls. Even though any single land transaction may yield a substantial gain, the position is quite different depending on whether such gains recur regularly or not. After all, it is normally held to be a disadvantage of a progressive income tax that it hits fluctuating incomes more than stable incomes when there is no averaging system. The general feeling that somehow land gains are of special character, and as such are an appropriate basis for heavy taxation, may owe something to the older idea among economists that economic rent was solely an attribute of land. Whether this explanation is correct or not, any reader of Parliamentary debates on the subject in the United Kingdom might be forgiven for thinking that land policy was a matter on which passion dominated intellect, giving rise to such gems of doubletalk as the proposition in the 1960s that a levy on land was not a tax on land.

Undoubtedly, neither discussion nor policy has been helped by a good deal of *confusion* in the land taxation area. As an example, we might take the distinction between a site value tax and a land value increment tax. Each of these taxes has been cited as a means of recapturing "unearned increment for the community" without much attention given to the various possible meanings of unearned or increment or community. In fact, the two taxes are likely to differ considerably in both coverage and timing, because a full site value tax would cover all land values (and not just those increments accruing after a certain date) and would also be on an accruals rather than a realization basis. Although the Layfield Committee (Local Government Finance 1976) did not make such an elementary mistake, its discussion of site value rating was clouded by the argument that the Community Land Act and Development Land Tax Act had made such rating irrelevant. This conclusion simply does not follow, as I have argued elsewhere (Prest 1978, p. 48).

More generally, there has been little discussion of the way in which particular land taxes should relate to more general taxes, e.g., a site value tax to a net worth tax and a land value increment tax to a capital gains tax. Nor has the interrelation between national and local taxation requirements received much attention.

Given this record of politically inspired proposals, emotional reactions, and confused thinking, it is not surprising that the economic

5. This sort of argument was put forward in the House of Commons by the chancellor of the exchequer in 1973 when advocating a change in land taxation arrangements. (*Hansard, Commons,* 17 December 1973, Col. 957)

arguments for differential land taxation, whether of an equity or efficiency character, have often disappeared from sight. It does not follow that we should have a better system of land taxation in the United Kingdom if economic analysis had not been buried under the avalanche, but at least we might have had a clearer idea of the arguments for and against it.

Conclusion

The main roles in land taxation in the United Kingdom today are played by the old rating system and the new land development taxation, although a number of other taxes have walk-on parts. The present tax mix-up was preceded by many years of academic and popular discussion, as well as a vast amount of activity at government level. However, for many years there have been conflicting motivations in demanding government action on land, although these underlying viewpoints have often been obscured by emotional outbursts or faulty reasoning.

References

Brocklebank, J., N. Kaldor, J. Maynard, R. Neild, and O. Stutchbury. 1974. *The Case for Nationalising Land*. London: Campaign for Nationalising Land.
Local Government Finance Report of the Committee of Enquiry. 1976. Sir Frank Layfield, chairman. Cmnd 6453. London: Her Majesty's Stationery Office.
Local Government Finance 1977. Cmnd 6813. London: Her Majesty's Stationery Office.
Marshall, A. 1926. "Memorandum on the Classification and Incidence of Imperial and Local Taxes." In *Official Papers by Alfred Marshall*, ed. J. M. Keynes. London: Macmillan.
Marshall, A. 1920. *Principles of Economics*. 8th ed. London: Macmillan.
Mill, J. S. 1848 Reprint 1969. *Principles of Political Economy*. New York: Kelley.
Pigou, A. C. 1947. *A Study in Public Finance*. 3d ed. London: Macmillan.
Prest, A. R. 1978. *Intergovernmental Financial Relations in the U.K.* Research monograph no. 23. Canberra: Center for Research on Federal Financial Relations, Australian National University.

9 *Mason Gaffney*

Two Centuries of Economic Thought on Taxation of Land Rents[1]

Professor Harry G. Brown often complained of a "conspiracy of silence" against the land tax idea. Certainly it has received more silence than its due, yet it would be hard to find a topic on which so many economists have rendered opinions and taken positions over the last two hundred years. I group these writers under five headings, according to their apparent sympathies towards the policy: (1) mainly negative; (2) mixed, or shifting and changeable; (3) noncommittal, detached, or supercilious; (4) positive but tentative, limited, partial, and remote; (5) mainly positive.

Many, indeed most, of those contributing to the debate had to be omitted to save space. On the affirmative side, some of these omitted are Henry George, Harry G. Brown, Thomas N. Carver, Eli Heckscher, Frank Graham, Lawson Purdy, Frederic Howe, Philip Cornick, Paul Alyea, Pierre Proudhon, Alfred R. Wallace, Joseph Schumpeter, Edward Polak, Philip Raup, Eli Schwartz, Arthur Becker, Raymond Richman, Marion Clawson, John Ise, F. F. von Wieser, Silvio Gesell, Charles Trevelyan, Walter Pollock, Thomas Paine, Thomas Jefferson,

1. Research support from the Robert Schalkenbach Foundation is gratefully acknowledged. Bibliographical help came from Paul Downing, Dennis Jesmok, Earl Bossard, and especially Peter Wells. I drew on the bibliography of Donald Ellickson, "A History of Land Taxation Theory," Ph.D. dissertation, Univ. of Wisconsin, 1966. A dissertation just completed by Terence Dwyer at Harvard has been very useful both bibliographically and conceptually.

and the Count Destutt Tracy, Louis Post, J. C. Stamp, and Josiah Wedgwood. On the negative side, some notable omissions are Frederic Bastïat, Gustav Cassel, Robert Harvey, Alexander Hamilton, John Hobson, Manuel Gottlieb, Yetta Scheftel, F. H. Finnis, Elmer Fagan, Carl C. Plehn, Dean Worcester, Ezra Mishan, Walter Morton, Raleigh Barlow, Albert Schaaf, Murray Rothbard, and George Hoxie. In the uncertain middle I have neglected Henry Aaron, John and Ursula Hicks, Arthur Weimer and Homer Hoyt, Donald Hagman, Arch Woodruff, Laszlo Ecker-Racz, Irving Fisher, Ernest Fisher, P. H. Clarke, Charles McLure, Abba Lerner, Benjamin Franklin, Kenneth Boulding, Charles Gide, Frank Taussig, Arthur Laffer, James Heilbrun, Carl Bye, Albert Hirschman, H. G. Hayes, and Erik Lindahl. No doubt I have also neglected to acknowledge all those neglected. But I have tried to cover the major issues.

Mainly Negative

Large numbers of economists have, over the years, articulated their opposition to the heavy and exclusive use of land as a tax base, particularly in the thoroughgoing manner advocated by Henry George. Some have attacked the land tax directly; others have worked on the conceptual structure of the argument. They are grouped here according to their most emphasized or most distinctive lines of argument.

Fusing Land with Capital: Theory

J. B. Clark in *The Distribution of Wealth* (1899) led the assault on George by undercutting the distributive basis of classical economics, the threefold division of inputs into land, labor, and capital. Clark's work marks the watershed between classical political economy and neoclassical economics. George himself believed that this quantum change was designed to undo his influence. While this might seem paranoid today, we must remember that George was the best-selling popular economist of the time, indeed of all time — Laffer, Thurow, Galbraith, Friedman, Heilbroner combined — and it was no more unusual for an establishmentarian at that time to be anti-Georgian than for one to refute Marx today. It is not hard to imagine that Clark was also gunning for Marx. However, J. B. Clark states it is George's marginal theory of wages that led him to develop his own (1899, pp. viii, xiii). Charles Collier (1979, p. 270) supports George's claim. He cites Simon Pattern: "Nothing please a . . . single taxer better than . . . to use the well-known economic theories . . . [therefore] economic doctrine must be recast . . . it must isolate itself more fully from history . . ." (Patten 1908, p. 219). Frank A. Fetter also believes the "single tax agitation" is what moved Clark to reformulate theory (Fetter 1927, rpt. 1977 pp. 126–28).

Clark's obliteration of land as a category takes two forms. One is the idea that all factors alike have marginal products, so the laws of production are symmetrical. Rent is not set apart as a "residual," due to "differential" fertility, location, or other qualities. Land is productive too, so land rent is no longer a "surplus," but a payment for a productive input. This payment is a real and legitimate social cost, an opportunity cost of taking land from the best alternative use.

Actually, none of this much affects the case for taxing land. Residual imputation of rent is reconciled with marginal imputation via Euler's theorem, and the productivity of land does not say anything about who should receive the income. But Clark's recasting of theory did serve to block the mental pathway via which classical political economy pointed so sharply towards land taxation by calling rent a residual surplus. One still hears Clarkogenic arguments levelled against land taxation.

Yet more was needed, to preclude permanently any clear distinction of inputs. Marginal productivity, after all, is the tool of those who want to impute specific contributions to specific inputs, and this could lead to peculiar treatment of land. Clark's other stroke (1883, 1895–96) was to essay a capital theory that would remove the quality of capital that distinguishes it from land, namely that capital is produced by labor, wears out, and is replaced. This is a different Clark from the crystalline logician of *Distribution of Wealth*. This is a mystic who creates ectoplasm in lieu of material capital.

Clark's ectoplasm is permanent; similar to land, it has no finite life. Clark engages the energies of Francis A. Walker (1888) and Bohm-Bawerk (1895–96), and Clark's follower Frank Knight (1946) engages Hayek (1936) in fruitless debates in their strange efforts to deny that capital turns over. The Austrians have no difficulty understanding the differences of land and capital; Knight believes the distinction can not be made, and he attacks it with vigor. George Stigler, Knight's disciple, indicates that the Austrian idea of a period of investment is objectionable because it presumes a distinction between capital and land (1941, p. 278). Stigler's only objection to Clark is that Clark made too many concessions (1941, p. 317). The strongest argument for untaxing buildings while "up-taxing" land is that it provides an incentive to replace and renew decrepit and obsolete capital, which, unlike land, is both reproducible and depreciable. Clark and Knight's concept of capital as an ether of immortal spirits is calculated to silence such arguments by destroying the very words in which they might be made.

Philip Wicksteed parallels Clark. All resources are fixed. "There is no such thing" as a supply curve — supply merely reflects the demand of those already possessing resources. The laws of distribution are symmetrical. Rent is erased. "There is no surplus at all" (1914, p. 15). Wicksteed deplores the misleading idea of diminishing returns because it is so intuitive to hold land fixed and let labor vary, resulting in a residual to land. He prefers to make land the variable: " . . . in practical problems . . . any individual can have as much land as he likes if he will pay the price. . . . " (1914, p. 23).

The modern usage of "variable proportions" in preference to diminishing returns, and indifference curves in preference to either, reflects Wicksteed and the extended flight from identifying rent as a surplus attaching to land.

Vilfredo Pareto (1897) is the progenitor of "transfer rent." The evident effort is to erase classical land rent and instead replace it with a new concept of the same name and a meaning analogous enough to lend plausibility to the switch. Transfer rent is just the surplus above opportunity cost; any factor may earn some, with land getting no more than any of the other factors. This destroys the classical contrast that human effort is a sacrifice of leisure, comfort, and often safety, while land comes free as a gift from Nature.

Alvin Johnson (1902) developed the idea in America, with emphasis on undercutting the case for taxing land. Land is mobile economically among competing uses, and so yields no more transfer rent than other factors.

Pareto's idea is subtly blended with Clark-Wicksteed's factor symmetry; it is hard to trace it explicitly for many years until the work of Frank Knight. More careful users of transfer rent, such as Alfred Marshall, Joan Robinson, and Hubert Henderson, have been scrupulous to distinguish the social viewpoint from the individual, and social distribution theory from exchange theory. Robinson writes, "From the point of view of society, land . . . is provided free, and the whole rent is a surplus and none of it is a social cost" (1933, p. 107). She uses only opportunity cost in partial analysis.

Knight, on the other hand, totally fuses the individual and social viewpoints. A cost to one is a cost to all. There is no aggregation problem, no fallacy of composition. Opportunity cost is social cost. There is no basis for distinguishing land from capital. "Killing off previous claimants" to land is merely an investment like any other; competition keeps the returns down to market levels (1924, rpt. 1952, pp. 167–69). It resembles a caricature of Chicago, but it *is* Chicago; it has been reprinted as a classic by the American Economic Association. Knight also argues (1953, p. 810) that slave-owners had just titles to slaves, because of society's sanction and open competition for capture of slaves. "Summary liberation" was unethical. "Society" was to blame and compensation was due. However, he does not say what tax should be used to finance the redemption. "Choice" is everything. "Apart from a necessity of choosing, values have no meaning or existence." " . . . The cost of any value is simply the value that is given up when it is chosen" (1924, rpt. 1952, pp. 167–69). Knight is quite clear that this undercuts classical ideas about taxing rent. George Stigler tracks Knight faithfully (1947, chap. 7); Milton Friedman brings Knight to the masses. In private correspondence Friedman occasionally refers to the land tax as "the least bad tax," but inconsistently reverts to Knight's and Pareto's concepts which impute rents to everything and everyone.

Frank A. Fetter is a persistent critic of Ricardian rent. He would erase all distinction between land and capital, and evidently also between social and individual viewpoints, and give a broader reading to rent. He does not, however, arrive at any clear alternative, and ultimately he mainly appears to have carped and nit-picked at the classics, as well as repeated J. B. Clark.

Fusing Land With Capital: Applied Economics and Law

Some real estate economists, students of R. T. Ely, have merged land with capital on practical business grounds. Richard Ratcliff writes that "Net Income Can't Be Split" between land and capital (1950). Dorau and Hinman were saying much the same in 1928: practical real estate men cannot "unscramble the omelette" and split income between land and capital. Yet one can wonder how, if we cannot split net income, we can know what net income is, or even if any exists, since net income is cash flow less depreciation, and land is not depreciable. The Internal Revenue Code is very clear on this point. Frederick Babcock's *Valuation of Real Estate* (1932), generally regarded as definitive, devotes several chapters to splitting income between land and buildings. His approach is followed by A. A. Ring, Morris Shenkel, and many others.

Henry C. Carey (1840) is better remembered today as a popular crusader than a seminal theorist, but he was influential in formulating protectionist and expansionist thought in Lincoln's day. Carey had no use for land taxation, nor for any taxation that might obviate tariffs. He is enjoying a modern revival at the hands of Lyndon La Rouche (former U.S. Labor Party candidate for president, now a Democratic primary candidate). As a proto-Keynesian (but Anglophobic) mercantilist, Carey regarded classical political economy with deep distrust and sought to discredit Ricardo by claiming that cultivation actually progressed from worse to better land. This principle alluded to Westward migration into the fertile corn belt lands, a part of The American System which he and Henry Clay promoted. This was supposed to weaken the idea of differential rent, but it has not received much of a following. His more enduring point is that western speculators made no more on their dollars than other investors — hence, no surplus.

Carey's theme is repeated later in a much-noted study by Shannon and Bodfish (1929) showing that land speculator returns were no more than, perhaps less than, returns on other investments during the 1920s. Shannon and Bodfish conclude from this that no differential tax is justified. Here, economic surplus is implicitly redefined from Ricardian rent to the increments received from buying and selling rents capitalized into land titles. Pareto's redefinition of rent makes it only a surplus over opportunity cost. Carey-Shannon-Bodfish make it a surplus over a normal return on the historical purchase price. For Ricardo and George, of course, land rent is the whole surplus above zero, because land is supplied by Nature, and they look at social issues from a social viewpoint.

Willford King (1921, 1924) fuses land and capital when he writes that capital itself would yield no profit above its costs were it not for the rise of land values. The speculative increase on land yields the return to capital. Evidently, he is describing investments in new buildings built on land already speculatively valued, and entered as a cost — a common situation today, where investors buy into "negative cash flows," and hold on. This is then a modified version of Carey-Shannon-Bodfish. Once one buys land at a speculative price, rising rents are necessary to yield a normal rate of return.

Frank Knight, we have seen, joined J. B. Clark in denying or obscuring in metaphysics the most distinctive qualities of capital vis-à-vis land, to wit its formation, migration, consumption, and replacement. Knight (1953) goes on to develop the doctrine of vested interest acquired by innocent purchase of land at advanced prices, a doctrine held by Francis A. Walker, J. S. Mill, and many others. Once society has let this happen it has endorsed and underwritten the contract, regardless of the origins of rent, and it would destroy confidence in contracts to act otherwise. Land becomes the moral equivalent of man-made capital. This presumably occurs some time after the first owner invests economically in "killing off previous claimants," as Knight puts it.

However one regards Knight the moralist, he is a bad lawyer. Few things are more basic to our Common Law than the underlying ownership by the sovereign of the regal estate — now called "real estate." This follows logically from the sovereign's monopoly of deadly force used to acquire land. Titles originate with the sovereign, who reserves paramount rights to condemn, police, regulate, zone — and tax. Titles are held subject to taxation, and tax liens are prior to private liens. That is the legal contract with the title holder. Anything more is based on sentiment and political clout, not contract. Still, the innocent buyer doctrine has put down many potential socializers of unearned increment. Granted, they say, that many landholders have grown rich in their sleep, yet there are others who bought in recently at high prices. It would be unfair to injure them, and so we must spare all.

It is ironic, then, to look at the detail of California's Proposition 13 of June 6, 1978, which applies exactly the reverse doctrine of innocence. Proposition 13 spares the ancient holder, he who innocently rode up the price escalator through no "fault" or desire of his own. High prices are the fault of recent buyers. The Proposition punishes these recent buyers by raising their assessments, while freezing others. Nor is this an inadvertent result; it was the major discussion point of Howard Jarvis, the measure's creator.

Equally ironic is the suppression of latent land values by low-density zoning. Many "innocent" buyers have lost out, as have their numerous lawsuits alleging inverse condemnation and demanding compensation. An equal confiscation of value by taxation would put billions a year into the fisc, to increase services or reduce other taxes. Yet, increasingly restrictive zoning blankets the country. The same developers who fight it where they build support it where they live. Only a few of Frank Knight's modern Chicago knights have raised a lance against it — it is easier to pick on rent controls.

We conclude that the innocent buyer doctrine is only a good debating point, but not a binding constraint in the real world of our institutions and cultural baggage. Law and custom say that land is different, and no buyer is presumed innocent or "lacking in worldly knowledge" about his risks. We never promised him a rose garden, and he probably knows it. He only plays dumb because it often works.

Fusing Land with Capital: Collectivist Approaches

Karl Marx is a strange bedfellow for Frank Knight. Although sometimes discoursing lengthily on land rent, he generally merges it with capital and its "mode of production." He often sacrifices consistency and clarity to sarcasm and invective, but the real Karl Marx stands up in *Capital* (1867, rpt. 1906, vol I, chap. 33). He attacks Wakefield's Australian scheme for locking up the frontier at high prices, in order to throw workers back into the arms of employers. This was a plan to create an artificial scarcity of land; its effect should be to increase rents, land values, and the bargaining position of landholders. But for Marx, the scarcity of land only increases the bargaining power of capital. He totally transfers the gains of land to the accounts of capital, even though "the old world constantly throws in capital" (1867, rpt. 1906, p. 843). Marxian distribution theory, like Clark-Wicksteed-Knight, thus fuses land and capital. But where Clark et al. simply stir them up, Marx subordinates land to capital. For Marx, capital has the superpowers of Mephistopheles; it seizes all surpluses, however generated, even though its supply is elastic.

When we ask what Marx means by "capital," we find Clark-Knight again. ". . . The value of commodities . . . in the circulation . . . of capital, suddenly presents itself as an independent substance . . . in which money and commodities are mere forms which it assumes and casts off in turn" (1867, rpt. 1906, p. 172). "Land as capital is no more eternal than any other capital" (1847, p. 138). It is fascinating to speculate on whether Clark the Rightist knew he was borrowing from Marx the Leftist. Certainly they shared a common purpose, that is, to destroy the case for land taxation as advanced by Clark's target, George, and Marx's target, Proudhon. One wonders, too, if they read the transcendentalists and Hindu mystics, for they both, like Knight later, seem to have enlisted the Hindu's Brahma for economic analysis. In any case, Marx, like Clark-Knight, uses these concepts to create a paradigm in which it is impossible to perceive the rationale for land taxation, a concept which to many neo-Marxists is simply meaningless.

Another strange bedfellow for Marx is Charles Spahr (1891) who has his own way of fusing land and capital. Spahr sees land value produced not by all men but by the good people collectively. Spahr identifies certain groups whose presence lowers land values, and who, therefore, have no claim to share in them. He mentions American Indians and "the most degraded negroes." Hungarians, Italians, and Bohemians are a wash at best. Anglo-Saxon laws recognize that land value results from improvements, public as well as private. The old owners paid for these individually and collectively, so they created the land value.

Spahr would then of course keep all wealth private, both land and capital; in contrast, Marx would socialize both land and capital. The common theme is a denial of George's effort to compromise by distinguishing land values, publicly created, from capital created by private effort and sacrifice. Together they sow the seeds of irrepressible conflict between Communism and Capitalism.

Let us end with the utopian socialists and others who say, "you cannot unscramble an omelette." Production is collective, they say, and imputation is futile (Russell 1945, rpt. 1967, p. 612). Better to drop the effort and distribute "to each according to his needs." There is a good deal of this in the advocacy of income taxation, too, "from each according to ability." In the long run this leads to collectivism, of the right or left, limited only by the emigration of those with high ability and low needs (as perceived by the authorities).

Inelastic Supply of Capital

C. B. Fillebrown (1907, 1914, 1916; see also Marling, pp. 40, 44), a George follower, published a sly argument based on Seligman's doctrine of tax capitalization. The doctrine said that land taxes serve to lower selling prices, so new buyers buy "free of tax," which all falls on sellers. Very well, says Fillebrown, let us go on from there. Owners of capital are paying taxes; owners of land are not, even though they appear to, because they bought free of taxes. To make landowners pay equal taxes, then, we may raise the rate each year by a surtax rate equal to the whole tax on capital. After a few years, *voilà!* We shall have the single tax.

This was too provocative to ignore. T. S. Adams (1916), H. J. Davenport (1917), and E. R. A. Seligman (1916) replied that if taxes borne by capital lower the after-tax return on capital, they divert investors into land until prices rise, equalizing the return on all investments. The new owner may buy clear of land taxes, but he is indirectly taxed by taxes on capital which lower the capitalization rate and raise the price of land. An old tax is a good tax because the market has adjusted to it; any change will hurt someone, and Fillebrown is rejected. One wonders what the world would be like today if all other new proposals, such as the Sixteenth Amendment, had to meet the same test.

Davenport and Seligman went on to adumbrate a theory that is hard to distinguish from what is now called the "Harberger thesis." In a closed economy, taxes on capital are borne by capital and are substantially neutral, provided the coverage is total, because capital has no escape routes. Total capital stock is virtually fixed in the short run because current saving is small next to the accumulated treasure of centuries. Besides, it is not known whether a lower net return after tax will raise or lower saving.

Where, says Seligman rhetorically to George, is all this capital to come from to fill the vacant lots? There is no fund of capital floating in the air — it can only come from other uses (Seligman 1895, rpt. 1923, chap. III, sect. 3). The metaphor and the idea both actually originate with Charles Spahr (1891, p. 632). There is the hand of J. B. Clark here, too. Clark assumed a "static" economy with "fixed" resources. Thus by assumption capital is fixed, like land. A "static" economy is akin to a closed economy: capital is fixed.

Jens Jensen, although not given to unequivocal affirmations, joins in this group: ". . . the property tax on producers' goods must rest largely on the owners of capital in general in the form of a lower interest rate . . ." (1931, pp. 61, 90). This is because the supply of capital is fixed.

It is easy to see the magnetism of this idea for the 1960 Chicago school, with its emphasis on scarcity, and allocation of fixed supplies. Only the

Utopian Keynesians thought you could pull new capital out of the air, and they saw investment, not saving, as the effective constraint on capital formation. It was natural for monetarist Chicagoans to differentiate themselves from Utopian Keynesians who promised suspiciously too much — higher employment, plus capital formation as a free lunch. Thus Chicago's Harberger replicated Seligman-Adams-Spahr-Jensen and supplied a rationale for taxing capital. Capital is as good a base as land, provided the tax be uniform, the supply fixed, the economy closed, and the flow of investment adequate. Chicago rejected the assumption of Netzer and Musgrave that capital taxes are shifted.

Meanwhile, the Keynesians of the '60s were rediscovering one, if not all, of the wheels on the carriage of Henry George. As had George, they pulled new capital "out of the air"; following George's ideas, they did it by favorable tax treatment. Unlike him, their vehicle was the income tax; and unlike him, they made labor pick up most of the revenue losses. Yet, there is a promise (or a threat) in their tax policies of converting the corporate income tax, and the property part of the personal income tax, into taxes on land income, with capital virtually exempt. It may not be coincidental that Walter Heller (1954) wrote in favor of taxing land in developing countries and studied at Madison where, we will see, John R. Commons advocated accelerated depreciation as a Georgian tool.

Jacob Stockfisch (1956, 1957), who with Earl Rolph (1954) kept Adams-Spahr-Seligman alive and anticipated Harberger, points out explicitly the Georgian implications of income tax loopholes. The effect of accelerated depreciation, investment tax credits, and expensing capital outlays is to exempt an increasing share of capital income from the tax base, leaving nondepreciable land bearing the brunt. While Georgist frontal assault waves were breaking against the rock of local property taxes, Keynesian subtlety was transforming the income tax. Stockfisch seems to view this transformation negatively. However, he identifies a tax development that Georgists let pass unrecognized as a move toward their preferred reform.

To be sure, Stockfisch overstates the case. Tax-cutting Keynesians who gave investment incentives for capital were also leaving many loopholes for land income. They were also piling up payroll taxes on workers, taxes George would have execrated. And yet, like George, they had a dream, a dream that untaxing capital could pull new capital out of the air, and spin off multiplied increased output and jobs. If the methods were different, the expansive optimistic spirit was alike, and quite at odds with the limited resources, competing ends, astringent skepticism, and expensive lunches of Chicago.

And so we find the "conservatives" Spahr, Jensen, Seligman, Adams,

Davenport, Knight, Rolph, Stockfisch, Harberger et al. rationalizing the taxation of capital. Meanwhile the "liberal" Georgists and Keynesians rationalize untaxing it, linking up with various right-wingers who must find their Chicago allies' position baffling, and alienating many left-wingers who view capital only as Robin Hood viewed the fat monk's purse. It is a confusing paradox that Chicago and other conservatives should line up with the Left on an issue so central to economic ideologies as the taxation of capital. One root of this paradox is the traditional reaction to the single-tax drive to replace capital with land in the tax base. In this context, taxing capital is the conservative position. Frank Knight is the pivotal figure. He dominates two generations at Chicago; his relentless antipathy to George lies between the lines of much of his work and locks his followers into a paradigm that guides them away from taxing rent.

If uniformity can make the taxation of capital efficient, so can it make other taxes efficient. We find much of the world accepting general income taxes for this reason, and now increasingly general sales taxes and next VAT. Forward shifting and the excess burden of indirect taxation are "excise tax effects," not the effects of general taxes. General equilibrium analysis, and theories of second-best all point toward this policy finding.

Ragnar Frisch (1939) used such a course of thought to attack Harold Hotelling's basic article on marginal-cost pricing. The attack was equally levelled against Hotelling's corollary case for taxing land to meet the deficits of marginal-cost pricing with decreasing costs – a case William Vickrey has adopted and developed. Yet a uniform sales tax applied indiscriminately both to increasing and decreasing cost producers is inherently inefficient, for reasons Hotelling gave: it is more efficient to subsidize the latter. Still, much of the later writing on welfare economics follows Frisch, undercutting Hotelling's principles and the implementation of marginal-cost pricing with theories of second-best and all that (Little 1950, rpt. 1960, appendix IV).

The other troubles with uniformity as a working guide are that there are not closed economies and there are no truly uniform taxes. Taxes on capital drive it away – the local supply is never fixed. In an open economy only one thing is closed, and that is the land supply. Tax jurisdictions are defined as areas of land; capital and people move in and out. So skeptics of the Harberger-Seligman-Spahr approach, such as Netzer, still have a lot to say about the excess burden of indirect taxation and the superiority of land as a tax base. As for Gaffney (1971), his reasons for believing the property tax to be progressive do not include a full subscription to the Harberger thesis, or any belief that the U.S. economy is more than partially closed.

The Social Functions of Land Speculation

Richard T. Ely advanced a theory of "ripening costs" to explain the function of land speculation. By holding land idle until the rise in value, he says, "I perform social service" (1920, p. 127). The service is to pre-empt land from premature underimprovement, while it ripens to a higher use. Holding costs — the unrealized latent rents — are the "costs of ripening." Land taxes force premature use at less than optimal intensity.

Ely's idea had a strong following in the 1920s, followed by a crash in the 1930s, after which Ely and Wehrwein ruefully accepted the revised metaphor of Simpson and Burton (1931, p. 44): "We speak of land ripening, but this is putting land into cold storage, and loading the community with the frozen assets that result." The pros and cons of the doctrine are easily subsumed today in the modern rule of planning the timing of a series of replacements over time so as to maximize discounted cash flow.

Ely's idea was briefly revived by Donald Shoup (1970) and Peter Mieszkowski (1970, p. 17), but not pushed. Roger Smith (1979) and Louis Rose (1971) have kept it alive, and John Krutilla has applied it to the pre-emption of scenic resources. But these modern statements are much more careful and limited than Ely's sweeping generalization; Krutilla's avoids tax issues entirely. It is not necessary to frame the question in the emotive pugilistic style of the 1920s. It is not a gut question of whether individual landholders serve any function, but rather how that function is affected by taxes. Shoup, Rose, and Smith suggest that land taxes motivate premature conversion. Gaffney (1970, 1973b), on the other hand, emphasizes that building taxes delay conversion. Ely's soul marches on in the political movement for preferential assessment of ripening land. Whether Ely originated the idea, or, like some composers, merely picked up an old folk tune, we may never know. Nevertheless the idea persists. It thrives in our times because urban sprawl has brought dreams or fears of ripening to so many more lands than ever before that every country Muzak box plays Ely's tune.

Ely also objected to calling land supply "fixed." A high price induces more supply, man-made. He interpreted many capital improvements, land use conversions, migrations, discoveries, and substitutions of capital for land as actually "increasing the land supply." Many neoclassical economists approve of this locution, which helps excuse them from rationalizing rent as a surplus. Orris Herfindahl (1974), the neoclassical mineral economist, saw mineral rents as mainly a return of discovery costs — a position I like to believe he would modify if writing after OPEC. He reflects the Chicago compulsion to rationalize markets so perfectly that there is no unearned wealth except by chance, and even then, it is a functional reward for taking chances (see Gaffney 1979).

J. B. Clark (1899, pp. 85–87), H. J. Davenport (1917), and B. H. Hibbard (1930) identify another function of land speculation, that of hastening the conquest of the frontier. "The lure of unearned increment" drew pioneers westward earlier than otherwise. Land taxation would put a damper on this "rent-seeking" behavior, which Clark and his followers regarded as beneficial, and slow down the early development of frontiers that were otherwise submarginal. Alvin S. Johnson claims the same effect in cities: unearned increments lead men to build in anticipation of future demand. Rising land values in boomtowns cause "overbuilding," a desirable outcome (1914, p. 35). At the same time, rising land values keep farmers from leaving for the city (1914, p. 34). B. M. Anderson (1914) refutes these positions, apologizing at the same time for siding with the single taxers.

To Ely, the function of land speculation is to delay use. To Clark et al. speculation serves to advance use. None of these economists sought to reconcile their polar positions, but instead united in their criticism of land taxation, which Ely said would bring on new land too soon, and Clark et al. said would delay it. George himself intended land taxes to act on the better lands, causing infilling and full use, and obviating premature recourse to marginal lands. *Progress and Poverty* is filled with complaints against urban sprawl and scattered rural settlement.

Davenport (1909) also raises the soil conservation issue. He believes that land taxes encourage soil mining, looting, and abandonment of erosive soils (and, by extension, of other extractive resources). This is also a theme of Seligman.

F. Y. Edgeworth writes that land taxes would inevitably bite into building profits, that builders' and buyers' fears would magnify the deterrent to build, and bankers' fears would doubly magnify the problem. The tax would hamper raising money on the "security of the premises." Edgeworth also objects to "forcing the market," and anticipates Ely's ripening cost doctrine – speculation is reserving land for a higher use. "In fine, the interest of monopolists is not always contrary to that of their customers" (1906, p. 73). The mood of Edgeworth's prose is more querulous than mordant, and he concedes some limited role for taxing unearned increments. The limits, however, are clearly his primary interest.

Edgeworth's point about land as collateral for loans is not found in other scholarly critics, and he himself gives it only a Parthian shot – and wisely so. It is clear in theory and experience that untaxing buildings improves the credit of builders as such; taxing land weakens the credit of holdout land speculators and helps shift land to builders. Yet, Edgeworth's point has an active life in political campaigns that touch anywhere near our subject. Lessees on Crown land in British Columbia, for example, successfully oppose the Crown's extraction of market rents by pleading their credit ratings, used to attract eastern capital "for the benefit of all."

Local Land Taxes as a "Tragedy of the Commons"

Alfred Marshall, who sees much merit in land taxation, also sees it as overcrowding central cities, and proposes that some land tax revenues be earmarked to a "fresh air fund" to offset this damage. Leonard Darwin (1907) carries this much further than Marshall. However, Edward Polak (1915) replies that cities generate more positive than negative spillovers.

A more challenging negative comes from Edwin Cannan. Cannan defends taxing buildings on the now familiar basis that they increase local public costs, and in proportion to building value (1907, p. 39). Buildings receive more services in large cities than small, so untaxing them will subsidize congestion in central cities. Free services to urban building create something analogous to a "tragedy of the commons," overcrowding cities and destroying rent (1907, p. 44).

Although Cannan's style is partisan, and much of his work unimpressive, this point is basic; he desperately wants an answer in light of today's exclusionary zoning and related policies. Cannan's argument needs adapting today when the suburbs outdo the central cities in their fear of fiscal parasites. Yet it is fiscal sharing more than physical congestion that concerns Cannan. His logic leads towards pooling tax revenues of whatever kind at higher levels of government, as proposed by Colin Clark. It is perhaps the great weakness of most Georgians that they have persisted in pushing land taxation purely as a local policy, thus leading right into Cannan's powerful rebuttal which currently is sweeping the field.

Inadequacy of Land as a Tax Base

Spahr (1891) and later Seligman (1895, rpt. 1923) write that marginal communities have little land value and hence no land value tax base. This is consistent with their belief that taxes on capital are borne by capital (for if local capital taxes come instead out of land rents, then a direct tax on land is simply a more efficient way of tapping the taxable surplus, which cannot exceed rent anyway [Andelson and Gaffney 1979]). It is at odds with their belief that farmers bear most of a tax on land values, a contradiction so glaring that Spahr and Seligman have little message for today. In retrospect, Edwin Cannan had a stronger point. He did not question the adequacy of rent, but the efficiency of locational incentives created by socializing rent through local taxation.

Many economists have questioned land's adequacy as a tax base. Ernest Kurnow is the most recent and quantitative of these (1959, 1960, and 1961). Gaffney has criticized his procedures elsewhere (1970, pp. 180–81).

Jens Jensen notes that land taxes are capitalized, but the value of capital has to remain at its cost of production. He sees capital therefore as able to yield "enormous revenue" compared to land (1931, p. 91). The opposite view is that local taxes on whatever base are shifted into land values. John A. Zangerle (1927) takes this view, tracing it back to John Locke (1692) and Jacob Vanderlint (1734). The physiocrats also held this view, as did Adam Smith. Gaffney has elaborated on this theme (1970), citing Paul Douglas, Bronson Cowan, and Ebenezer Howard, among others. A curious twist is that the arch-critic Alvin S. Johnson sees land rent as much more than adequate to cover all public needs (1914, pp. 29, 30).

Wide Distribution of Landownership

Alvin S. Johnson's major theme is that single tax is "a device for the spoliation of the middle class" (1914, p. 30), because they own most of the urban land, and all the farmland. Charles Spahr (1891) had earlier sounded the same note. E. R. A. Seligman (1895, rpt. 1923) takes relish in quoting Voltaire's satire *L'Homme au quarante écus,* accusing the physiocratic land taxers of a regressive proposal, hitting the poor people who own all the land. It is fascinating to read these pre-econometric economists who issue facts on their own authority without data.

General Francis A. Walker (1883a, rpt. 1898), director of the U.S. census, president of M.I.T., and first president of the American Economic Association, did have data. He pointed out that the average size of farms in 1880 was small, and growing smaller, contrary to George's allegation of increasing concentration. George objected to the use of a simple mean; he wanted to know how much was held by the largest few. He never used the term "Lorenz Curve," but that was the idea. Walker, trapped in an untenable position, tried to shoot his way out in an exchange that must have embarrassed him (Walker 1883a, rpt. 1898, May, June). It is perhaps due to this exchange that in 1900 the census began collecting data on farms ranked and grouped by size. There was no retroactive count, but the trend from 1900 to the present is one of rising concentration.

Later critics have avoided this issue, other than mentioning it incidentally in connection with the question of whether the *general* property tax is regressive. Here the main germane issue becomes the corporation. Several studies show corporate shares to be held more closely than "real

estate." Many property tax opponents conclude from this that property
taxes exempt the wealthiest. I am not aware, however, of any systematic
study refuting the belief that corporations are our major landholders, as
documented in Gaffney (1970).

Mixed, or Shifting and Changeable Positions

Francis A. Walker thought that George overstated his case inex-
cusably. We have discussed Walker on his feelings about concentration.
He also attacks George's forecast that rents will continue to rise with increased population, because the evolution of technology is labor-saving
and resource-using, and because higher incomes lead to higher demand
for land. Walker cites M. Leroy-Beaulieu, "an economist and statistician
of eminence," who said that rent "will soon disappear altogether"
(Walker 1883b, p. 147). Chicagoan Theodore Schultz (1953) says much
the same.

In truth, the periodic collapse of land values in our history of cyclical
territorial expansion has weakened support for land taxation; George's
forecasts were overdrawn and premature. But now, one hundred years
later, land values are looming up as George warned.

Walker's hostility to George is more stylistic and personal than
substantive. Walker remains a Ricardian, and tackles J. B. Clark for
treating capital as though it were fixed, like land (1888, pp. 417–35). In
Land and Its Rent, after a furious attack on George, Walker still says in
regard to the rights of property, "property in land stands lower, much
lower in the hierarchy than property in capital" (1883b, p. 198). Before he
is through, the eminent M. Leroy-Beaulieu "can command little conviction" (1883b, p. 191).

Five years later, Walker has mellowed so far as to accept land taxation
as reasonable in principle but impracticable in implementation (1888, pp.
415–17).

Alfred Marshall (1920, rpt. 1947) improves upon Ricardo by contributing a new concept, the "public value of land," to help define the
desired tax base. Ricardo wrote mainly of farmland and fertility
differences and perverse readers persisted in taking this narrowly. Marshall's public value is what George means by "community-created" value,
the joint product of nature, location, public works and services, settlement, and community synergy. Marshall realizes that urban location
values are outgrowing farm values, and he provides an appropriate concept.

Marshall also develops a lucid statement of how high urban land costs
cause intensive land use by actuating substitution of capital for dear land

(1920, rpt. 1947, chap. XI). Marshall is also clear that "from the economic and from the ethical point of view, land must everywhere and always be classed as a thing by itself" (1920, rpt. 1947, appendix G). He seems to favor a kind of creeping land tax.

But Marshall is ambivalent and cautious, the very type of Harry Truman's two-handed economist. For every proposal there is a caveat, for every aid to one side, comfort to the other. Any change should be slow — during one 1883 lecture, he discusses the merit of nationalizing land interests after one hundred years (1883, rpt. 1969). It is a sobering thought that that centennial is now only two years away.

Marshall also contributes new concepts for the Omelette School, which resist unscrambling land and capital. Durable capital earns "quasi-rents," in the short run just like land rents. Big land developers consciously create values that spill over onto neighboring lands that they own. The supply of *national* capital is fixed, so a uniform national tax on building values is neutral, and not shifted (this is the "new view" Harberger thesis again).

Marshall distinguishes "onerous" and "beneficial" local taxes. An "onerous" rate is one which taxes property to provide services to people — for example, "a poor-rate levied on the well-to-do" (1920, rpt. 1947, p. 794) — and so fails to give back to property a service equal to what it pays for. This is cousin to Cannan's tragedy-of-commons case against taxing local land values to provide services that attract immigrants and congest cities. But where Cannan focuses on people moving in, Marshall sees the wealthy moving out to the suburbs. Having raised the issue, however, Marshall characteristically minimizes it — he says that the rich cannot escape because tax jurisdictions are widened to catch them in their new locations.

Still, Marshall provides the framework for today's mischievously potent slogan, that property should pay only for services to property. These are "beneficial"; services to people are "onerous." The viewpoint is clearly that of the local landholder.

Marshall resented Henry George's influence in England, and in 1883 he took the stump against him. As with Walker, differences of style overrode substance, and no doubt George seemed a cocky intruder in Marshall's nation and profession. George developed his attitudes in a land that either belonged to the national government or was only freshly granted to private holders; Marshall's England had its own history. Marshall mainly objected to the immediacy of George's reforms.

The mature Marshall never published these immature polemics, and wisely so. George Stigler (1969) has exhumed them, possibly in the belief they show the real Marshall. But yet another George (Prime Minister

Lloyd) did win Marshall's support for a British land tax when he proposed it in 1909 (Hutchison 1969, pp. 248–49, n. 50). The real Alfred Marshall is probably the one who stood up when push came to shove in his native land. Hostility to an invader is one thing: conviction on principle is another.

A. C. Pigou (1949) takes a fairly clear stand in favor of using Marshall's public value of land as a tax base, "a moderate tax assessed at a moderate percentage," in a family of "different imposts." Its strong point is its perfect "announcement aspect," i.e., its unavoidability and unshiftability. It rates poorly on horizontal equity (Pigou takes "income" as the base of reference for "equity," without regard to sources); but rates well on vertical equity. An added attraction is automatic recoupment of betterment.

Pigou contributes the important concept of "announcement effect." Some prior economists wrote simply of taxing rent, without usually specifying much about the actual method. Pigou likes the tax because we can "announce" it to the taxpayer as a lump sum for the year, based on an outside assessment, independent of taxpayer activity. It is not clear if some earlier writers always had this in mind, or would tax rent as realized, ex post. Today, most discussion, pro and con, premises Pigou's concept of a tax on presumptive or "notional" rent, as revealed by assessed land value. This unfortunately confuses two questions, because there also are income taxes on rent, and there is a case for letting taxes vary with short term changes in realized rent (as when prices widely vary). It is too bad Pigou never pursues this lead further. It has been left to analysts of leasing methods to choose among different ways for a landlord to "announce" rent to a tenant, and the field is beginning to yield a vigorous literature. Among land taxers, we will see John R. Commons emphasizing the use of income taxation to collect rent.

Karl Marx wavers in a love-hate relationship with land taxation. Mostly it is hate. The *Manifesto* (Marx and Engels 1848, rpt. 1959), demands "application of all rents of land to public purposes" (Plank 1), but the means is never explained. The allied demands include forced labor (Plank 8), the reverse of what land taxers intend. Still, the unfinished posthumous vol. III of *Capital* (1867, rpt. 1906), pieced together by Engels, is half about ground rent. However, in *The Poverty of Philosophy* (1847), Marx attacks Proudhon for pushing a tax on rental income. He marshals technical problems of separating land and capital, but more basically he objects to a reform so easily accommodated within the capitalist system of market pricing. He suggests that rent might better be distributed by lowering consumer prices — a process familiar enough to domestic producers of "old" oil and gas today, and consistent with

Marx's disdain for conservation. Marx also is leery of a proposal animated by a decentralist bias, his own being the reverse. Marx seems at times to say that only farming yields rents, because of diminishing returns, while manufacturing yields none, because of increasing returns — he is careless about distinguishing scale and proportions.

Finally, he opposes any reform that would make capitalism more tolerable, and that would delay the apocalypse of his heart's desire (whatever that is — we know what Marx is against, but not what he is for).

E. R. A. Seligman (1895), like Francis Walker and Alfred Marshall, followed the catharsis of a no-holds-barred attack on George by a partial agreement on the desirability of at least some special taxation of land (Andelson and Gaffney 1979).

There are countless other economists who have touched on one or another aspect of the land tax case and then shifted as they aged and changed. I leave to philosophers the case of Herbert Spencer. I do not attempt a comprehensive catalogue, but hasten on to cover the more prominent or currently relevant cases.

Noncommittal, Detached, or Supercilious Economists

David Ricardo, whose contributions to analytical method tower over our subject, does not take an advocate's role. He merely explains in short and simple terms that a tax on rent is not shifted (1817, chap. X). Nothing suggests that he cares if this intelligence is put to use.

That it was put to use by others is some kind of tribute to the power of conceptualization in guiding behavior, a power clearly understood by Clark et al. as they went about undoing Ricardo.

My guess is that Ricardo doubted the adequacy of rent for taxes, because his treatment of other taxes has them all shifted forward, never back into rent. He even rebukes Adam Smith on this point. Believing this, he would not see that most taxes in an open economy come from rent anyway.

Other and more sophisticated aspects of rent were defined by Heinrich von Thünen, founder of location theory; and Martin Faustmann (1849, rpt. 1968) who mastered the mathematics of defining ground rent in forestry when yields are slow and periodic. Both care about economizing on land, but are not known to have written about taxing it.

Location theorists, urban land economists, and regional scientists in large numbers deal constantly with location rents and the importance of pressing landholders to economize on land in the measure indicated by its rent in order to economize on transportation. They are allied with professional city planners, many of whom follow the lead of Ebenezer Howard (1965) in promoting special taxation of situation rents. But the theorists, oddly, have avoided tax policy questions. William Alonso (1964) extends himself beyond the norm of this reference group when he devotes one half of page 116 to note that a tax on land rent is neutral.

Paul Samuelson, in various editions of his text, gives statements as lucid as any heart could desire of land rent as a taxable surplus – and there they rest. We cannot attribute this quiescence to a reticent disposition, or to qualms against melding positive and normative economics. He simply is detached from this issue.

Herbert Simon's article on the incidence of a tax on urban real property (1943) is a fine piece of thread-the-needle reasoning that suggests a general equilibrium approach to tax incidence along lines pioneered by Harry G. Brown, and shows that a tax on "house rental" is separable into a tax on land and building, with different effects. He spikes Edgeworth's incipient fallacy that a given capital adds more to value on a more highly rented site – an approach that could arrogate the land value to the capital value, in the manner of Marx. There are ideas launched about housing as a composite service combining location and building, and it is regarded as a contribution to demand theory. Yet, if it was anything for Simon but an intellectual game, there is no sign. In 1979, however, Simon played a role in a successful campaign to place more of Pittsburgh's graded property tax on land, and less on buildings.

Frederick Babcock's classic *Valuation of Real Estate* covers most of the topics on separating land and building values over building life, on different shaped lots, and so on (1932, see esp. chaps. 23, 30). Babcock does for urban real estate what Faustmann did for forestry: he applies capital theory to separate land and capital values over the long life of durable capital. Richard Hurd (1903) earlier did for urban real estate what von Thünen did for regions; he showed the power of location over land values. Anyone constructing a map of land values relies heavily on Hurd's work because it shows the spatial continuity of urban land values, which is the basis for interpolating and extrapolating. While Hurd attempts no formal theory, it would be hard to fault his penetrating observations of real life on any theoretical ground. Perhaps it is just as well that Babcock and Hurd wrote for the trade, and pronounced nothing on public policy. They illustrate that the needs of economic life demand separate valuations for land and capital, regardless of ideologies.

It is altogether remarkable that Babcock and Homer Hoyt (1933) were writing their classics on land values in Chicago right by Knight's temple. George Olcott was issuing his annual *Blue Book of Chicago Land Values*. Herbert D. Simpson (1933) was studying property taxation and land value cycles, and attributing the banking collapse to the collapse of real estate – a point never entertained by Friedman. Chicago sociologists Park and Burgess (1925) were pioneering their ring hypothesis of land value, and Hoyt (1939) was developing his sector hypothesis. Wallace Atwood was founding the discipline of economic geography, the study of how land determines the location of human culture. They drew on the rich and instructive experience of the vital city around them. However, University of Chicago economists were hewing to Simon Patten's counsel that "economic doctrine must isolate itself more fully"; for them the land market was ruled out of this world. The brilliance of their work in other fields has only compounded the mischief by spreading theories from which land was exorcised.

Friedrich Hayek (1941, pp. 87–94) like other Austrians rejects the classical reason for distinguishing land and capital as backward-looking and based on origin. He insists on maintaining the distinction in Austrian economics for an appropriately forward-looking reason: ". . . capital . . . needs replacement and in consequence leads to investment." He rejects Clark, Cassel, and Knight on the capital fund as "pure mysticism." "The distinction between capital and land is surely not an invention of the economists. . . ."

Yet, having kept the concept pure he lets it languish, and no Austrian has been conspicuous as a land taxer. Nor do they even enter land rent among the carrying costs of durable capital in their treatments of replacement timing, a matter near the heart of their theories.

Positive, but Tentative, Limited, Partial, and Remote

Developing Nations

Haskell Wald (1959) gathers together many arguments for land taxation, although the style is skittish. He anticipates one modern domestic trend in recommending some "personal allowances" in the land tax, to remove the regressive stinger (John Shannon's term) and allow a higher overall rate. He suggests the wisdom of adjusting levies for year-to-year changes in economic rent due to weather and prices. However, after marshalling a persuasive case for a tax that sharpens incentives, distributes wealth more equitably, and is administrable and richly yielding, he suggests that land taxation is a transitional tool that can be phased downwards after developing countries acquire the accounting skills needed for income taxation.

John Due (1963) is much more the observer-analyst than advocate. He finds and records a land tax being implemented in many cities of east Africa. He brings out the importance of land registry, surveys, and clear

titles. In West Africa he generally finds that titles are so obscure, boundaries so unspecific, and extended families so complex that a land tax base
can hardly be defined, so property taxes concentrate on buildings. In
rural east Africa, likewise, the cadastral tradition is lacking. He might
have added that in precommercial societies community interests in land
are expressed in nonpecuniary ways.

In East African *cities,* however, European concepts of tenure have
been applied. Land has been commercialized, making land taxation
possible – and, he might have added, more appropriate, in order to compensate for extinguishing ancient communal rights.

Due writes glowing reports of the modernity of land-tax
cities – Nairobi and Salisbury receive specific praise – and of high standards of administration, among both Africans and Europeans. Due
remains the careful technician, mainly discussing nuts and bolts, eschew-
ing ideologies, except when he attributes land taxation in East Africa to
"a spread of ideas of the single tax . . . from Great Britain through South
and Central Africa and gradually into Kenya." One gathers that the ideas
traveled in the natural way, by indigenous grapevine without benefit of
A.I.D., World Bank, Ford, U.N., or Colombo Plan, and are the firmer
rooted for it.

Due contributes to theory the cultural relativity of land taxation: it fits
where land is under tenure. On Crown and unsurveyed lands, he notes,
charging for the *use* of land is "the same as a program of land value rates
under freehold." The idea is germane in our own commercial culture
where so many resources (such as highways and waters) are still without
adequate tenure control. Due also echoes Cannan's concern about
distorting locational incentives by distributing central city rents. We still
see that Colin Clark has a solution to this.

Robert M. Haig (1915a) is both a keen observer and a theoretician. In
1915 he writes, on behalf of the city of New York, "The Exemption of Improvements from Taxation in Canada and the U.S.," mainly discussing
western Canada. The title is carefully chosen. Property taxes were so low
in that part of Canada, both absolutely and relative to other revenues,
that the experience was more with exempting buildings than taxing land,
as he points out. His meager raw data on building volumes demonstrate
no clear effect on the policy. Cautious and detached though he is, he
reasons a priori and from extensive interviews that the policy has a
substantial effect in stimulating building and reducing lot sizes. As a
political observer, he notes that the policy is pushed by real estate men, in
the booster spirit. The region is growth oriented, quite the reverse of
Cannan's England. He notes the net effect on land values is positive, and
the zeal of the boosters is not utopian, but wealth-maximizing. There is

no drying up of loanable funds, as Edgeworth feared. In a few smaller towns, taxes have been high enough utterly to destroy "speculation" (construed as holding vacant land for the rise). Ever circumspect, Haig offers a left-handed conclusion: "Under certain circumstances" improvements can be exempted "without disastrous consequences."

Haig contributes a practical sense of the importance of credit rationing — a factor neglected by most theoreticians. He observes that banks are loathe to lend on raw land, so some owners must build in order to borrow. He conjectures that this may stimulate building, where holders keep land for the "lure of unearned increment," a topic that bemused him. He feels that *present* land taxes hasten building, but *anticipated* taxes dampen the lure of increments. The increment is not the direct cause of stimulus: "It is rather the necessity of preserving title to that increment" (1915b, p. 837). He does not determine whether this is an economically efficient stimulus, or another "tragedy-of-commons" misuse of rent as a stimulus, as modern economists would sense, and Harry G. Brown replied. He likes to define contervailing forces, and to leave us with country lawyer wisdom: "Circumstances alters cases." Like Due, however, he contributes a strong sense of the importance of tenure institutions in determining the effects of land taxation.

Harold Groves contrasts Canadian and American property taxation. Canada has narrowed the base more than we have, partly exempting improvements and nearly wholly exempting personal property, following the British custom. Groves says ". . . exempting improvements . . . strikes a responsive chord in those who, like the author, hold that land is an especially suitable subject for taxation and that little, if any, rational ground can be found for taxing improvements" (1948, p. 29). However, there it rests, since he devotes his main strength to institutional matters.

American, English, and Canadian economic missionaries to LDCs have been legion during the last 35 years of Pax Americana. I cannot possibly name all those who have smiled on land taxation abroad, but a representation includes Richard Bird (1974), William Rhoads (1969), Albert Berry (1972), Erwin Johnson (1970), Richard Musgrave (1969), Daniel Holland (1969), Robert Hardie (1952), Richard Lindholm (1965), Richard Goode (1970), Peter Dorner (1972), John Strasma (1969, 1965), Orville Grimes, Jr. (1977), George Lent (1967), John R. Hicks (1959), Milton Taylor (1965), and Walker Heller (1954). Reform may be easier to comtemplate at a distance, but dreams of far away may come to life. We have seen Marshall shorten the count-down from one-hundred years to "Blast off!" in 1909. Lindholm, for one, has also promoted domestic land taxation. Heller, a student of Groves, has engineered major exemptions of domestic capital from income taxation. John Strasma has skillfully guided a tax on net proceeds of mineral extraction — read "rent" — through the Wisconsin legislature. Others, too, may yet bring their messages home.

Advocates with Unresolved Reservations

J. S. Mill, like the early Marshall, would limit rent taxes to future increments only. The problem turns out not to be so simple, since in a rising market, future increments for all future time are already reflected in land prices paid by "innocent" buyers. He recognizes fleetingly that present land values include discounted future increments, but dances calisthenically around this, concluding it is all right to tax future increments to rent (1872, book V, chap. II). In later passages he returns to the attack without the qualification. The existing land tax is not a tax burden at all, but a reservation of ancient feudal rights. Landowners should bear it silently, *plus* their share of general taxes. He says profits of capital should be taxed at a lower rate than land rent (1872, chap. III; para. 2). The long run supply of capital is elastic because of international flows. (He also anticipates Domar and Musgrave by noting that taxes on profits increase risk-taking.) ". . . among the very few kinds of income which are fit subjects for peculiar taxation, these (urban) ground-rents hold the principal place." A house-tax, so far as it falls on the ground-landlord, "is liable to no valid objection." For Mill the moralist and logician, that is strong language.

In later years, Mill becomes active in the Land Tenure Reform Association, but only after his autobiography is finished and his main energies spent; it is almost a posthumous activity.

Most poignant is Paul Douglas' (1972) comment in his autobiography, concerning what might have been. Looking back, he regrets his failure to support land taxation more vigorously. Knight's Chicago was hardly a hospitable matrix for a young professor so inclined, and anyway Douglas had been trained at Columbia by J. B. Clark and nurtured on Philip Wicksteed. Later as a U.S. Senator he did push the National Commission on Urban Problems to recommend land taxation (1968). He hopes "St. Peter may forgive my silence . . . and accept my later efforts as at least partial atonement" (1972, p. 446). There is no suggestion of how St. Peter should deal with Clark and Wicksteed, who conditioned the young mind against those efforts. To the very end Douglas calls Wicksteed "one of my favorites . . . from whom I had learned the coordination of the laws of production and distribution" (1972, p. 123). One could argue that the Cobb–Douglas production function, which came from Wicksteed (Douglas 1972, p. 46), helps condition even more minds, if not against, then away from those efforts. As used by Wicksteed and Douglas there are just two factors of production, labor and capital. The enclosure movements, in which capital drives labor off the land and which actuated the radicalism of both Marx and George, cannot be fitted to any Cobb–Douglas function.

Advocates for Special Industries or Conditions

There are repeated proposals to exempt specific kinds of capital from taxes. In forestry, Ellis Williams (1974) renews the call for a tax based on site productivity. Fred R. Fairchild (1935) and many others have preceded Williams on this topic. The problem is that there has been no effort to calculate the equivalent rate necessary to compensate others whose capital remains taxable. In effect, these proposals involve preferential treatment for one industry.

Ebenezer Howard (1965) has led generations of planners toward an ideal city financed solely from ground rents. However, Howard's interest in taxes is incidental, and stops at the local level.

Harold Hotelling (1938) is prominent for his marginal-cost pricing proposals. While Marshall and Pigou launched the same balloon in the abstract, Hotelling got right down to the case of regulated utilities, reviving and crediting Jules Dupuit (1844). To meet the deficits of marginal-cost pricing with declining average costs, Marshall and Pigou suggested taxes on increasing-cost industries (with the sideshow of some confusion in defining increasing cost). Hotelling suggests meeting the deficit by taxes on income, inheritance, or land. Land is an even better tax base than increasing cost industries, says Hotelling, because there is some deadweight loss in taxing even them; the vertical supply curve of land, however, means there is *no* deadweight loss at all. As he warms to his subject, Hotelling gives the strong impression that the ideal tax base for meeting deficits is the land benefited by a utility or new bridge, and he therefore forgets the income and inheritance taxes.

He recognizes that it is hard to measure benefits exactly from each project, but urges us to more "communal spending in ways beneficial to the public at large" — perhaps not realizing what a Pandora's box he was opening! At any rate, this could be interpreted to mean that land taxes need not be limited to benefits demonstrably received from specific projects.

Hotelling's seminal article is filled with insights on the nature of rents and costs and congestion. In spite of immediate and recurrent attacks by neo-Leibnitzians[2] such as Frisch and Little, Hotelling launched a whole

---

2. Leibnitz is the original for Dr. Pangloss in Voltaire's *Candide*, who counsels that reform is futile anywhere because the world is imperfect everywhere else, and all is interconnected. It is hard to distinguish Leibnitz' philosophy from "second-best" theories of welfare economics.

new field of utility economics and forward-looking marginal-cost pricing.

Hotelling also contributes to defining the rent of exhaustible mines. However, here, as with his bridges, Hotelling never makes it crystal clear what all his assumptions and conclusions are, and in the end there are those nagging doubts over how far he is advising us to carry the land tax policy.

William Vickrey carries Hotelling's ideas much further to the logical conclusion of a thoroughgoing general shift to the land value tax base. To Vickrey, urban land rents are a reflection of all the economies of urban scale. Efficiency requires that these land rents "be devoted *primarily* to financing the intramarginal residues" or deficits of marginal-cost pricing (1969, p. 19).

The rent of mines, including oil and gas wells, is a topic of wide interest. Where forest economists have sought taxes on sites only as an incident to preferential exemption of timber capital, other economists have seen mineral rents as a particularly good tax base, with only incidental, if any, mention of exempting capital. This biased treatment could be a reaction to the preferences achieved by mine owners *de facto,* and/or to widespread absentee ownership. Otherwise it is anomalous, because the rent of mines is harder to separate out, and easier to defend as socially functional, than other rents. One can blend mine rents with a return on discovery costs, call it a fund for replacement, and so on. We have seen Herfindahl (1974) taking this tack. Economists leaning the same way include Henry Steele (1967), Paul Bradley (1977), and Stephen McDonald (1963, 1967, 1971). And yet, their differences from others are only those of emphasis, not of analytical technique or concept. All four of them expound and use the concept of resource rent. McDonald has even praised a property tax on oil deposits (1966). It is a fascinating development in economic thought that "rent" has become the universal usage in mineral economics, where it is most vulnerable.

A pioneer analyst of mine rents is Lewis C. Gray (1914), who also draws together and discusses the sparse earlier treatments in Marshall, Ricardo, Böhm-Bawerk, and Sorley. Gray divides mineral rents into two parts, a pure income and a depletion charge, the latter variously referred to by others as "user cost" and "royalty." Gray insists that both are part of rent, which he defines as the surplus above social costs. Depletion, he says, is simply the present value of future rents foregone by present use, and therefore part of rent. He has in mind resources which are replaceable without high discovery costs. He does not fully face up to the problem of long run replacement; or he may simply be taking implicit note of the empirical fact that the bulk of replacement costs consist of payments made to other landowners.

John Ise (1925) joins Gray's inclination to socialize mineral rents, but is more conservation-minded. Ise favors policies to retard the rate of use, a position later reached by Gray as well. Ise is the intellectual idealist, appalled at the vulgar materialism of sovereign consumers, and not at all disturbed at making them learn the character-building discipline of waiting. This message, of course, would be ridiculed by Joe Hill, whose preacher tells the slave, "There'll be pie in the sky in the sweet bye and bye," and by John Keynes: "In the long run we are all dead."

Harold Hotelling (1931) supplies a classic mathematical model of mine rents, one rightly admired by modern modelers for its rigor, but with more than a touch of exclusionary esoteric obscurity. Hotelling tells us we must master the calculus of variations in order to understand depletion. One senses an element of pedantic ostentation, and we are grateful that he was not also vaunting Greek and Sanskrit. The basic reasoning and the findings are in fact much like Gray's.

Warren Roberts (1944, 1967) reinforces the emerging Gray-Hotelling model of resource rents. The presence of rent in mining is implied by sharply rising marginal costs, with average cost therefore well below price. Although Roberts is by trade a political scientist, he favors the economic model of defining rent, and the economic solution of taxing it. ". . . Other means, such as exchange control, tend to confuse issues and lead away from, rather than toward, optimum understanding" (1967, p. 215). "Accounting is not without political meaning. It educates and puts in gear the rationality of men. . . . The practical importance of the concept of rent lies in its near universal validity and in the ability of intellectuals to give it proximate definition." (1967, pp. 207–8.)

Mason Gaffney (1967) writes favorably of taxing mine rents, but not in a discriminatory way. To him, land rents of all kinds are the tax base of choice. As to mineral rents he treads more cautiously than Gray, seeing a need to reward and finance replacement, in principle. Yet, in pursuing this principle he finds such a weight of institutional bias favoring excessive and premature discovery that he sees little need for current concern about adequacy of motivation. He seeks to devise a tax scheme which would motivate exploration optimally while raising revenues as well. He sees much potential rent dissipated in interest on premature effort and emphasizes the benefits of an industry operating with leaner advance reserves. Gaffney also sees rent taxation as a reform of extended economic and social consequences, with benefits to equity, competitive structure of industry, employment, efficiency, and social harmony.

Absentee ownership of minerals gives a fillip to our subject where intellectuals find themselves in colonial settings. Canadian economists have responded in force. Lewis C. Gray originated as a Canadian. Anthony Scott (1976) assembles a number of them in his *Natural Resource Revenues: A Test of Federalism.* Contributors include Thomas J. Courchene, W. D. Gainer, John Helliwell, J. Clark Leith, Milton Moore, T. L. Powrie, Donald Smiley, and Irene Spry. Milton Moore writes, "I shall take as my first principle that economic rents belong to the community" (1976, p. 241). Only Paul Bradley, an American by origin, shows major doubts. But it is characteristic of this Canadian group that they focus solely on the rent of mines. There is no hint of extending the taxation of rents to the commercial land of Toronto, the political land of Ottawa, the docks of Montreal, or the fields of Manitoba.

Another Canadian writing on mineral rents is Meyer Bucovetsky of Toronto (1972). Later, he joins with Malcolm Gillis of Harvard (1978). Their locations may demand more circumspection than the colonial spokesmen's. They by no means dispute the case for taxing mineral rents, but look at it mainly from the taxpayer's viewpoint.

Economists are also giving great attention to collecting mineral rents from lessees on public lands. Few challenge the old practice of giving away water rights free, and hardly any have taken up Delworth Gardner's (1962) evidence of a need for higher grazing fees. But economic writers and policy makers are vigorously pursuing the mineral rents. Even the "conservatives" in this field, such as Mead (1977), Sorenson (Mead and Sorenson 1980), McDonald (1979), and Kenneth Dam (1965), do not dispute the meaning of resource rent, or the public right to receive it. On the contrary, they proclaim it. They simply prefer leases to be written with low royalties, no intermeddling, and a high emphasis on the front-end bonus as the bid variable and allocating device. Others prefer leases with more deferred payments, and "participation." These include Ross Garnaut and Anthony Clunies-Ross (1977), Michael Crommelin (1977), Mason Gaffney (1977a, 1977b), Gregg Erickson (1977), Arlon Tussing (1977), and Robert Kalter and Wallace Tyner (1975).

The subject of rent pervades and transcends all of economic life and policy, inescapably. ("They reckon ill who leave me out; when me they fly, I am the wings.") Hundreds of economists recognize rent when capitalized into the value of taxi medallions and liquor licenses, of all things. It is a strange quirk that so many economists recognize and condemn these as petty while resting so taciturn on the gross ones.

The rent of water manifests another anomaly. Hardly anyone has responded to Gaffney's call (1969a, 1973b) for public charges on reserving and withdrawing water, but legions have joined Allen Kneese's (1962) effort to promote effluent charges for polluting water and air. But neither movement has made much headway compared to community collection of the rent of mines.

There is an active literature on collecting rent from the radio spectrum, a valuable resource now allocated without any price going to the owners, viz. the public (Levin, 1971). As with all these "exotic" resources, there quickly emerge three camps. The first wants to collect rent publicly. The second dismisses distributive equity and focuses on firming up existing tenure rights. The social goal of this is to allow commercialization and easy transfer, leading to efficient allocation. The third camp is solely concerned with asserting the public right, regardless of efficiency. The beauty of taxing rent, of course, is to achieve and harmonize the (professed) goals of the second and third camps. It would have prevailed long since, were the second and third camps more aware and respectful of the validity and sustained power of each others' half-share of truth.

Mainly Positive

Several economists have dedicated major efforts to promoting land taxation. I pass over the most dedicated advocates, Henry George and Harry G. Brown, because their positions are so well known, so total, and so easily referenced. Beyond these, it is often thought there is only an eccentric band of true believers. These eccentrics include, however, Léon Walras, John R. Commons, Colin Clark, Dick Netzer, William Vickrey, Lowell Harriss, Ralph Turvey, François Quesnay and the physiocrats, John Zangerle and a large group of assessors, Knut Wicksell, and Adam Smith.

The appearance of Léon Walras (1896) here may be a surprise to those who know him through Jaffe's translation of selections that emphasize abstruse techniques. Walras is a thoroughgoing land taxer, who writes with the passion of a Gallic Henry George. A few passages give the flavor.

" . . . In order that the total of personal faculties and their products should belong to the individual, the State must own the land and find in its rent the means to subsist and the source of capital it needs. The assignment of land to the State solves the question of taxation by erasing it" (1896, book II, section 8).

"Lands do not belong to all the men of one generation; they belong to humanity, that is, to all generations of men" (1896, book II, section 6). (Rawlsians take note.)

"In relieving the feudal aristocracy of its public duties, we neglected to take back the soil, the enjoyment of which constituted the compensation for these duties" (1896, book II, section 6).

Walras regards himself as the carrier of the truths of Quesnay and Turgot, "and for this to have been excommunicated from the science by those who have led it to the point of sinking and discredit where it finds itself today" (1896, book II, section 9). He assails Bastiat, leader of the "Chicago School" of France. "One reaches the top by persuading himself that lands which sell at 2000 francs the square meter have no value" (1896, book III, section 36). Henry George never impugned the motives of courtier economists more bitterly than Walras.

Walras devotes great care to a detailed plan of transition to land taxation, beginning from earlier compensation proposals of James Mill and Hermann-Henri Gossen. Mill would compensate present holders at a price capitalized from current income (similar to modern "use-value" assessments), taking development and speculative value for the State. Gossen would compensate at a higher price discounted from future higher rents, relying on the State's superior credit and lower capitalization rate to let the State amortize the debt from future rents, and eventually own it clear.

Walras rejects Gossen's rationale, finding his mathematics imprecise, and observing (with Adam Smith) that the State's discount rate must be higher than that of its creditors — who also can buy land. From here he becomes a bit vague, suggesting that when political economy has been rescued from its venal traducers, the State could carry out such a project and make it pay as successively higher industrial stages raise rents, aided by a State that guides social organization better, advised by honest and right-thinking economists. (Wicksteed expresses the same hope, from the other side!)

Walras also treats the practical problem of separating land from capital (1896, book IV). He refutes the idea that farmland is so fused with fertilizers and "buried" improvements that land and capital are indistinguishable — he treats the capital as a revolving fund, recovered in crop sales. He scores economists who "declare insoluble all questions which strike them as difficult." Walras is fun to read. "God, according to them, in creating man said to him, 'You will discover the compass, the railroad, the electric telegraph, constitutional government, but you will never discover a satisfactory tax.' Strange malediction!" For Walras the land tax is not a tax but co-ownership of land by the State, and the perfect source of public revenue.

John R. Commons (1922, 1934) is another devoted land taxer, more politically involved than most. The 1921 Grimstad Bill in Wisconsin embodies his proposals. Commons urges us to modify "ability to pay" as a canon of taxation. Social utility is also important; taxes are part of the police power. Even if not so intended, "taxes nevertheless regulate, . . .

they say to the businessman: Here is profit; there is loss." So taxes should vary *directly* with ability to pay, but *inversely* with service and contributions to the common wealth. Landowners as such only take from the common wealth without returning anything. Land and its rent income should therefore pay at the highest rate.

"Institutional doctrines" are utilitarian, looking to the future, disregarding the "dogma of natural rights." Institutionalism says we should give "inducements to individuals to acquire wealth by increasing the commonwealth." It sounds as though Commons is arguing in favor of incentives and against excess burden, but he has his own way of putting things.

Like Walras, Commons is absorbed in the question of soil conservation, and equally involved in the institutional problem of winning farm votes. He proposes a rough-and-ready 50 percent exclusion of farm land values from the tax base, to allow for capital mixed with the soil — a proposal that overlooks entirely the differences among soils, which is the basis of Ricardo. This was really a political strategem. It mollified "the farmers," he claims — but the Grimstad Bill fails.

Commons writes with especial favor of "the American invention of Special Assessments"; Marshall much earlier wrote of their use in England, but Commons traces them to 1830 in New York. Unlike Hotelling, Commons likes the idea of limiting the assessment to the cost of the public works, and limiting public works to those thus financeable. But even more he prefers the limitation of these assessments to land values. He likes the common sense of early courts in seeing that public works enhance only land values, not capital values. The legal distinction between taxes and assessments has a renewed life in post-Proposition 13 California. Many lawyers believe that "assessments" for benefits to land fall outside the 1 percent limitations of Proposition 13; some one-fourth of all property revenues in California are from assessments of special districts (Zion 1979).

Commons likes rules of reason rather than absolutes: "There is a diminishing validity of truth." "A single truth, like a single tax, ends in its own destruction." So he proposes to blend the two canons of taxing the ability to pay and untaxing the service to the community by a three-tier income tax rate: a low rate on wages, a medium rate on capital, and a highest rate on land income.

Unlike most Georgians, Commons sees the Federal income tax as one tool for socializing rent. He would dispute Paul Douglas, who kept silent on land taxation as a senator because "the issue involved local and state governments, rather than national" (Douglas 1972, p. 446) and who lumped accelerated depreciation together with the depletion allowance and capital gains under the titles of "abuses" and the "citadel of privilege" (1972, p. 452). Commons notes the L. H. Parker Committee (1931) is proposing higher rates on unearned income, but failing to distinguish land and capital. Commons proposes favoring capital by accelerated depreciation. That wish has come true, but not the rest of the package. He would not like today's confiscatory rates on ordinary wage income, nor 60% exclusion for unearned increments.

Commons ends by refuting Willford King's (1921) attempt to fuse land and capital. It is the same issue we have met several times. King wrote from the individual view, and failed to see that "if our canon . . . be . . . that of the economic effects of speculation on the wealth of the nation," then land income has no social function. Creating capital adds to the common wealth. Acquiring land is merely a zero-sum game, as we would say today, and worse than that if speculation and credit rationing interfere with economic allocation, as George alleged.

Many assessors have become land taxers, or vice versa. We have already cited John Zangerle. Some others are Moody of San Diego, A. A. Pastoriza of Houston, Lawson Purdy of New York (1929), Percy Williams of Pittsburgh, W. W. Pollock (1926), William A. Somers of St. Paul, John Rackham of Washington, D.C., John McCutcheon of Johannesburg, J. F. N. Murray of Australia (1969), Ted Gwartney of British Columbia, and Hector Wilks and P. H. Clarke of England. Purdy, Pollock, Somers (1901), and Murray in particular wrote extensively on techniques of separate land valuation, fully understanding the necessity for demonstrating the practicability of this art.

François Quesnay (ca. 1760, rpt. 1963), the founding physiocrat, royal physician to Louis XVI, and precursor of input-output analysis (the *Tableau Économique*) was of course a land taxer (possibly to save his patient's health?). He defines the *produit net* or rent of farm land as that which the state may tax without damage. In his zeal to discourage the taxation of capital, he doesn't even allow that it receives net income, but only a recovery of principal, so any taxation will diminish the stock, and thus also reduce *produit net*. This is a primitive apprehension of excess burden. It is hard to be sure if Quesnay actually believes that capital has no income, and that only agriculture is productive; he may be overstating his case in a desperate effort to penetrate the slow wits who mismanaged France. His follower Pierre Samuel du Pont de Nemours, who later fled the Terror and helped his son Éleuthère Irénée found the powder mill in Delaware, believed the main idea was to keep the State from taxing capital. Perhaps that was du Pont's main interest. In any case, Quesnay and Victor de Mirabeau framed a reasonable definition of land rent, and a rationale for taxing it. Some others of the school were Mercier de la Rivière and N. Baudeau. Its political spokesman was Baron A. R. J. Turgot.

Knut Wicksell's (1896) case for taxing land resembles Hotelling's, only Wicksell begins more timidly and ends more boldly. He begins with the narrowest of benefit theories of taxation, the purpose being to put an upper limit on spending. All public spending should have a positive benefit/cost ratio at the margin; the proof of this is to be unanimous consent of those taxed (at least the theoretical possibility of unanimous consent) or nearly unanimous consent. Evidently, Wicksell is not thinking here of purely transfer taxation, but of public works and services.

He deplores the use of hidden taxes, which yield such ample revenue that States spend it wastefully, without needing to ask how to fund each project.

Then he turns moderate. His principle will let legislatures pass proposals that might otherwise fail because non-benefiting citizens will not be taxed, and so not oppose them. It sounds like "Public Choice" — and was indeed translated by J. M. Buchanan (Wicksell 1896).

But next he seems like Hotelling. The simple pricing or fee principle will not do for public works, because marginal cost is far below average cost. He is much more specific than Hotelling, though, about how to meet deficits. The specific *beneficiaries* can pay, in fixed fees.

Finally, he arrives at Henry George's ideas. Everyone knows you never get unanimous consent from landholders to pay for public works — but Wicksell's unanimity rule applies only to those who hold their wealth justly. Landholders are to have no veto. "I agree . . . wholeheartedly with the special taxation, or better confiscation . . . of . . . the increase in land value. . . ." Private rights to land are ". . . in open contradiction with modern concepts of law and equity . . . society has both the right and the duty to revise the existing property structure" (Wicksell 1896, p. 7). So we have the benefit principle construed as a tax on land values, but with no suggestion that *this* tax be limited to benefits. There is a suggestion, but not much more, that it be limited to future increases. "The tax should be increased in steps to the point where the unearned windfall profits are in principle absorbed . . ."

The tax should be levied currently — the Haig-Simons principle — and not as a transfer tax, which would "hinder the flow of commerce." It should be levied not just on urban land or farmland, but all land.

Last, Wicksell declares that private land rights be narrowly limited to those qualities of land contemplated by the original grantors; and future resources discovered or made valuable, such as mineral rights, should be reserved to the Crown. Think of all the natural goods that were "free" in 1896, and even 1933, and precious today.

Ralph Turvey's (1957) analysis is characteristically terse, tight, and practical. He never actually says he favors land taxation, but only that the claims of the advocates are "in general correct." He shows no interest in even bringing up the various doubts we have noted in other writers. He writes in the English context where rates fall on occupiers, not title holders, but he has no difficulty distinguishing impact from incidence. He emphasizes the stimulus to urban renewal and to improved quality of building, using simple diminishing returns concepts and marginal equation of costs and receipts. Ever practical, he discusses liquidity effects. He notes the removal of excess burden and the resulting increase of taxable surplus. This is physiocracy renewed, only this time for a nation of shopkeepers in the cities. His only reservation is a faint doubt about taxing ripening land on its capital value — the Ely idea — but he does not pursue this.

Lowell Harriss (1968) also emphasizes the excess burden of taxing buildings. However, where Turvey posits diminishing returns as we add capital to land, Harriss, like Walter Morton, emphasizes decreasing unit costs per square foot as buildings get larger (he does not say what this does to lot size). Of course, this would redouble the excess burden of taxing buildings. Like Marx however, he may have failed to distinguish variable scale from variable proportions.

Harriss meets part of Cannan's argument for taxing buildings by noting that public costs are not in proportion to building values when we compare old and new ones. Costs are, if anything, inversely proportional to values. As for the distortion of locational incentives that disturbed Cannan, Harriss writes that taxing buildings leads industries to cluster in low-tax enclaves. The result is a centrifugal bias, a major cause of sprawl in American metropoles, and a self-reinforcing process that keeps getting worse.

Harriss deplores the property tax on utility capital, using a muted Hotelling-Wicksell rationale, and ends by suggesting the replacement of all capital taxes with land taxes.

Colin Clark (1965) repeats the now familiar idea about lack of excess burden of the land tax, in contrast to other taxes. Then he launches a simple and original scheme for preventing the distortion of locational incentives caused by local taxation: " . . . land values per head of population should first be ascertained; then the state would impose a land tax which exempted altogether those local authority areas where per-head land values were low, and which rose in a progressive scale for those with higher land values per head. Each local authority would then also impose its own tax . . . ." Gaffney (1973a, p. 33) has also written in a similar vein, and it seems sure that local exclusionary zoning will slowly strangle us if we fail to move along such lines.

Dick Netzer (1966) systematically disposes of the various cases against land taxation surveyed in our "Mainly Negative" section above, save for some residual doubts about adequacy of base; these doubts subsequently have been dropped. Netzer meets the Cannan argument by proposing to supplement the land tax, not with a building tax but with a "family of user charges" geared to marginal congestion costs, in the style of William Vickrey. He recognizes that this does not address the larger question of how to handle Marshall's "onerous" taxes, for "services to people" – that is, transfers.

Conclusion

We end where so much economics begins, with Adam Smith (1776, rpt. 1937). Smith likes land as a revenue base first because it is stable and permanent. Few great nations or sovereigns, looking back, have subsisted without it – many by direct ownership of crown lands. Smith thinks that sovereigns do a dreadful job when they try to manage land directly; he advises them to sell it and tax it.

Smith accuses the physiocrats (rightly or wrongly) of favoring a land tax that varies as a function of realized rather than potential rent. He points to the excess burden of such a tax, and the lack of burden in the fixed English land tax. Yet the English tax is out of date, so Smith proposes a regular reassessment of the rental value, exempting improvements. Before a landlord's improvement, Smith would assess his land and "rate him at this valuation for such a number of years as might be fully sufficient for his complete indemnification." Data for updating values are to come from a public register of lease terms, a Venetian practice. A "general survey and valuation" is also possible, but Smith thinks this to be painful; he prefers the Venetian method.

Smith, like Ricardo, opposes "Tithes," or any tax on gross output. But unlike Ricardo, he sees such taxes shifted to landowners, along with their excess burden (Ricardo saw them shifted forward). Smith does not need Marshall to teach him about supply and demand; he uses it as a tool.

Smith believes housing to be a superior good and is not dead set against a tax on house rents. However, he says, "Ground rents are a still more proper subject of taxation than the rents of houses." There is no shifting, no decline of supply. The owner is always a "monopolist" who charges what he can. (It is interesting how often critics like Stigler deride George for this classical usage, as though it were peculiarly his.)

Place a tax on rent, and "no discouragement will thereby be given to any sort of industry. The annual produce . . . of the society . . . might be the same after such a tax as before. . . . Nothing can be more reasonable than that a fund which owes its existence to the good government of the state, should be taxed peculiarly . . ." (p. 796).

If you tax stock (capital), on the other hand, it will be concealed or removed. Worse, some forms of capital are more concealable than others, so a tax is necessarily nonuniform. Knowing the quantity of capital requires a deep inquisition "as no people could support" (p. 800). How he would boggle at the inquisitions "supported" today — but capital is never uniformly taxed. Place a tax on stock, and "not only the profits of stock, but the rent of land and the wages of labor, would necessarily be diminished by its removal" (p. 800). The last thought epitomizes a fair share of both Georgian and Keynesian economics. May economics progress faster in the next two hundred years than in the last, or at least stop retrogressing from the necessary and sufficient wisdom of the great Adam Smith.

References

Adams, T. S. 1916. "Tax Exemption Through Tax Capitalization — A Fiscal Fallacy." *American Economic Review* 6: 271–87.

Alonso, William. 1964. *Location and Land Use: Toward a General Theory of Land Rent.* Cambridge: Harvard Univ. Press.

Andelson, Robert V., and Mason Gaffney. 1979. "Seligman and His Critique form Social Utility." In *Critics of Henry George,* ed. Robert V. Andelson. Rutherford, N.J.: Fairleigh Dickinson Univ. Press.

Anderson, B. M., Jr. 1914. "'Unearned Increments,' Land Taxes, and the Building Trade." *Quarterly Journal of Economics* 28: 811–14.

Babcock, Frederick. 1932. *The Valuation of Real Estate.* New York: McGraw-Hill.

Bahl, Roy W. 1968. "A Land Speculation Model: The Role of the Property Tax as a Constraint to Urban Sprawl." *Journal of Regional Science* 8, no. 2: 199–208.

Baker, John A. 1945. "Toward a Theory of Land Income." *Journal of Land and Public Utility Economics* 21: 160–66.

Berry, Albert. 1972. "Presumptive Income Tax on Agricultural Land." *National Tax Journal* 25: 169–81.

Bird, Richard M. 1960. "A National Tax on the Unimproved Value of Land: the Australian Experience, 1910–1952." *National Tax Journal* 13: 386–92.

Bird, Richard M. 1974. *Taxing Agricultural Land in Developing Countries.* Cambridge: Harvard Univ. Press.

Bradley, Paul. 1977. "Some Issues in Mineral Leasing and Taxation Policy." In *Mineral Leasing as an Instrument of Public Policy,* ed. Michael Crommelin and Andrew Thompson. Vancouver: Univ. of British Columbia Press.

Bradley, Paul. 1976. "Governments and Mineral Resource Earnings." In *Natural Resource Revenues: A Test of Federalism,* ed. Anthony Scott. Vancouver: Univ. of British Columbia Press.

Bucovetsky, Meyer. 1972. "Tax Reform in Canada: The Case of the Mining Industry." Ph.D. diss. Univ. of Toronto.

Bye, Carl R. 1940. *Developments and Issues in the Theory of Rent.* New York: Columbia Univ. Press.

Cannan, Edwin. 1907. "The Proposed Relief of Buildings from Local Rates." *Economic Journal* 17: 36–46.

Carey, Henry C. 1840. *Principles of Political Economy*. Philadelphia: Carey, Lea & Blanchard.

Carver, Thomas N. 1915. *Essays in Social Justice*. Cambridge: Harvard Univ. Press.

Clark, Colin. 1965. "Land Taxation: Lessons from International Experience." In *Land Values,* ed. Peter Hall. London: Sweet and Maxwell.

Clark, J. B. 1883. *Capital and Its Earnings*. Publications of the American Economic Association, vol. 3, no. 2: 1–61. See the discussion with E. v. Bohm-Bawerk, *Quarterly Journal of Economics 1895–96,* vols. 9, 10.

Clark, J. B. 1899. *The Distribution of Wealth*. New York: Macmillan.

Collier, Charles. 1979. "Clark and Patten: Exemplars of the New American Professionalism." In *Critics of Henry George,* ed. Robert Andelson. Rutherford, N.J.: Fairleigh-Dickinson Univ. Press.

Commons, John R. 1922. "A Progressive Tax on Bare Land Value." *Political Science Quarterly* 37: 41–68.

Commons, John R. 1934. *Institutional Economics: Its Place in Political Economy*. New York: Macmillan.

Cornick, Philip H. 1934. "Land Prices in a Commodity Price System." *Journal of Land and Public Utility Economics* 10: 217–31.

Crommelin, Michael. 1977. "Concluding Note: Economic Rent and Government Objectives." In *Mineral Leasing as an Instrument of Public Policy,* eds. Michael Crommelin and Andrew Thompson. Vancouver: Univ. of British Columbia Press.

Dam, Kenneth. 1965. "Oil and Gas Licensing in the North Sea." *Journal of Law and Economics* 8: 51–75.

Dam, Kenneth. 1970. "Pricing of North Sea Gas in Britain." *Journal of Law and Economics* 13: 11–44.

Darwin, Leonard. 1907. "The Taxation of Site Values with Reference to the Distribution of Population." *Economic Journal* 17: 330–44.

Davenport, H. J. 1909. "Exhausted Farms and Exhausting Taxation." *Journal of Political Economy* 17: 354–62.

Davenport, H. J. 1917. "Theoretical Issues in the Single Tax." *American Economic Review* 7: 1–30.

Dorau, Herbert, and Albert Hinman. 1928. *Urban Land Economics*. New York: Macmillan.

Dorner, Peter. 1972. *Land Reform and Economic Development,* Harmondsworth: Penguin Books.

Douglas, Paul. 1972. *In the Fullness of Time*. New York: Harcourt Brace Jovanovich.

Douglas, Paul. 1968. "Supplementary Views on the Taxation of Land Values." In *Building the American City*. Report of the National Commission on Urban Problems. Washington, D.C.: United States Government Printing Office.

188 LAND AS A TAX BASE

Due, John. 1963. *Taxation and Economic Development in Tropical Africa.* Cambridge: The Massachussetts Institute of Technology Press.

Edgeworth, Francis Y. 1906. "Recent Schemes for Rating Urban Land Values." *Economic Journal* 16: 66–77.

Ely, R. T. 1920. "Land Speculation." *Journal of Farm Economics* 2: 121–36.

Ely, R. T. 1922. "The Taxation of Land." In *Proceedings of the 14th Annual Conference of the NTA.* 241–54. Harrisburg, Pa.: National Tax Association.

Erickson, Gregg. 1977. "Work Commitment Bidding." In *Mineral Leasing as an Instrument of Public Policy,* eds. Michael Crommelin and Andrew Thompson. Vancouver: Univ. of British Columbia Press.

Fairchild, Fred R., et al. 1935. *Forest Taxation in the United States.* United States Department of Agriculture, Miscellaneous Publication 218. Washington: The department.

Faustmann, Martin. 1849. Reprint 1968. "Calculation of the Value which Forest Land and Immature Stands Possess for Forestry." In *Martin Faustmann and the Evolution of Discounted Cash Flow,* ed. M. Gane, trans. W. Linnard. Oxford: Commonwealth Forestry Institute: The University.

Fetter, Frank A. 1927. Reprint 1977. *Capital, Interest, and Rent.* Kansas City: Sheed Andrews & McMeel.

Fillebrown, C. B. 1907. "The Single Tax." *National Tax Association Bulletin,* Vol. 1, pp. 286–93.

Fillebrown, C. B. 1910. "The Taxation of Privilege." *The Outlook* 94:311–13.

Fillebrown, C. B. 1914. *Taxation.* Chicago: A.C. McClurg.

Fillebrown, C. B. 1916. *The ABC of Taxation.* 4th ed. Garden City, N.Y.: Doubleday, Page, & Co.

Frisch, Ragnar. 1939. "The duPuit Taxation Theorem." *Econometrica* 7:145–50.

Gaffney, Mason. 1967. "Editor's Conclusion." In *Extractive Resources and Taxation,* ed. Mason Gaffney. Madison: Univ. of Wisconsin Press.

Gaffney, Mason. 1969a. "Economic Aspects of Water Resources Policy." *American Journal of Economics and Sociology* 28:131–44.

Gaffney, Mason. 1969b. "Land Rent, Taxation, and Public Policy." *Papers of the Regional Science Association* 23: 141–53.

Gaffney, Mason. 1970. "Adequacy of Land as a Tax Base." In *The Assessment of Land Value,* ed. Daniel Holland. Madison: Univ. of Wisconsin Press.

Gaffney, Mason. 1971. "The Property Tax is a Progressive Tax." In *Proceedings of the National Tax Association,* 1971. Columbus, Ohio: The association.

Gaffney, Mason. 1973a. "A Critique of Federal Water Policy." In *The Political Economy of Federal Policy,* eds. Robert Hamrin and Robert Haveman. New York: Harper & Row.

Gaffney, Mason. 1973b. "Tax Reform to Release Land." In *Modernizing Urban Land Policy,* ed. Marion Clawson. Baltimore: Johns Hopkins Univ. Press.

Gaffney, Mason. 1977a. "Objectives of Government Policy in Leasing Mineral Lands." In *Mineral Leasing as an Instrument of Public Policy,* ed. Michael Crommelin and Andrew Thompson. Vancouver: Univ. of British Columbia Press.

Gaffney, Mason. 1977b. "Oil and Gas Leasing Policy: Alternatives for Alaska." A Report to the State of Alaska, Department of Natural Resources.

Gaffney, Mason. 1979. "Review and Recollection Related to Resource Economics: Selected Works of Orris C. Herfindahl." *Natural Resources Journal* October: 1006–1010.

Gardner, Delworth. 1962. "Transfer Restrictions and Misallocation in Grazing Public Range." *Journal of Farm Economics* 44: 50–63.

Garnaut, Ross, and Anthony Clunies-Ross. 1977. "A New Tax for National Resources Projects." In *Mineral Leasing as an Instrument of Public Policy,* ed. Michael Crommelin and Andrew Thompson. Vancouver: Univ. of British Columbia Press.

Gillis, Malcolm, et al. 1978. *Taxation and Mining.* Cambridge, Mass.: Ballinger.

Goode, Richard. 1964. "Reconstruction of Foreign Tax Systems." *Readings on Taxation in Developing Countries,* ed. Richard Bird and O. Oldman. Baltimore: Johns Hopkins Univ. Press.

Gillis, Malcolm, et. al. 1978. *Taxation and Mining.* Cambridge, Mass.: Ballinger.

Goode, Richard. 1964. "Reconstruction of Foreign Tax Systems." *Readings on Taxation in Developing Countries,* eds. Richard Bird and O. Oldman. Baltimore: Johns Hopkins Univ. Press.

Gray, Lewis C. 1914. "Rent under the Assumption of Exhaustibility." *Quarterly Journal of Economics* 28: 464–89.

Grimes, Orville, Jr. 1977. "Urban Land and Public Policy: Social Appropriation of Betterment." In *Local Service Pricing Policies, etc.* ed. Paul Downing. Vancouver: Univ. of British Columbia Press.

Groves, Harold. 1948. "The Property Tax in Canada and the United States." *Land Economics* 24: 23–30; 120–28.

Groves, Harold. 1949. "Impressions of Property Taxation in Australia and New Zealand." *Land Economics* 25: 22–28.

Hagman, Donald. 1978. "Land Value Taxation." In *Windfalls for Wipeouts,* ed. Donald Hagman and Dean Misczynski. Chicago: Planners Press.

Haig, Robert M. 1915a. *The Exemption of Improvements from Taxation in Canada and the United States.* New York: The Committee on Taxation.

Haig, Robert M. 1915b. "The Effects of Increment Taxes upon Building Operations." *Quarterly Journal of Economics* 29: 829–40.

Haig, Robert M. 1915c. *Some Probable Effects of the Exemption of Improvements from Taxation in the City of New York.* New York: Press of Clarence Nathan.

Hall, Peter, ed. 1965. *Land Values.* London: Sweet and Maxwell.

Hardie, Robert S. 1952. "Philippine Land Tenure Reform." Special technical and economic mission, U.S. Mutual Security Agency, Manila. Lithographed and bound.

Harriss, Lowell. 1968. "Economic Evaluation of Real Property Taxes." In *Municipal Income Taxes,* ed. R. H. Connery. New York: Academy of Political Science.

Hayek, Friedrich. 1936. "The Mythology of Capital." *Quarterly Journal of Economics* 50: 199–228.

Hayek, Friedrich. 1941. *The Pure Theory of Capital.* London: Macmillan.

Hayes, H. Gordon. 1920. "The Capitalization of the Land Tax." *Quarterly Journal of Economics* 34: 373–80.

Heilbrun, J. 1966. *Real Estate Taxes and Urban Housing.* New York: Columbia Univ. Press.

Heller, Walter W. 1954. "The Use of Agricultural Taxation for Incentive Purposes." In *Papers and Proceedings of the Conference on Agricultural Taxation and Economic Development,* ed. Haskell Wald and Joseph Froomkin. Cambridge, Mass.: Harvard Law School.

Herfindahl, Orris. 1974. *Resource Economics: Selected Works of Oris C. Herfindahl,* ed. David Brooks. Baltimore: Johns Hopkins Univ. Press.

Hibbard, Benjamin H. 1930. "A National Policy to Conserve Land Values." *Annals of the American Academy of Political and Social Science* 148: 115-19.

Hirschman, Albert. 1964. "Land Taxes and Land Reform in Colombia." In *Readings on Taxation in Developing Countries,* ed. Richard Bird and Oliver Oldman. Baltimore: Johns Hopkins Univ. Press.

Hobson, J. A. 1920. *Taxation in the New State.* New York: Harcourt Brace and Howe.

Hobson, J. A. 1931. *Poverty in Plenty: The Ethics of Income.* New York: Macmillan.

Holland, Daniel. 1969. "A Study of Land Taxation in Jamaica." In *Land and Building Taxes: Their Effect on Economic Development,* ed. Arthur P. Becker. Madison: Univ. of Wisconsin Press.

Hotelling, Harold. 1931. "The Economics of Exhaustible Resources." *Journal of Political Economy* 39: 137-75.

Hotelling, Harold. 1938. "The General Welfare in Relation to the Problems of Taxation and of Railway and Utility Rates." *Econometrica* 6: 242-69.

Howard, Ebenezer. 1965. *The Garden City of Tomorrow.* Cambridge: The Massachusetts Institute of Technology Press.

Hoyt, Homer. 1933. *One Hundred Years of Land Values in Chicago.* Chicago: Univ. of Chicago Press.

Hoyt, Homer. 1939. *The Structure and Growth of Residential Neighborhoods in American Cities.* Washington: Federal Housing Authority.

Hutchison. T. W. 1969. "Economists and Economic Policy in Britain after 1870." *History of Political Economy* 1: 231-55.

Ise, John. 1925. "The Theory of Value as Applied to Natural Resources." *American Economic Review* 15: 28-91.

Jensen, Jens P. 1931. *Property Taxation in the United States.* Chicago: Univ. of Chicago Press.

Johnson, Alvin. 1902. *Rent in Modern Economic Theory.* AEA Publications. Third Series 3, no. 4.

Johnson, Alvin. 1914. "The Case Against the Single Tax." *The Atlantic Monthly* 113: 27-37.

Johnson, Erwin. 1970. "Land Tax and Its Impact on Use and Ownership in Rural Japan." *Economic Development and Cultural Change* 19: 49-70.

Kalter, Robert; Wallace Tyner; and Daniel Hughes. 1975. "Alternative Energy Leasing Strategies and Schedules for the Outer Continental Shelf." Department of Agricultural Economics, Cornell University.

Keiper, Joseph, Ernest Kurnow, et al. 1961. *Theory and Measurement of Rent.* Philadelphia: Chilton.

King, Willford I. 1921. "Earned and Unearned Income." *Annals of the American Academy of Political and Social Science:* 240-60.

King, Willford I. 1924. "The Single-Tax Complex Analyzed." *Journal of Political Economy* 32: 604-12.

Kneese, Allen. 1962. *Water Pollution.* Baltimore: Johns Hopkins Univ. Press.

Knight, Frank. 1924. Reprint 1952. "Some Fallacies in the Interpretation of Social Cost." In *Readings in Price Theory,* ed. G. Stigler and K. Boulding. Chicago: R. D. Irwin.

Knight, Frank. 1946. "Capital and Interest." *Encyclopedia Brittanica* 4: 779-801.

Knight, Frank. 1953. "The Fallacies in the 'Single Tax.' " *The Freeman,* 809-11.

Kurnow, Ernest. 1960. "Land Value Trends in the United States." *Land Economics* 36: 341-48.

Kurnow, Ernest. 1961. "Distribution and Growth of Land Values." In *Theory and Measurement of Rent,* Joseph Keiper, et al. Philadelphia: Chilton.

Lawrence, Elwood. 1957. *Henry George in the British Isles.* East Lansing: Michigan State Univ. Press.

Lent, George E. 1967. "The Taxation of Land Value." *I.M.F. Staff Papers* 14, no. 1: 89-123.

Levin, Harvey. 1971. *The Invisible Resource.* Baltimore: Johns Hopkins Univ. Press.

Lindholm, Richard. 1964. *Economic Development Policy.* Eugene: Univ. of Oregon Press.

Lindholm, Richard. 1965. "Land Taxation and Economic Development." *Land Economics* 41: 121-30.

Little, I. M. D. 1950. Reprint 1960. *A Critique of Welfare Economics.* London: Oxford Univ. Press.

Marling, Alfred E., chairman. 1916. *Final Report of the Committee on Taxation of the City of New York.* New York: The O'Connell Press.

Marshall, Alfred. 1883. Reprint 1969. "Three Lectures on Progress and Poverty." *Journal of Law and Economics* 12: 181-226.

Marshall, Alfred. 1920. Reprint 1947. *Principles of Economics.* 8th ed. London: Macmillan.

Marx, Karl. 1847. *The Poverty of Philosophy.* New York: International Publishers.

Marx, Karl. 1867. Reprint 1906. *Capital,* trans. Samuel Moore and Edward Aveling. Chicago: Charles H. Kerr.

Marx, Karl, and Friedrich Engels. 1848. Reprint 1959. "Manifesto of the Communist Party." In *Marx and Engels,* ed. Lewis Feuer. Garden City, N.Y., trans Samuel Moore: Doubleday.

McCulloch, John. 1979. "Site Value Rating in Johannesburg, South Africa." In *The Taxation of Urban Property in Less Developed Countries,* ed. Roy W. Bahl. Madison: Univ. of Wisconsin Press.

McDonald, Stephen. 1963. *Federal Tax Treatment of Income from Oil and Gas.* Washington, D.C.: The Brookings Institution.

McDonald, Stephen. 1966. "The Effects of Severance vs. Property Taxes on Petroleum Conservation." In *Proceedings of the National Tax Association, 1965.* Columbus, Ohio: The association.

McDonald, Stephen. 1967. "Percentage Depletion, Expensing of Intangibles, and Petroleum Conservation." In *Extractive Resources and Taxation,* ed. Mason Gaffney. Madison: Univ. of Wisconsin Press.

McDonald, Stephen. 1979. *The Leasing of Federal Lands for Fossil Fuel Production.* Baltimore: Johns Hopkins Univ. Press.

Mead, Walter. 1977. "Cash Bonus Bidding for Mineral Resources." In *Mineral Leasing as an Instrument of Public Policy,* ed. Michael Crommelin and Andrew Thompson. Vancouver: Univ. of British Columbia Press.

Mead, Walter, and Philip E. Sorenson. 1980. "Competition and Performance in OCS Oil and Gas Lease Sales and Lease Development, 1954–69." Final report, USGS contract no. 14-08-0001-16552.

Mieszkowski, Peter. 1970. "A Critical Appraisal of Land Value Taxation." Draft, pp. 1–37.

Mill, John S. 1872. *Principles of Political Economy.* People's ed. Boston: Lee and Shepard.

Moore, Milton. 1976. "The Concept of a Nation and Entitlements to Economic Rents." In *Natural Resource Revenues: A Test of Federalism,* ed. Anthony Scott. Vancouver: Univ. of British Columbia Press.

Murray, J. F. N. 1969. *Principles and Practice of Valuation.* 4th ed. Sydney: Commonwealth Institute of Valuers.

Musgrave, Richard. 1950. "A Graduated Land Tax." In *The Basis of a Development Program for Colombia,* pp. 384–87. Washington, D.C.: The International Bank for Reconstruction and Development.

Netzer, Dick. 1966. *Economics of the Property Tax.* Washington, D.C.: The Brookings Institution.

Olcott, George C. 1910–1979. *Land Values Blue Book of Chicago and Suburbs.* Chicago: G.C. Olcott. Annual Volumes.

Pareto, Vilfredo. 1897. *Cours d'Economie Politique.* Lausanne: Librairie de l'Universitie, vol. 2.

Park, R. E., and Burgess, E. W. 1925. *The City.* Chicago: Univ. of Chicago Press.

Parker, L. H. 1931. *Preliminary Report on Earned Incomes.* Report of the Joint Committee (on Internal Revenue and Taxation) to the Committee on Ways and Means of the House of Representatives.

Patten, Simon. 1908. "The Conflict Theory of Distribution." *Yale Review,* 17: 156–84.

Pigou, A. C. 1949. *A Study in Public Finance.* 3d rev. ed. London: Macmillan.

Pilack, Edward. 1915. "Reduction of Tax on Buildings in the City of New York." *Annals of the American Academy of Political and Social Science* 58: 183–88.

Pollock, Walter William, and Karl W. H. Scholz. 1926. *The Science and Practice of Urban Land Valuation: An Exposition of the Somers Unit System.* Philadelphia: Manufacturer's Appraisal Co.

Purdy Lawson. 1929. *The Assessment of Real Estate.* 4th ed. New York: National Municipal League.

Quesnay, Francois. ca. 1760. Reprint 1963. Various works. In *The Economics of Physiocracy,* trans. R. Meek. Cambridge, Mass.: Harvard Univ. Press.

Ratcliff, Richard. 1950. "Net Income Can't Be Split." *Appraisal Journal* 18: 168–72.

Rhoads, William, and Richard Bird. 1969. "The Valorization Tax in Colombia." In *Land and Building Taxes: Their Effect on Economic Development*, ed. Arthur P. Becker. Madison: Univ. of Wisconsin Press.

Ricardo, David. 1817. *Principles of Political Economy and Taxation*. London: J. Murray.

Roberts, Warren. 1944. *State Taxation of Metallic Deposits*. Cambridge, Mass.: Harvard Univ. Press.

Roberts, Warren. 1967. "Mine Taxation in Developing Countries." In *Extractive Resources and Taxation*, ed. Mason Gaffney. Madison: Univ. of Wisconsin Press.

Robinson, Joan. 1933. *The Economics of Imperfect Competition*. London: Macmillan.

Rolph, Earl. 1954. *Theory of Fiscal Economics*. Berkeley: Univ. of California Press.

Rose, Louis A. 1971. "Taxation of Land Value Increments Attributable to Rezoning." Honolulu: Economic Research Center, 1–61.

Russell, Bertrand. 1945. Reprint 1967. *History of Western Philosophy*. London: G. Allen and Unwin.

Schultz, Theodore. 1953. *The Economic Organization of Agriculture*. New York: McGraw-Hill.

Scott, Anthony. 1967. "The Theory of the Mine under Conditions of Certainty." In *Extractive Resources and Taxation*, ed. Mason Gaffney. Madison: Univ. of Wisconsin Press.

Scott, Anthony. 1976. "Who Should Get Natural Resource Revenues?" In *Natural Resource Revenues: A Test of Federalism*, ed. Anthony Scott. Vancouver: Univ. of British Columbia Press.

Seligman, E. R. A. 1895. Reprint 1923. *Essays in Taxation*. New York: Macmillan.

Seligman, E. R. A. 1916. "Tax Exemption Through Tax Capitalization: a Reply." *American Economic Review* 6, 790–807.

Shannon, H. L., and H. M. Bodfish. 1929. "Increments in Land Values in Chicago." *Journal of Land and Public Utility Economics* 5: 29–47.

Shoup, Carl. 1940. "Capitalization and Shifting of the Property Tax." *Property Taxes*. Symposium conducted by the Tax Policy League. New York: The League.

Shoup, Donald C. 1969. "Advance Land Acquisition by Local Governments." *Yale Economic Essays* 9, no. 2: 147–202.

Shoup, Donald C. 1970. "Optimal Timing of Urban Land Development." *Papers of the Regional Science Association* 25: 37–39.

Simon, Herbert. 1943. "Incidence of a Tax on Urban Real Property." *Quarterly Journal of Economics* 57: 398–420.

Simpson, Herbert D. 1933. "Real Estate Speculation and the Depression." *Proceedings of AEA* 23 (supplement): 163–71.

Simpson, Herbert D., and E. R. Burton. 1931. *The Valuation of Vacant Land in Suburban Areas.* Evanston: Northwestern Univ. Press.

Skouras, A. 1977. *Land and Its Taxation in Recent Economic Theory.* Athens, Greece: Papazissis.

Smith, Adam. 1776. Reprint 1937. *The Wealth of Nations,* 5th ed. New York: Modern Library.

Smith, Rogers. 1979. "The Effects of Land Taxes on Development Timing and Rates of Change in Land Prices." In *The Taxation of Urban Property in Less Developed Countries,* ed. Roy W. Bahl. Madison: Univ. of Wisconsin Press.

Somers, William A. 1901. *The Valuation of Real Estate for the Purpose of Taxation.* St. Paul, Minn.: Rich and Clymer.

Spahr, Charles B. 1891. "The Single Tax." *Political Science Quarterly* 6: 625–34.

Steele, Henry. 1967. "Natural Resource Taxation: Resource Allocation and Distribution Implications." In *Extractive Resources and Taxation,* ed. Mason Gaffney. Madison: Univ. of Wisconsin Press.

Stigler, George. 1941. *Production and Distribution Theories.* New York: Macmillan.

Stigler, George. 1947. *The Theory of Price.* New York: Macmillan.

Stockfisch, J. A. 1956. "Capitalization, Allocation and Investment Effects of Asset Taxation." *Southern Economic Journal* 22: 317–29.

Stockfisch, J. A. 1957. "Investment Incentive, Taxation, and Accelerated Depreciation." *Southern Economic Journal* 24: 28–40.

Strasma, John. 1969. "Property Taxation in Chile." In *Land and Building Taxes,* ed. Arthur Becker. Univ. of Wisconsin Press.

Taylor, Milton, et al. 1965. *Fiscal Survey of Colombia.* Baltimore: Johns Hopkins Univ. Press.

Turvey, Ralph. 1957. *The Economics of Real Property.* London: George Allen and Unwin.

Tussing, Arlon. 1977. "The Role of Public Enterprise." In *Mineral Leasing as an Instrument of Public Policy,* ed. Michael Crommelin and Andrew Thompson. Vancouver: Univ. of British Columbia Press.

Vickrey, William. 1969. "External Economies in Urban Development." *Proceedings of The American Real Estate and Urban Economics Association,* ed. Stephen Messner.

Wald, Haskell. 1959. *Taxation of Agricultural Land in Underdeveloped Economies.* Cambridge: Harvard Univ. Press.

Walker, Francis A. 1883a. Reprint 1898. Letters to *Frank Leslie's Illustrated Newspaper.* In George, Henry. *Social Problems.* New York: Doubleday and McClure.

Walker, Francis A. 1883b. *Land and Its Rent.* London: Macmillan.

Walker, Francis A. 1888. *Political Economy.* 3d ed. New York: H. Holt.

Walras, Léon. 1896. *Studies in Social Economics.* Lausanne: F. Rouge and Co., Inc. Unpublished trans. M. Gaffney, 1967.

Wicksell, Knut. 1896. "A New Principle of Just Taxation," trans. J. M. Buchanan. In *Classics in the Theory of Public Finance,* ed. R. A. Musgrave and A. T. Peacock. New York: Macmillan, 1958.

Wicksteed, Philip. 1914. "The Scope and Method of Political Economy." *Economic Journal* 24: 1-23.

Wieser, F. F. von. 1909. Reprint 1960. "The Theory of Urban Ground Rent." In *Essays in European Economic Thought,* ed. L. Sommer, New York: Van Nostrand.

Williams, Ellis. 1974. "Site Value Taxation." *National Tax Journal* 27: 29-44.

Zangerle, John A. 1927. *Principles of Real Estate Appraisal.* 2d ed. Stanley McMichael Publishing Organization.

Zion, William. 1979. "Special Districts: A Special Tax Limitation Problem." *The Urban Interest* Spring: 75-80.

10 *Arlo Woolery*

The Fairhope, Alabama, Land Tax Experiment

The very name "Fairhope" sparkles with a promise of a brighter tomorrow. Fairhope, Alabama, was founded in November 1894 on the east shores of Mobile Bay about 25 miles from the city of Mobile. The founders were "single taxers" who chose the site in Stapleton's pasture for their experiment in testing the economic theories of Henry George. Those theories recommended placing a community's total tax burden upon the land. In February of 1894, prior to coming south, the single tax group had incorporated in Des Moines, Iowa, as the Fairhope Industrial Association. Ten years later they were reincorporated as the Fairhope Single Tax Corporation.

The constitution of both corporations contained the following article: "Purpose: Its purpose shall be to establish and conduct a model community or colony, free from all forms of private monopoly, and to secure to its members therein, equality of opportunity, the full reward of individual efforts, and the benefits of cooperation in matters of general concern."

In 1894, the Fairhope Single Tax Colony purchased its first land, some 150 acres at a price of $6 an acre. This purchase included about one-half mile of frontage on Mobile Bay. An additional 200 acres was purchased about the same time for only $1.25 an acre.

The eastern shore of Mobile Bay between Montrose and Battle's

197

Wharf was chosen because of its climate, its beauty, and the cheapness of the land. There are conflicting versions of how the name Fairhope came about. The oldest version states ". . . As plans were being discussed, a member remarked, 'There is a fair hope that we will succeed.'" Thus, the name Fairhope was chosen for the proposed new community.

The Colony

The first Fairhope settlers included 25 men, women, and children. Two families came by covered wagon and the remainder came by boat. These early settlers faced a true series of obstacles. The land chosen for the Fairhope location was to a certain extent submarginal. The settlers were strangers to each other and they had different cultural and social outlooks. They were not acquainted with the agriculture of the region and had little money for the purchase of the large tracts of land that they felt were needed to demonstrate the single tax principles. They were also troubled by a band of Socialists who became attached to the community. This Socialistic group had ideals that were mostly antagonistic to the Henry George principles of the founders.

Development

The determined band of single taxers faced a bleak immediate future. The survival forecast was a gloomy one because other colonies had tried to implement the single tax theory and had failed. However, the "Fairhopians" were sustained by their strong dedication to the basic economic principles of Henry George. By 1917 the colony owned 4,000 acres of land. There were 125 homes in place and the population had reached 500. They had erected bath houses on the beaches, built a school and a library, and the community had the only public waterworks in Baldwin County. The business district had a dozen stores, three hotels, a sawmill, a brickyard, a blacksmith shop, and a printing shop. The previous dozen years had been busy ones. In 1895 a public well and pump were put in use; in 1896 a wharf was built in Mobile Bay, and a public school was built and put into operation by the colony with no outside financial assistance.

In the days before highways and motor transportation, bay boats were the important means of transport and continued to be until the late 1920s. The colony bought its first boat (called *Fairhope*) in 1900. In one of a series of early misfortunes, the boat burned in 1905. The second *Fairhope* was then built and continued in use until the 1920s.

Problems

Dissentions began early in the Fairhope experience. Joseph Fels, the wealthy soap manufacturer, social reformer, convinced single taxer, and philanthropist of Philadelphia and London, advanced money to the colony to construct a telephone system. The initial expense of installing a telephone service was $457.42. However, criticism of the telephone system revolved around two points: (1) Many thought the service was being provided much too far in advance of public demand, and (2) many felt that the colony had already strained its resources in providing an adequate water system, a public service much more in demand than a telephone system.

The phone system began operation in Fall 1904 with 12 subscribers. Each user furnished his own equipment and received free service. In practice, the upkeep of the system did prove costly. There was growing unhappiness among the lessees, an increasing proportion of whom were not members of the corporation and had no official vote in Colony matters. These people felt that the small group of telephone users were benefitting at the expense of a large number of rent payers who were paying unnecessarily high rents and receiving inadequate water, public school, and other facilities.

Problems reached crisis proportions in late 1904. These problems were so severe and so well publicized that throughout the country, single taxers began to talk about "the Fairhope controversy." The basic principle at issue was whether the single tax doctrine necessarily demanded that an attempt be made to collect the full annual use value of the land irrespective of the desires of the community for public services.

Paul and Blanche Alyea in their book *Fairhope 1894–1954* detail other areas involved in the controversy. There was the basic principle concerning the propriety of characterizing as "single tax" a plan that actually operated within the framework of state and local taxation, and that included structures and personal property in the tax base. Also in dispute was the degree of democracy in government or management of the Colony which would be necessary to square the experiment with Henry George's emphasis on the importance of freedom. In addition, a major controversy arose because the Fairhope group owned and managed the land through leases rather than through the issuance of deeds.

Rent Level Opinion Differences

Like so many arguments of principle, the Fairhope controversy actually may have revolved about money. Generally when people say it's not the money, it's the principle, they mean that it is the money. Tenants complained bitterly about rent increases running as much as two-thirds between the years 1903 and 1904. Their principle questions and objections included "why any raise at all?" And, if any raise, why such a large one? Also, was it desirable to increase rents if rental income could be used to refund the taxes paid by lessees on their improvements, stock of goods, and so on. At least one member did not object to the rent, but he simply objected to the way the money was spent. He thought it had been squandered.

Another member, who had served as a Colony officer, asserted that it was not part of the single tax to "rack rent." As he understood it, George had proposed that the landowner/holder would be left a small portion of rental value in order to cover the services rendered by him and also to prevent loss on the sale of his improvements in the event that increasing taxes made it necessary for him to move.

Colony officials, in defense of their rent policies, countered with statements that (1) rental values of Fairhope lands had not increased by two-thirds in 1903, they had simply been too low in the past and now it was necessary to catch up with the market; (2) the agricultural value of the land was irrelevant because they should be assessed not as farmlands, but for other purposes that currently are in demand; (3) rentals charged in Fairhope had caused county tax officials to raise assessed valuation.

Then the council went on to state that Fairhope rents afforded no proper basis for assessing taxes. The Council was also concerned that county tax officials might be discriminating against the colony. Apparently the officers were persuasive. At the close of their meeting, the question of rent levels was put to a vote and only one person stood to object and stated that they were too high.

In November of 1904 the Executive Committee again made its annual rent appraisal and recommended further substantial increases in rent. The lessees immediately organized and requested a special meeting of the membership to hear complaints on the proposed rentals. At this time the tenants argued that rents on leasehold lands had become a real burden and that reasonable capitalization of proposed rentals would show values of Fairhope land equal to that of city and suburban properties in the North. The tenants also called for detailed financial statements and information on all transactions affecting the corporation.

Rights of Lessees

This background is important because the same scenario is being re-enacted at the present time. During the past year a group of tenants was successful in getting legislation passed by the Alabama State Legislature which imposed binding arbitration on the single tax corporation and the tenants in matters of rental dispute.

In late April 1979, the Fairhope Single Tax Corporation was named the defendant in a suit filed by nine lessees in the United States District Court of the Southern District of Alabama. The suit charges that the plaintiffs were deprived of "their civil rights under color of State law." The suit charges that the application of the single tax economic theory "deprives the plaintiffs of their rights, privileges, and immunities secured to them by the Constitution of the United States."

The complaint goes on to state that "the defendant has adopted and applied a rental formula in such a manner as to discriminate against the plaintiffs." (Lessees have charged that the rental rates vary greatly within a small area and that they are significantly different for land that shares the same natural advantages.) "The defendant has adopted a rental policy and is charging plaintiffs rental rates that are confiscatory." Defendant actions toward the plaintiff have "violated their trust," and "the aforementioned lessee leases provided for arbitration rental disputes."

In an effort to redress the lessee's grievances, the State of Alabama enacted an arbitration statute Title 10-4-194 which applies to the defendant. The defendant has willfully refused to obey the provisions of Title 10-4-194 although the demand has been made upon it to do so. Single tax members have said they find Title 10-4-194 particularly offensive since it requires the corporation to recognize and deal with the lessee's association. They argue that the lease agreements were entered into with individuals.

However, the lessees feel that they need to be able to deal with the corporation jointly on matters of their common interest. They brought another suit to court. The suit asked the court: (1) "To declare that the rental charges would violate the plaintiff's property rights"; (2) "To require 'the defendant to adopt and apply' a nondiscriminatory formula"; and (3) "To require and direct 'the defendant to obey Title 10-4-194.'"

Class Action Suit

There also is a class action suit against the single tax corporation which was filed in 1977. This suit deals with the corporation's use of rental monies collected in excess of taxes paid by the corporation. Apparently the corporation has had a continuing concern about the issue of rent levels. As early in 1914 the corporation lessees unanimously adopted a report submitted by W. A. Sommers recommending a system for determining rents. The Alyeas' book has a chapter on the Sommers system and quotes the Sommers report in its entirety.

Sommers System

Essentially, the Sommers system recognizes the need for a land value map and the importance of establishing benchmark parcels for value comparison. Sommers started with the most valuable inside lot as his 100 percent land. Then other lots were scaled in value based on Sommers' judgment of their relative value compared to the 100 percent lot. The same general procedure was followed in establishing rents for farmland. That is, the best and most valuable tract outside of the town line was marked "100" and from this every tract was marked proportionately.

In 1914 the gross rent for the Colony lands was established at $6,500. This amount was prorated by the Sommers formula over the street units and acre units as indicated on his land maps. At the time, the Sommers system was well accepted by the lessees and there was relative harmony between the lessees and the single tax corporation. However, the system did not address itself in ensuing years to changes in relative value. This meant that the Colony's appraising officials had to address this point, and thus they were forced to make decisions on changes in the amount of rents annually assessed on Colony lands in terms of: (1) the algebraic sum of increases in some street unit values and decreases in other unit values, (2) changes in the level of general demand for colony land, and (3) the amount of Colony land actually under lease.

It would appear that until recently there have been very few changes in relative street values for the Colony lands. This would indicate that until the current round of rent increases (land user charges) rents may have been too low. However, the large amount of increase in the short time period is what most upsets the present tenants.

Dissolution Attempts

Colony officials are not strangers to litigation. In 1913 Alexander J. Melville established a group called "kickers" to attend a meeting. The purpose was to develop community sentiment to mount an appeal to the courts to dissolve the Fairhope Single Tax Corporation and define the right of the lessees. The Mobile Chancery Court found in favor of Melville and his adherents. The Single Tax Corporation brought an appeal in the Supreme Court of Alabama.

The ruling of the Mobile Chancery Court fully stirred the single taxers into action. Several members of a prominent Memphis law firm joined in filing a brief as friends of the court. Fiske Warren of Boston brought with him William H. Dunbar, a law partner of Lewis E. Brandeis. Dunbar acted as a consultant and also filed a brief. The Joseph Fels estate employed two attorneys to appear in both oral and written argument.

The force of so many high powered attorneys must have had some effect on the State Supreme Court of Alabama, because that body sustained the legality of the Fairhope Single Tax Corporation. The Court readily conceded "that any legislative attempt to apply or to enforce the 'single tax system' would be absolutely void under the constitution of Alabama." The Court also addressed the question of the single tax corporation dissolution because it "has failed and must fail of its purpose." The Court held that it could not be affirmed or denied that the stated purpose is impossible to attain.

Survival Expectations of the Colony

Aside from the current problems with the lessee association, what are the survival prospects for the Single Tax Corporation? A clue may be found in the publication of the counsel proceedings of the Fairhope Single Tax Corporation's meeting of August 16, 1976.

Be it resolved by the Executive Council of the Fairhope Single Tax Corporation that Daphne V. Anderson as president and Ruth E. Rockwell as secretary be — and they are hereby — authorized and directed to exercise and deliver for and in the name of this Corporation (including those located under dedicated streets) to Amerada Hess Corporation comprising 4290.74 acres for a term of five years and for so long theralter as oil, gas, and minerals are produced therefrom for a consideration of $125 per acre for the first year and $1 per year thereafter at the option of the lessee to defer drilling operation during the term of the lease with the reservation of a royalty of three/sixteenths of all oil and gas produced, one-tenth of all other minerals except on sulphur mined and marketed the royalty shall be $2.50 per long ton and with the following provisions: (1) all rights above a depth of 1,500 feet beneath the surface of the earth shall be excepted, (2) no operation shall be commenced on any land without the express consent of the surface lessee or lessees of the corporation of the tract or tracts on which the lessee desires to commence operations, (3) no drilling operations will be conducted within the corporate limits without prior consent of the city of Fairhope, Alabama, (4) the lease will contain no warranty of title.

The terms of this lease would indicate a first year payment of $536,342.50 to the Single Tax Corporation by Amerada Hess. This is more than twice the rents collected in 1977.

If our country's drive for self-sufficiency in petroleum products continues and Fairhope's lands yield significant oil, that income will so greatly overshadow surface land rents that the windfall riches may be a source of embarrassment to the 110 members of the Fairhope Single Tax Corporation. The lessees come back into the picture because they could place a high price on their consent for the drilling companies to begin operations. The stage may be set for another round of disputes between the lessees and the Corporation but this time for the highest stakes ever. In fact, this may be the final round of "show down" in which all the chips are on the table.

Alyea Opinion

Paul and Blance Alyea concluded their book on Fairhope with an opinion on the survival value of the Fairhope Single Tax Corporation. They state that the corporation should not be judged entirely on its past accomplishments and failures or on its present importance to those directly affected — the members and lessees. In assessing the survival value of the Fairhope experiment, the Alyeas make the following observations:

(1) "The urban community of Fairhope has outdistanced many small American cities, both in material achievements and in those intangible imponderable qualities which make a community worthwhile."

(2) "Fairhope has neither unearthed any windfall — such as striking oil — nor has it benefitted directly from an industrial development in the immediate vicinity. The oil might come, but a major industrial development is unlikely."

Conclusion

The prophetic words were penned 25 years ago. For the moment, major industrial development has bypassed the eastern shores of Mobile Bay. However, successful oil drilling is a very real possibility in Fairhope and the surrounding area. Depending upon its timing and degree of success, Fairhope's single tax colony may be little more than an interesting historical footnote to a century of discussion about George and his land and tax theories. On the other hand, the valuable natural resources of the land controlled by the Fairhope Single Tax Corporation may ignite new popular support for general distribution of the income arising from exploitation of location and land's productiveness.

11 *Matthew Edel*

Capital, Profit, and Accumulation: The Perspectives of Karl Marx and Henry George Compared

The centenary of *Progress and Poverty* follows by only a few years that of Volume I of Marx's *Capital*. These two great works of radical economics both appeared in a period of economic turmoil — a long-swing downturn marked by disruption of existing economic relationships, depression, and the rise of new industrial monopolies. Both books proposed systems for analysis of economic conditions and advocated revolutionary changes. Both were based on the classical writings of David Ricardo, although their systems and proposals differ in many ways. Both won adherents, and both still have them, although Marx has had more impact on policy.

In the present paper, I explore some of the differences between the economic analyses of Marx and George. Centenaries are a time for ecumenical dialogue. More important, the modern world's challenges require greater theoretical precision and cross-fertilization of ideas. I shall focus on the treatment of capital, profits, and accumulation in the two theories.

The relationship between Marxist economics and the economics of Henry George has often been an antagonistic one, notwithstanding certain common themes. Rival schools often treat each other only with studied ignorance or calumny. Mutual learning and a clarification of fundamental axioms through confrontation are foregone.

Both Karl Marx and Henry George were capable of careful and penetrating analyses of their predecessors in political economy. Whatever the
merits of a description of either man as a "post Ricardian" (surely
Samuelson's "minor" is unwarranted), both knew and could explain their
differences with Ricardo (1821), Malthus (1798), Wakefield (1849), or Mill
(1848). But neither gave the other serious attention. Their followers did
even less.

Control over Economic Rents

In *Progress and Poverty,* Henry George presented a cautious attitude
toward Socialism. He was skeptical of "demagogues" who argue, "there
is a necessary conflict between capital and labor", or that the market
should be restrained by government (1879, rpt. 1929, p. 11). Yet he stated
that a regulated socialism (as in ancient Peru) might be a better social
state "than that to which we now seem to be tending (1879, rpt. 1929, p.
220). Essentially, he felt the scheme was utopian:

Socialism in anything approaching such a form, modern society cannot successfully attempt. The only force that has ever proved competent for it — a strong
and definite religious faith — is wanting and is daily growing less . . . . Our governments, as is already plainly evident, would break down in the attempt. . . .

The ideal of socialism is grand and noble; and it is, I am convinced, possible of
realization; but such a state of society cannot be manufactured — it must grow.
Society is an organism, not a machine. It can live only the individual life of its
parts . . . (George 1879, rpt. 1929, p. 321).

With the reduction of inequality and the "free and natural development"
of society, such socialism might come about. However, George believed
that it could not be implemented in his time (1879, rpt. 1929, p. 321).

After the breakdown of the 1886 political coalition of Single Taxers
and Socialists, George's attitude toward Marx hardened. In *The Science
of Political Economy* he classifies Marxism as a branch of German pro-
tectionism, as a "learned bureaucratic and incomprehensible" system
(1897, p. 197). But his only analyses of *Capital* are a claim that wealth is
never defined (1897, p. 124) and the following comment:

Without distinguishing between products of nature and the products of man,
Marx holds that there are two kinds of value — use value and exchange
value — and that through some alchemy of buying and selling the capitalist who
hires men to turn material into products gets a larger value than he gives. This
economic proposition of Marx . . . can hardly be called a theory (1897, p. 197).

The comment suggests that he had read *Capital* but had not grasped the definitions and concepts contained in the early chapters of volume I.

Marx, on his part, suggests a scheme similar to that of George. Some Georgist adherents might be attracted to Marx's comments, primarily directed at Mill's weaker land value increment tax, included in his notebooks on *Theories of Surplus Value:*

Assuming the capitalist mode of production, then the capitalist is not only a necessary functionary, but the dominating functionary in production. The land-owner, on the other hand, is quite superfluous in this mode of production. Its only requirement is that land should *not* be common property, that it should con-front the working class as a condition of production, not *belonging* to it, and the purpose is completely fulfilled if it becomes state property, i.e., if the state draws the rent . . . The radical bourgeois (with an eye moreover to the suppression of all other taxes) therefore goes forward theoretically to a refutation of the private ownership of the land, which, in the form of state property, he would like to turn into the common property, of the bourgeois class, of capital (1905, rpt. 1963, p. 44).

Unlike George, who argued that the single tax would allow access to self-employment or the equivalent in benefits for all, Marx argued that tax on landed property, or even its nationalization under capitalist condi-tions, would not amount to access to the conditions of production for all:

The Ricardian law would prevail just the same, even if *landed property* were *non-*existent. With the abolition of landed property and the retention of capitalist pro-duction, this excess profit arising from the difference in fertility would remain. If the state appropriated the land and capitalist production continued, then rent . . . would be paid to the state, but rent as such would remain. If landed property became *people's property* then the whole basis of capitalist production would go, the foundation on which rests the confrontation of the worker by the conditions of labor as an independent force (1905, rpt. 1963, pp. 103–4).

Later, when commenting on the 1886 political situation in the United States, Engels applied such a view directly to George, arguing that historically the separation of people from the land did not always mean liberation (e.g., feudalism). Engels claims that George's proposed remedy left the present mode of social production untouched and had, in fact, been anticipated by the extreme section of Ricardian bourgeois economists who also demanded the confiscation of land by the state (1887, rpt. 1973, pp. 17–24). However no analysis was offered to explain why George argues that only land values need be expropriated to allow access to land.

All of this does not add up to a careful critique of each school by the other.

Comparative Positions

The Henry George movement influenced American socialism more than is generally recognized. The dominant, reformist branch within the socialist movement of the turn of the century – the so-called "sewer socialists" – appropriated much of George's program for urban use. The leader of the opposed tendency, Daniel DeLeon, had passed through the Single Tax movement in his political trajectory. There were many occasions, such as the 1893 A.F.L. convention, where Single Tax and Marxist positions on property directly opposed each other; yet there were also cases of mutual participation in local alliances over the next two decades (Edel 1977, pp. 1-15).

I have argued also that these influences and alliances were possible, and sensible from a Marxist viewpoint, because there is considerable formal overlap between the theories of Marx and George on the question of rents. Both argue that rent is not merely confined to a "natural" Ricardian differential. George's treatment of speculative land values and Marx's of absolute rent show that certain elements of land ownership can be a barrier to economic development through capitalist investment. Both argue that ownership of land is also a factor holding labor in low-wage employment (although for Marx there are other factors as well). Both suggest cases in which the removal of land monopoly might allow improvements (short run in Marx's view, but nonetheless real) in labor's conditions. Where there are differences in detail, Marxists can learn from George's analysis (Edel 1977).

Wages and Profits

Underlying these similarities in theoretical position (allowing some alliances over specific reforms) there is also a convergence of some aspects of wage theory. Both repudiate the Malthusian population theory and the doctrine of the fixed wages fund. Indeed, their critiques of these theories overlap and reinforce each other, being based on similar optimism about the creative potential of human labor to increase production, if it is unfettered by social institutions. This radical optimism is the strongest bond between the two schools, and their prime difference with conventional "iron law" economics of their century.

There are, to be sure, major differences in their treatment of the specific mechanisms of wage fixing. George, as will be shown, relies on marginal productivity of labor (in a unique way) and Marx on a concept of socially determined subsistence levels. There are even some differences in their projection of the future course of rents under capitalism. George saw them as rising with technical advancement, while Marx suggested they might fall as the "forces of production" advanced. How these differences relate to the theoretical core of the two analyses must still be examined. They do not, as will be shown below, rest on ad hoc assumptions.

It is not in the treatment of rents and wages that the differences between the theories is most apparent. To understand the basis of their differences, it is useful to focus on the determination of the third major "factor income" — interest or profit, and upon the related, more general question of the nature of capital and its role in economic development or accumulation. This treatment of capital reflects the most fundamental differences between Marx and George; these are differences in the vision of which classes are in conflict with each other in society, and about the economic form of society that should exist in an ideal state. These differences are substantial and in many ways cannot be reconciled.

Marx writes from the perspective of the organizations and experiences of an industrial labor force, long separated from the land, which was confronted by large enterprises. He sees a return to farming or artisan activity as an undesirable and, more important, impossible goal. The individual proprietor, peasant, or petty bourgeois enters into his analysis only in a secondary position.

George writes with the conditions of the frontier constantly in mind. An individual alone, if unfettered by monopoly, can be an important producer. Farming, mining, and even artisan industry do not inevitably need large enterprises, although George is second to none in his praise for agglomeration. The individual proprietor or petty bourgeois, for George, is not an anachronism — in fact, he is the central actor in many ways. No antagonism is necessary between such proprietors and the wage worker; the two classes, in a better system, would indeed merge.

How these differences in perspective underlie and are exposed in the two theories is apparent if we look closely at several questions. First, what is the definition of capital? Is it a thing or a relationship? What forms of wealth or means of production are defined as not being capital? Second, what determines the rewards received by capital? Are they part of a surplus value? Are interest and profit rates uniform for all forms of capital? What is the relationship between normal and monopoly profit conditions? Third, what role does capital play in economic development?

The differing positions of the two authors on these questions will be explored in the following section, with more general aspects of contrast and connection saved for the final section.

Defining Capital

George

The attempt to define capital formally is one of the most confusing sections in Henry George's work, due to the multiplicity of specific definitions offered. In George's simplest definition, capital refers to a subset of the category "wealth," and wealth is defined as "labor impressed upon matter in such a way as to store up, as the heat of the sun is stored up in coal, the power of human labor to manifest to human desires" (1879, rpt. 1929, p. 42). Capital is only a part of wealth — that part, namely, which is devoted to the aid of production" (1879, rpt. 1929, p. 42). This definition is close to the notion of produced means of production in Marx. George also defines capital in terms of saver's motives ("that portion of wealth which its owners do not propose to use directly for their own gratification, but for the purpose of obtaining more wealth") (1879, rpt. 1929, p. 45). Capital is also defined as "wealth in course of exchange, understanding exchange to include not merely the passing from hand to hand, but also such transformations as occur when the reproductive or transforming forces of nature are used for the increase of wealth" (1879, rpt. 1929, p. 48).

There are some discrepancies here, in that the first definition would seem to exclude inventories of consumer goods held for sale; while the latter two would include them. More fundamentally, George is torn between considering capital as a set of things, and realizing that a definition ought to be oriented to a description of social relations. Thus having stated his first definition, he is forced to exclude some items used in production not owned by capitalists. As he states:

If we must consider as capital everything which supplies the laborer with food, clothing, shelter, etc., then to find a laborer who is not a capitalist we shall be forced to hunt up an absolutely naked man, destitute even of a sharpened stick, or of a burrow in the ground — a situation in which, save as a result of exceptional circumstances, human beings have never been found (1879, rpt. 1929, p. 45).

This consideration leads him to exclude not only laborer's own tools, but also human capital and consumers' durables from the definition. It is for this reason that the production definition must be qualified by consideration of exchange. As will be shown, when George comes to treat *profits* he defines as capital those assets which yield returns after a delay and which are exchanged *in very specific* markets for one particular subset of capital goods. A working definition, in terms of an enumeration of examples, is thus possible. However, it includes some problems, which emerge precisely because the return to capital, in George's model, may be determined by what goes on in a subsistence sector of the economy that may not fully meet his terms for the definition of capital.

Marx

Marx's route to definition of capital is, in a sense, the reverse of George's. Rather than starting with a definition of capital as a set of assets or things, he defines it initially as a social relationship. Although George apparently missed the point, there is a concept in Marx's argument that is equivalent to George's "wealth" (produced means of production), as well as a broader wealth concept of "forces of production," which would include both produced and natural means of production, as well as technology, human capital, and the like. This second concept is closer to Smith's ideas. However, these concepts are kept separate from the notion of capital.

Capital is defined as such only within capitalist systems, or those with some capitalist elements. Assets are capital only insofar as they exist opposed to things that are not capital; industrial capital can be defined as such only if there is a proletariat to be hired by capitalists. Even merchant capital requires for its existence either a capitalist system or a dominant noncapitalist system with whose producers or exploiters the merchants can trade (Marx 1867, rpt. 1967, part II; see also Ollman 1974 and Sweezy 1964).

This definition is rather abstract. Yet only in a concrete setting can one enumerate those goods or assets that are capital. Then it becomes clear that some goods are capital sometimes and not capital other times. Financial assets, which George excludes from the definition of wealth or capital, are also part of capital, according to Marx, at least at certain points in their circulation. Therefore any attempt to measure a real capital stock in Marx's categories becomes problematic, and indeed Marx makes no attempt to measure such a stock. Operationally, capital is handled in terms of flows when capitalist economies are modelled. As a result, any linking of Marx's definitions for rates of profit with the common definition is subject to much controversy. But its form is useful for concentration on the economic flow and its interruption, and on a capital-labor relationship. In Marx's view, also, it is important to make the definition historically specific, to avoid trying to explain the complexities of modern society by appeals to Robinson Crusoe's island or some other presumed state of nature. Rules for the determination of profits, as well as for the governance of production, will be different economic systems or "modes of production" (Marx 1867, rpt. 1967; Hindess and Hirst 1975).

Role of Profits

If Marx and George differ on their definitions of capital, they are even more clearly apart when explaining the reasons that capital should receive a profit, and what determines the magnitude of this profit. Essentially, Marx sees profit as being determined at the aggregate or macroeconomic level by the extent to which a capitalist class can extract surplus labor (or surplus value) from a proletariat, with some allowance for the distribution of surplus value among capitalists and from them to other nonworking classes. For George, profit is determined by the productivity of capital, not in the aggregate but on a (very literal) margin. Like Marx, George has a theory of surplus value, but he does not see competitive capital as participating in that surplus. In both theories, complications arise from the presence of different capitals with greater or lesser monopoly positions. In their descriptions of monopoly, however, the two writers are closer together in position. To some degree their differences in profit theory are determined by their assumptions as to which fraction of capital (monopolist, competitive, or family level) is most characteristic of capitalism.

Marx

Marx's analysis of the determination of profit focuses on capitalist firms large enough to employ workers but (in the first instance) small enough to be affected by competition. (Application to larger-scale monopolies is a simple extension.) However, the analysis is actually carried out at an aggregate level. For Marx, the value of goods is based on the labor required to produce them, including direct labor in the act of production and the additional labor required to replace the raw materials and depreciating equipment used up in production. The labor used is performed, in a typical capitalist operation, by proletarians who sell their "labor power" (the ability to work) to employers at its value. The value of "labor power" is a cost of production, based on the amount of labor used in producing the consumer goods and services that go to reproduce the labor force. This cost is not determined by physiological subsistence, but rather by social "historical and moral" elements, including the ability of the workers to enforce a decent standard of living through class struggle. As long as the productivity of labor in society is great enough that only a portion of the potential labor time of society can provide the consumption required to reproduce labor power, a gap between the value of labor power and the value produced by labor exist, as long as capitalists can make workers work hard enough (Marx 1867, rpt. 1967, chap. 7, and 1968).

In this model the definition of capital *in terms of a relationship to labor* is central. The relationship actually is that of control over production. If "alchemy" is involved, as George claims, it is in production, not in "buying and selling." The surplus is created by the gap between the *productivity* and the *cost of production* of the laborers. Thus anything that has been produced which adds to that productivity — whether through engineering efficiency, or through stricter discipline — is part of the capitalist class's capital (Marx, 1905, rpt. 1963).

Surplus value is, initially, acquired by the capitalists who direct the labor process, hiring workers to produce goods. Portions are drawn off as rents, interest, merchant's profits, and taxes. One complexity arises because in developed capitalist systems, competition among capitalists and the mobility of investment funds between sectors of the economy require equalization of profit rates among these sectors.

If all goods sell at their values, and if the ratio of constant capital expenditures (materials and depreciation) to variable capital (wage expenditures) is different in different industries, rates of profit (surplus value as a proportion of total capital) will be unequal unless rates of surplus value (as a proportion of value produced) also vary. This assumption would require differential wage rates to apply in many cases. Marx holds that untrue. Marx resolves this difficulty by arguing that the price of commodities is determined by what he calls *prices of production:* costs including payment for wages, constant capital replacement, and an average profit on capital (1867, rpt. 1967).

This theory is sometimes considered contrary to the labor theory of value used in Marx's introductory chapters, but as presented it is not inconsistent if surplus value is thought of as an *aggregate* economic concept. At the level of the economy as a whole, the wage rate is still determined by the value of labor power, total produced value is still determined by the amount of labor the capitalists can force from their employees, and total surplus value is still determined by the gap between total value produced and value of labor power. The individual values and profits are a transformed function of this total, as modified by intercapitalist competition and the power of renters to take part of surplus (Laibman 1973-74).

George

George's analysis has similarities to that of Marx at some, but not all, levels. In his attack on the wages fund doctrine George argues that all production is the result of direct or indirect labor. A portion of the product, that received by landlords or certain monopolies, is treated as an unearned value, accrued *because* the social cooperation of individuals (or, in George, small capitals) produces more than they would produce in isolation from each other, and *because* the market does not return all of the social gains from agglomeration to individual producers. But the determination of wages and competitive profits is based not on an asymmetrical relationship (social subsistence vs. aggregate surplus value) as in Marx. Both are determined competitively by marginal processes.

The institutions of the American frontier permeate the assumptions of George's model. For George, labor's share is not governed by physiological or social subsistence minima. A floor is set to wages by the amount a worker can earn going to the margin of cultivation and working without prior wealth on available and free land:

Wages depend upon the margin of production, or upon the produce which labor can obtain at the highest point of natural productiveness open to it without the payment of rent (1879, rpt. 1929, p. 213).

Competition of employers will keep wages from sinking below this point.

Similarly, the return to capital is given by frontier conditions. Capital here is thought of as real equipment (or livestock) and not, as in Marx, an abstract social concept represented by the market value of assets. Its productivity, too, is governed by the frontier's location:

The general rate of interest will be determined by the return to capital upon the poorest land to which capital is freely applied — that is to say, upon the best land open to it without the payment of rent (George 1879, rpt. 1929, p. 201).

But how can capital be conceived as being "applied" to land? Herein lies one problem of George's theory. If capital is indirect labor, frontier conditions do not in themselves determine how much above the initial labor cost investment capital will receive in returns. Some reward for waiting must be applied if a non-zero markup is to be justified. Yet George does not take this tack. Instead he conceives of some capital as increasing on its own:

It is true that if I put away money it will not increase. But suppose, instead, I put away wine. At the end of a year I will have an increased value, for the wine will have improved in quality. Or supposing that in a country adapted to them, I set out bees; at the end of a year I will have more swarms of bees, and the honey which they have made. Or supposing, where there is a range, I turn out sheep, or hogs, or cattle; at the end of the year I will, upon the average, also have an increase (1879, rpt. 1929, p. 181).

If some investments increase on their own, their rate of increase must set a floor to other investments, for why would an investor put money into some assets that do not grow in value if other assets grow naturally?

George's explanation of interest as ruled by such natural forces, which he sees as operating more strongly as the extent of land available for their operation increases, allows a certain symmetry between his theories of rent, wages, and interest. All are set by the location of "the margin of cultivation," with wages and interest rising together and rent falling, as the margin of cultivation "rises" (1879, rpt. 1929, p. 219). This also allows him a theory with no innate conflict between labor and capital. However, even in George's explanation, there are qualms about this "natural" theory of capital.

In the first place, not all capital investments are in assets that will increase on their own. How, then, does George treat the others? Here George comes rather close to Marx's labor theory of value. He writes, following an example of one carpenter lending a plane to another for interest, that such lending could lead the borrower to the point where his whole product was owed to the other, making him "virtually his slave" (1879, rpt. 1929, p. 179). What is loaned here, he says, is not the tool's productivity:

The power which exists in the tool to increase the productiveness of labor is neither in justice nor in fact the basis of interest . . . And I am inclined to think that if all wealth consisted of such things as planes and all production was such as that of carpenters — that is to say if wealth consisted but of the inert matter of the universe, and production of working up this inert matter into different shapes, that interest would be but the robbery of industry and could not long exist (1879, rpt. 1929, p. 180).

In other words, George feels that it is only a particular subset of capital which through the "interchangeability of wealth" sets a general rate of interest. Without this special case, no positive interest would be justifiable. Like the rent of land, it would then, if it persisted, be considered part of the unearned surplus.

In the second place, even if some profits are justified as equivalents to the natural increase of wine, hives, trees, or cattle, these profits do not exhaust the category popularly thought of as profit. George devotes a chapter to "spurious capital and . . . profits often mistaken for interest" (1879, rpt. 1929, book III, chap. 4). Assets seized by force or threat (including political privilege) and by monopoly power he equates *not* to assests accumulated by indirect labor or by their own natural increase but rather to a monopoly such as landownership. He writes:

The belief that interest is the robbery of industry is, I am persuaded, in large part due to a failure to discriminate between what is really capital and what is not, and between profits which are properly interest and profits which arise from other sources than the use of capital. In the speech and literature of the day everyone is styled a capitalist who possesses what, independent of his labor, will yield him a return while whatever is thus received is spoken of as the earnings or takings of capital (1879, rpt. 1929, p. 189).

Their returns, George argues, are not returns to capital.

Thus, George reads out of the category *capital* those assets most characteristic of the portfolios of capitalists:

Now, taking the great fortunes that are so often referred to as exemplifying the accumulative power of capital — the Dukes of Westminster and Marquises of Bute, the Rothschilds, Astors, Stewarts, Vanderbilts, Goulds, Stanfords, and Floods — it is upon examination readily seen that they have been built up, in greater or less part, not by interest but by elements such as we have been reviewing (1879, rpt. 1929, p. 194).

It is of course, precisely such fortunes, made initially in the course of the "primitive accumulation" of assets by force (and the concurrent dispossession of workers from access to the means of production), which Marx finds most characteristic of capitalism (1867, rpt. 1967, part I). The difference between capital theories stems, to a great extent, from differences about whose capital is being described.

Although Marx's typical capitalists are not capitalists in George's view, there is no real disagreement that these people do receive surplus value. Disagreement remains concerning the basis of their monopolies — George relates it to control of land and proposes to cure it by fiscal land reforms, while Marx relates it to control over labor and suggests that land reform or the single tax, if it did anything, would strengthen the major capitalists. But this disagreement itself stems from different appreciations of the role of self-employed petty capitalists in the economy. By making them the typical capitalist of his model, George is reaffirming his basic populist position that these are the economic beings who should be the backbone of the economy (Marx 1905, rpt. 1963, part II, p. 43-44).

Of course, not all small proprietors were out of business, even in Marx's Europe. In George's frontier California, they were quite important. George took them as the norm for capitalism, and Marx did not ignore them completely. He recognized, as did George, that the small proprietor might not have the same profit rate as the larger operator. Yet this did not mean for Marx that the system in which the working proprietor functioned was not exploitive capitalism. In Marx's eyes, the artisan, peasant, storekeeper, and other petty capitalists were theoretical hybrids who embodied aspects of workers and capitalist in one person (or family unit). The capitalist side of the unit sought a competitive return on investment in vain (because of inefficient scale, low capitalization, state favoritism, and so on). In the process, the "capitalist" side was forced to drive the "laborer" side to the utmost to avoid bankruptcy. Hence the "self-employed" often worked harder and longer than did wageworkers, even though they earned less profits than other capitalists.

Sources of Accumulation

The process of economic development is a major concern of both Marx and George. This, indeed, is one factor that sets them apart from their contemporaries, who were turning from the classical dynamics to marginalist statics. Both place some emphasis on the role of capital in the development process (Marx refers to development as the accumulation of capital), but neither sees development as simply the piling up of capital goods.

George

In treating development, George is much in the tradition of Adam Smith, when he considers the wealth of a nation to consist of its productive potential in the broadest sense. Agglomeration effects achieved through the extension of the market, through development of techniques and ideas favorable to growth, and through efficiency of labor are all more important than the accumulation of a stock of capital goods. True, George states that to speak of a community increasing in wealth means "an increase of certain tangible things — such as buildings, cattle, tools, machinery, agricultural and mineral products, manufactured goods, ships, wagons, furniture, and the like." However, once he is past the establishment of definitions, he insists several times that this physical wealth is relatively unimportant. Citing several natural and man-made disasters, George shows that a developed society can rebuild this physical stock of capital quickly — a forecast of the rapid development of Germany and Japan after the destruction of World War II.

Note that there is nothing in this picture to prohibit development by a community of petty proprietors. Large production units play a small part in progress; machinery is useful but not central. Urban growth, population increase, and increasing communication allow small businesses to contribute fully to progress.

Marx

For Marx, too, development is defined as more than just the piling up of physical capital. The development of the forces of production, defined abstractly, involves much more than construction and the making of machines. All of the elements cited by George play some role. Yet there is also an historical progression involved. The division of labor between trades leads to a division of labor within branches of industry and firms. The scale of cooperation and of complexity in production increases. This historical tendency toward a socialization of the productive process makes the role of small-scale operations marginal. In addition, tendencies toward centralization and concentration undermine small proprietor competitiveness. Thus, apart from any relation of scale to the use of capital equipment, the process of development undermines the sorts of firms thought normal by George.

Indeed, in Marx's presentation of the basic dynamics or "general law" of capitalist accumulation, the process of growth in a capitalist system is described as involving *both* the growth of a stock of capital goods (arising from technical composition of capital) and the expansion of the proletariat, as increasing numbers of people are pushed out of positions of small proprietorship. For both Marx and George, development under unreformed capitalist rules involves a growing surplus, combined with increasing poverty; some of this surplus is invested in capital equipment. However, whereas for Marx it is inevitable and progressive that this process squeezes out the petty capitalist, for George such a squeeze is regressive but reversible.

Conclusion

The previous three sections have analyzed some key points of difference between George's and Marx's theories of capital. Some aspects of those theories have been shown to be less divergent than they first appear: both theories involve inventory and social relationship concepts of capital; both suggest that there are differences in returns to petty, large competitive, and monopoly capitals; both accept the notion of surplus value accruing to at least some capitalists. Their differences, however, seem irreconcilable on other key points, notably the role of small capitalists in the formation of the profit rate, in the growth process, and in the class composition of society. Putting the matter most simply, George's theory reflects in its structure the implied unity of workers and working petty capitalists; Marx sees capital and labor locked in eternal conflict, even within the same individual.

This conclusion gives some perspective on the reasons that, at certain times in history, collaboration between proponents of the two theories has been possible. There are historical conjunctures in which, even from a pure Marxist viewpoint, alliance between labor and small-scale capitalist is desirable. Opposition to landlord or monopoly interests is the basis of such an alliance. However, when conflict with landed property or monopoly is not a principal problem, the latent conflict emerges. Urban land policy at the turn of the century was one field in which such alliance was beneficial; present-day monopolization of energy-producing resources may be the occasion for another such alliance.

In any such alliance, greater awareness of similarities and fundamental differences between the paradigms of the participants is, I believe, desirable. While ignoring fundamental differences may lead to greater enthusiasm in the short run, in the long run it leads to disillusionment. Yet, clarification of differences and exploration of tactical collaboration is not the only proposal for dialogue that emerges from a confrontation of the two theories of capital. Rather, the confrontation suggests to both theoretical camps certain areas in which self-examination may be necessary.

While I am not optimistic of any easy solution, I think relationships between the theories should be explored. The economics of Henry George is directed toward the preservation of a highly decentralized system, faced with internal pressures to decompose. It would be ironic if, having grown obsolete through the decline of its original frontier world, it found a new life in some future socialism. This is not to say that the single tax is alive and well and living in Yugoslasvia, but perhaps it should be.

References

Edel, Matthew. 1977. "Rent Theory and Labor Strategy: Marx, George and the Urban Crisis." *Review of Radical Political Economics* 9, no. 4: 1–15.

Engels, Frederick. 1887. Reprint 1973. "Preface to the American Edition." In *The Condition of the Working Class in England.* Moscow: Progress Publishers.

George, Henry. 1879. Reprint 1929. *Progress and Poverty.* New York: Modern Library.

George, Henry. 1897. *The Science of Political Economy.* In *Complete Works of Henry George,* vol. IV. Garden City N.Y.: Doubleday, Page.

Hindess, B., and P. Hirst. 1975. *Precapitalist Modes of Production.* London: Routledge and Kegan Paul.

Laibman, David. 1973–74. "Values and Prices of Production: The Political Economy of the Transformation Problem." *Science and Society* 37, no. 4: 404–36.

Malthus, T. R. 1798. *An Essay on the Principle of Population.* London.

Marx, Karl. 1905. Reprint 1963. *Theories of Surplus Value,* trans. Emile Burns. Moscow: Progress Publishers.

Marx, Karl. 1867. Reprint 1967. *Capital,* trans. Samuel Moore and Edward Aveling. New York: International Publishers.

Marx, Karl. 1898. Reprint 1968. "Wages, Price and Profit." In Karl Marx and Frederick Engels. *Selected Works.* New York: International Publishers.

Mill, John Stuart. 1848. *Principles of Political Economy.* London: J. W. Parker.

Ollman, B. 1974. *Alienation.* Cambridge: The Univ. Press.

Ricardo, David. 1821. *On the Principles of Political Economy and Taxation.* London.

Sweezy, P. 1964. *The Theory of Capitalist Development.* New York: Monthly Review Press.

Wakefield, E. G. 1849. *England and America.* London.

Comment Centered on Economic Reform and Future TRED Topics

William S. Vickrey: I want to go back to George Break's point. He spoke of rent as a gift of nature. Rent is, of course, generated by public facilities, i.e., infrastructure, but more than that, there is rent from a particular property as a creation of buildings on neighboring property. In effect, if you put up a nice big office building in the center of town and then you attract tenants to that office building, this raises the rents on the residential area that is tributary to that office building. It might be desirable policy not to tax the construction of this nice new office building; perhaps you ought to subsidize it because of the benefits conferred on the surrounding property owners.

George F. Break: No comment. I agree.

Vickrey: You spoke of Mexico and California. I think the real place to look is New Zealand, which is perhaps one of the areas of latest settlement and where perhaps land value taxation has been more thoroughly applied than anywhere else, even in Australia. In Australia there is a peculiarity; you do not subject improvements to the property tax, at least in some areas, but instead you declare that under the income tax. Under the income tax real property cannot be depreciated. In this way, you impose in effect an extra burden on improvements under the income tax that merely offsets what you removed by land value tax. So the results are not as strong as they might be otherwise, even considering that the amount of

221

local services financed by local taxes in Australia is much smaller than it is in many other places. Also, the property tax is generally heavier in New Zealand than in Australia.

Roy W. Bahl: Just a small note to Mason Gaffney. You were classifying proponents for land value tax (LVT) when you talked of the long ago and far away academic people who were in favor of land tax as long as it was across the ocean. Far be it from me to attack that list of people you named, but I think there may be a bit more to it. It may have to do with the setting for a land value tax; at least in my reading of the evidence, if LVT is to be established anywhere it will be in the urban areas of developing countries. It is in these areas where there has been a movement to levy a higher tax on the land component of the property tax base. The reason for this I would argue is partly because of the setting.

The set of functions that the local governments were responsible for in LDCs was fairly new. These cities were just developing as true urban areas, and there was much more than normal interest in questions concerning the allocation of land.

Real Estate Tax in Holland

William Deyll: I would like to spend a few minutes to summarize the new land tax developments that have taken place in Holland during the past several years.

Arlo Woolery: I had been hoping you would do this. After you have completed your brief description of the recent developments in Holland, I may want to ask you a few questions.

Deyll: In 1970, the Dutch decided not to continue beyond 1979 a group of taxes used by urban centers to meet a traditional group of government services financed at the local level. A new type of real estate tax was made available to municipalities to replace the unrenewed revenue sources. The new real estate tax can be levied either on a value basis or on the surface basis of land only.

Woolery: How rapid has progess been made toward adopting the new approach to urban land taxation?

Deyll: By 1977, many municipalities had changed to the new revenue source and abandoned their old sources. (The former taxes included a land tax, duty on houses, street tax, building site tax, insurance tax, and entertainment tax.) About 17 percent of all the municipalities, including both Amsterdam and Rotterdam (which include 27 percent of the total population), adopted the new surface real estate tax. This approach is based on dividing the urban area into sections that have been given tax payment levels per square meter according to the location and use of the real estate.

Woolery: Could you describe the procedure used in arriving at the tax-due figure?

Deyll: The total square meters within a real estate holding is reduced by 300 square meters of land not covered by the structure; this exemption is meant to encourage small gardens. The next step establishes the number of square meters covered by a building and the additional square meters of bare land.

The tax per square meter of land is calculated from a table developed by the Union of Netherlands Municipalities — that is, the Bouwcentrum foundations. Each square meter of land is included within blocks that are given a single location coefficient. The taxable surface is divided into two parts — land on which structure rests and land not covered by a building.

The number of square meters of land not covered by a structure is multiplied by three coefficients based on desirability of the area. The result is the adjusted number of meters used to apply the rate established in that city.

The meters covered by a building is adjusted by application of the same coefficient of location as on bare land. In addition, it is multiplied by the coefficient of the kind and use of the building and the coefficient of the building quality.

The total meters of bare land plus the square meters covered by a building, as adjusted, are taxed separately on the basis of the adjusted square meters. The tax per adjusted square meter of surface in Rotterdam is about $1.00 and in Amsterdam about $1.50 (in 1975 figures). The substantially higher tax in Amsterdam is partially the result of exemptions of many historical buildings and the greater revenues Rotterdam collects from its port.

Woolery: How is the tax burden allocated?

Deyll: The total tax levied on the property is divided into two parts, based on the concepts of legal user tax rate and the legal owner tax rate. The legal owner's tax rate is typically several times higher than the legal user tax rate. Both taxes are paid by the same tax payer on owner-occupied property.

The revenues provided by the new tax approach are proving to be adequate. The varying rate applied to legal owners and legal users has permitted Amsterdam to favor legal users (renters) to a greater extent than does Rotterdam.

Woolery: Now, I would like to ask Mr. Deyll several questions that will help provide some additional background on the property tax system employed in Amsterdam. My first question is: What is the coefficient for vacant land in Amsterdam?

Deyll: In Amsterdam we have the lowest coefficient for vacant land. It is .01. This low coefficient applies to land that is not served with streets, electricity, or water. This was the last type of property that we dealt with in setting up our table of coefficients. Since there isn't a great deal privately owned, and most is owned by the municipality itself, we weren't too concerned about the coefficient for this particular type of property.

Woolery: Then I would like to ask as a second question: What is the tax status for public buildings and what is the coefficient for the Councertgebouw?

Deyll: We actually do tax the public buildings in the city of Amsterdam and the Concertgebouw is one building that is at a very high level due to its use coefficient. Last year the coefficient for the Concertgebouw was 3; this year that has been reduced to 2.9.

Woolery: What about the actual tax rates and how are the tax payments divided between the owner of the property and the user of the property?

Deyll: I'll answer the second part of that question first. The taxes fall about 75 percent on the owner and about 25 percent on the user. Where the user and the owner are the same person, that person pays 100 percent of the property tax. The tax rates are set by a municipal ordinance each year; recently the owners have been paying about 30 guilders for each ten square meters of taxable area, while the users have been paying about ten guilders for each ten square meters of taxable area.

Woolery: What kind of limitations are imposed on municipalities concerning the amount that they may raise from the property tax as a percentage of the revenues received from the central government?

Deyll: There is definite limitation on the amount that local municipalities can levy on the owners and the users of property. The total municipal tax on owners is limited to 15 percent of the total grants we get from the central government, and the total local municipal tax on users is limited to 12 percent of the amount we receive in advance from the central government. As you can see, the absolute amount of money that local municipalities can raise from the property tax is determined by the amount of money that each municipality receives from the central government; until recently, the users of the tax have not been taxed anywhere near the 12 percent limit.

The Fairhope and Other Single Tax Corporations

Kenneth C. Back: I would like to shift back to Fairhope. First, is the school system of Fairhope a public school system? And second, what are your own views of whether that experiment is working or not working?

Wooley: What is called the organic school was established quite early in Fairhope. It is more than an adult educational center that is devoted to teaching George's theory. In order to become a member of the single tax colony you have to take this course in George's economics and pass the examination. Paying your $100 membership isn't enough. You have to be convincing to your oral committee that you are indeed a dedicated single taxer before you can become a member of the corporation.

The county and city do levy taxes and school taxes, and they do have a public school. Only 15 percent of the land in the actual incorporated area of Fairhope is owned by the colony. What it does is collect the rents and then pays all of the taxes on the land and improvements out of those rents.

As far as my own viewpoint, I think part of the current controversy is centered on the strong possibility of successful oil exploration. The tenants group told me that the reason the Fairhope corporation is raising the rents now is to force the tenants off the land so the 110 members of the corporation will have all of the oil revenues at their disposal. I guess if I were a tenant and my rent were going up, I would take that viewpoint because it would be to my interest.

The people at the corporation whom I interviewed never once alluded to these oil leases. They were extremely cagey and I really felt that the answers I was getting from them were pretty much self-serving and unfavorable to the tenant group's position.

As far as I can see, Fairhope is held together out of the pure dedication of these people to George's economics and the single tax theory. In addition, they were a very select group. Here was a group of highly intelligent people and, like the Mormons going to Salt Lake, this is the place and this is the philosophy. That is the impression I got.

Mathew Edel: I want to comment on Roy Bahl's point on taxation in developing countries. Certainly, in Columbia, a country I have studied most, there is a good deal of discussion on land value tax — some use of property assessment that unofficially at least is heavily weighted toward land. However, it struck me that Bahl's key question was "Why a tax on real estate?" Obviously, when an income tax cannot be administered, you turn to a real estate tax. The real question that he should have asked is: "Why site value rather than land plus buildings?" My guess is that you are dealing with a situation in which it is not so much a matter of how revenues should be raised, but rather a feeling that land speculation is holding land back from uses that are really crucial elements in whether or not development occurs.

Haskell Wald was mentioned this morning; his discussion of agricultural land tax in developing countries centers around the above point. I suppose in a way it is parallel to the pro-urban-renewal argument for site value tax in urban developed countries. I would guess it is more a great fear of the harm the speculator could do, rather than anything else, that brings the site value tax to the fore in urban planning.

H. Clyde Reeves: I believe that Alan Prest and William Deyll both indicated that in their countries something approaching site value taxation was imposed but that agricultural lands were exempted. I want to raise this question: Were you specifically talking about municipalities where there is no agricultural land or is it a matter of national or widespread policy to exempt agricultural land from the site value tax?

Alan R. Prest: In England the exemption dates back to the agricultural depression in the nineteenth century when it was thought reasonable to exempt agricultural land. That is when it started. At first this land was partially exempt, then in the 1920s it became completely exempt and it has been exempt ever since. There is no justification for it, but once having done it, it just goes on. The use is fixed and betterment taxes at very high rates have been levied when a higher use is decided upon.

Deyll: Agricultural land is exempt in our country (Holland) too.

Gaffney: I wish to go back to Bahl's observation relative to LDCs and their use of the land tax. Australia or East Africa, which are new countries and yet highly developed compared with what I suspect Bahl had in mind, make a widespread use of site value taxation.

Bahl: Take a city such as Nairobi. Near the center of the city you find a great deal of vacant land. This makes the problem of assessing the land easier. On the other hand, the level of services the government is now providing are fairly new services made necessary by the rapid urbanization. For example, in recent years water supply has been extended to all of the population.

Gaffney: I'm not sure I follow you on the implication of that.

Bahl: Typical local/municipal services were not being produced. Now that they are being provided the taxation of land has been seen as an appropriate financing procedure.

Kenneth E. Boulding: I would like to return to Fairhope. There are some similar communities in Canada. I think there was one near Vancouver, a place called Westminster. There are a couple.

Woolery: Arden in Delaware.

Boulding: I wonder if anyone has made comparative studies.

Woolery: All I can say is that the tenants group told me in Arden that the lessees who are nonmembers of the corporation still had voting rights, which is something the members are quite put out about because there are approximately 900 tenants in Arden and only 110 members of the corporation. The corporation members feel that on the sheer weight of the numbers of the tenants they are getting discriminatory treatment.

Boulding: I don't know whether the lessees at Arden agree with Henry George or not. There is a reward for successful pioneering, but to me it seems to be awfully hard to value. If your name is Gladwyn and your grandfather was in the Revolution, you are not going to reverse the action taken. You have this business of — the biologists have a name for it — the founders of fact. It seems to me extraordinarily hard to avoid. If it doesn't take one form, it somehow seems to take another. It is an awful feeling. The whole social world is full of traps for the virtuous. If they don't catch you one way, they will catch you another.

C. Lowell Harriss: In Arden, Delaware, there is an active George's group and the head of that is the daughter of the mayor of Arden, Delaware.

Boulding: The local squire stood on tradition and my ancestors fought for land ownership. My grandfather squared away and said to the squire, "Okay, I will fight for it." Somehow or other it wasn't an offer that the squire would accept.

Harriss: Apropos of the long ago and far away, I believe it was at a meeting some years ago that Ursula Hicks recommended a book which I bought and have never read. The British utilitarians in India in the nineteenth century tried to levy some kind of a tax on land values. Maybe when I retire I will read it.

Communities and Land Taxation

Gaffney: It might be useful to look at the question of marginally worthless land that would have no tax base if only land values were used.

Vickrey: Yes, but what are the public services being provided on this submarginal land?

Gaffney: Unless the community generates enough rent, it had better not exist. It had better join itself onto a larger community and enjoy the services from the larger community.

Vickrey: Not necessarily. The community that is located on the periphery of the larger community enjoys the services but not the cost of access to the larger community. One really has to say why are communities, especially large cities, large? And, in effect, my answer is that they are large because there are activities accountable to scale and there are transportation costs. If there are no transportation costs, you might just as well have a one-industry town.

228

Gaffney: Well, the second reason why large cities are large is that they start generating rents, then the public spends this on services, and these services in turn attract employment to the extent that these services are free or low-cost.

Vickrey: They can be priced below average cost. If they are below marginal costs, that is something else again. If they are priced below marginal cost, that is wrong. They should correspond to marginal cost.

Gaffney: We are raising the question of the way in which the surplus should be collected and spent. This raises the interesting question how George would rationalize this. He never faced it.

Vickrey: If you are the first community to become a Georgist community, then you benefit from the greater efficiency which the Georgist doctrine enables you to enjoy. You become larger and more efficient than the rest of the communities and you have a surplus because you are, in effect, selling products that cost you less than they cost other communities because your community is more efficient. There is a surplus which I suppose accrues to the people who had the brains to persuade everybody to become Georgists.

Daniel M. Holland: And this shows up in a higher value for land and a higher tax base.

Vickrey: In such a community there will be an excess of LVT collections over the cost of maintaining the community. This surplus will be available to government if conventional tax rates are maintained.

In fact, what you might say is that in a perfectly competitive equilibrium theory, if you have a country where all of the cities are general property tax cities and then one city elects to become a Georgian city instead, the surplus will be generated. In fact, surplus will be equal to what the landlords are currently getting, so this is one city that can convert to Henry George without any disadvantage to the current landlords. What happens if all the other cities follow suit is another thing. But in effect there should be, at least in theory, an advantage accruing to the first cities that go single tax.

Edel: I think the problem comes down to what one means by productive. As I read Marx, I would agree with him on this. What he is saying is that the productivity of different factors is not commensurable. Based on his own theory of how the world works, Marx decides that what is relevant for the analysis of human social relations is the labor that people expend. In the common use of the word productive, certainly he agrees that nature is productive. At times he uses the works of Leibitch to argue that it is in a sense nature that is exploited when nutrients are being taken from the soil and not returned to the soil. Marx, however, makes no attempt to measure this exploitation of land productivity against the exploitation of the human productivity of labor. Capital to Marx is essentially an indirect form of labor; its productivity is an additional contribution of labor to a product.

The definition of value stems from the purpose of the analysis. I think that there are only very limited purposes for partial equilibrium analysis in which one can judge the relative contribution of one factor of production versus another. One has to take too much as given to extend that up to the economy-wide level that he is talking about.

So I don't think you can apply what Marx refers to as the trinity formula, the attempt to get land, labor, and capital compared with each other in terms of productivity. Certainly labor-using equipment is more productive than labor that has to go out there and scratch in the wilderness. That is obvious.

That society has to make arrangements for inducing people to produce is also true. These arrangements may take the form of profits which go to a wide range of ownership, as opposed to other conceivable relationships that are historically specific. All in all, I think that Marx's way of aggregating things is useful.

Gaffney: Suppose I spend $50,000 to build a house and then rent it out. In ten years the cash flow I get back is equal to $50,000; it goes on for another sixty years and adds additional cash flow. Does that additional cash represent productivity of capital or productivity of labor?

Edel: I think it is an illegitimate question to pin it down to one specific property in the Marxist framework. Your example means that labor has been expended in a way that yields greater returns over time than if it were used to build a house that would last a shorter amount of time. It doesn't answer the question about the extent that those returns should go to you who put out the money or about the extent that it should be kicked back to the original labor. Nor does it address the extent that the original price should be reduced and the benefits spread throughout the society by price reduction. Those are social questions. Certainly I am not going to debate that the building is more socially advantageous. It certainly shows that capital works to produce goods over a long period of history. That is not at issue either.

What is at issue is whether the system builds continuous inequalities by virtue of having that system.

Harriss: Did any of the other people that you read, Mason, attempt quantification of land grant potential? I believe Alfred Marshall did.

Gaffney: Well, yes, Colpepper did that for one, and then in a much cleaner way Seal of the early authors did.

Harriss: Did Wilfred King?

Gaffney: Yes. His presentation actually may have been better, but I haven't looked at it.

Harriss: I must say I got very impatient as I was reading Henry George because of his refusal to take a sympathetic or even potentially sympathetic view of the newly-developed capital theory. He had his answers and that was that.

Gaffney: I suppose one reason that the question of capital and land productivity never loomed as important to Henry George was that he felt if you removed taxes from other things, this would increase the rental of land, so that the size of land rental as it exists today is not really the bone of the question.

Prest: I think Liddel Brown did some extensive computations on the value of land rent in Britain.

Break: Back to Marshall; yes, he did do some quantification. I can't remember the basis of his conclusion, but the result came out to be that nationalizing all the land in England would reduce taxes by a ha'penny or something, some very small amount. He remarked that he was appalled that George was willing to have a social revolution in the ownership of land for this pittance.

The Land Tax in Developing Nations

Lindholm: Bahl, you made some comment on the helpfulness of the Marxist and Georgist revolution in underdeveloped countries.

Bahl: I don't think I know anything about that. But I bet Hartojo Wignjowijoto does.

Hartojo Wignjowijoto: I'd like to comment on Lindholm's inquiry regarding the Georgist and Marxist positions. Both have radical elements, but the radical elements of George attract those who hold the power of the establishment, or the radical elements of the establishment. Marx attracts more of the people, the masses. In developing countries such as Indonesia, for example, those who own land are those who are in power. Both contain radical elements but different audiences.

Becker: It seems to me that people who own land would oppose Marx. It seems to me neither has much chance to make headway unless you get masses of people behind you one way or the other.

Wignjowijoto: Well, as we know, George is more of a gradualist than Marx. Marx attracts those wanting overnight change/revolution. Those in power will favor a gradual evolutionary change, while the Marxist doesn't have anything and wants to have everything right away.

Philip Finkelstein: I don't pretend to know anything about the developing countries, but certainly George would have very little appeal to people who identify themselves as a mass because that whole notion is absent in George. The masses or the proletariat is a concept that goes by the boards and George places stress on the individual. In such societies where the revolutionary fervor is on a class basis, the attraction has to be elsewhere than in George's philosophy.

Prest: One answer to this question is that in a number of countries there has been effective land reform but there are very few with an effective land tax.

Lindholm: Do you have any idea why this is true? Is it the British that ruined this?

Prest: You may accuse them of many things, but I am not sure you can accuse them of that one.

Holland: One of the few places where there is an effective land tax is an old British colony.

Prest: That is correct.

Holland: The Jamaicans have a land tax and even a passion for it, but they came to it without benefit of close reading of Henry George. They have had an interest in land value tax way back to the early 1900s; they see it in almost a revolutionary light. They see large land holdings as one aspect of their society that requires substantial change because they see vast inequalities. If your grandfather was a descendant of Oliver Cromwell, you may own one-tenth of the island. Without any literary back-up, they consider this to be an inappropriate state of affairs, and they consider taxation of land values a possible way of remedying that.

Bahl: I've spoken with many people around the world who are responsible for the tax policy; they have had no exposure to Henry George but have acted like good Georgians. South Korea is a good example. It is a country growing rapidly and really a great success story; they reshaped the property tax five or six years ago, worked on the assessment process, assessed land separately from improvements, and then taxed improvements at one-half the rate applied on land. In the Philippines and Egypt, they have done the same thing.

Future TRED Topics

Arthur D. Lynn, Jr.: What would be a good topic for a future TRED session?

Reeves: We are living in a society that is heavily dependent for its socio-economic viability on growth, be that economic development or something else. This kind of growth that we now seem to be dependent on to keep our country viable is not going to be maintainable over a long period of time. I don't mean to imply that I am a no-growther, but; I don't think we can continue to grow as in the past. Availability of energy will see to that. We need some thoery building on the ways of maintaining a viable economy under conditions somewhat less than an optimum growth situation. As I see us at the present time, we are basically sterile concerning ways to operate under conditions other than what we consider optimum growth. Is there any possibility in examination of this area?

This gets a little away from Henry George although I think there are some overtones in it. However, it is thoroughly in keeping with what the letters "TRED" represent.

Gaffney: I think that is a marvelous idea and I see lots of Georgian overtones. Something concerned with an effective land value tax on input and a more intensive labor to land ratio, i.e., how to accommodate a growing population on a limited resource base. I am not sure that is what you had in mind.

Reeves: I think we are headed in the same direction.

Lynn: I am glad to have that subject. Are there further comments?

Bahl: I think there is a lot to the growth subject. The question of determining the proper way to tax in a period of economic decline needs attention. New York City is a good example of what I have in mind. The rhetoric on the people's side tells us we must cut back welfare spending, and that on the revenue side tells us we must cut back on the high marginal tax rates. There hasn't been an awful lot done on this. I don't know if it is a good topic, but it is a good idea.

Gaffney: That is a twist on Reeves' original idea. The way I look at it, what is involved here is not accepting decline or adjusting to it, but reversing it and giving it a different character, or giving growth a different character, or giving stability a different character, or what have you.

Bahl: I am not so sure. Reeves may be looking at it through Kentucky glasses. Through Kentucky glasses they are not doing as well as they thought they were a decade ago. The Kentucky economy isn't suffering but the national economy is going to go slower and this will affect Kentucky.

Vickrey: It may be premature, but the concept of going up at an exponential rate, onward and upward forever, leads to the mass or perhaps a falling ball expanding at the speed of light. Somewhere it has got to stop.

Lindholm: Maybe it has already stopped.

Reeves: Well, this problem has regional, national, and global overtones that are quite different, but the mere analysis of them, differentiation between them, and information on the parameters around them might be a wholesome exercise.

Lynn: Are there other suggestions?

Edel: Yesterday Lindholm and I were discussing the great scarcity of studies on the ownership of land, which is obviously relevant to the distributional implications of a land tax. I don't know if there are enough papers in the works for a conference on this as soon as next year or not, but it is certainly an appropriate topic.

Finkelstein: May I point out with regard to this topic that there is supposed to be some additional data in the 1980 census. John Behrans of the Census Bureau has been talking about adding some wealth data. I don't know if it will be in the questionnaire, but I know there was some strong discussion a couple of years ago about getting property ownership data. Maybe that would be a good topic after we have a little more information than is now generally available. Also, a national research group is supposed to be applying for an NSF grant to move itself in this direction.

Wignjowigoto: Speaking of land ownership, or wealth distribution, I believe there has not been much of a change in the distribution of wealth. There is a paper that proves that there has been a change in the distribution of income, but not in the distribution of wealth.

Lynn: Thank you. Other comments along this line?

Welch: I believe I have a subject that lends itself to this group. We have been baffled by the effect that income taxes, corporate and personal, have on property values. There are a lot of angles to this that aren't apparent on the surface that I would like to see explored somewhere. If anybody knows of any such exploration that has occurred in the past that has been published, I would like to hear about it. Sometime I hope to interest somebody in doing it.

Woolery: Land use doesn't seem to be dictated simply at the land action level. Welch is saying to the tax administrators, "To what extent is the land tax a property tax or an income tax.?"

Reeves: I don't know if this question has been addressed.

Gaffney: Well, we have never really done a job on income tax treatment of land income. We have treated our subject as if the property tax was the only tax that is on land income and we pretty much neglected the income tax.

Holland: Welch, while you are here, can you elaborate?

Welch: Well, I am not really prepared to interest you in the subject I suppose. But in California we have had a long-standing argument with the assessors who say that income taxes have no effect on property values. In the State Board of Equalization our view has been that corporate income taxes should be recognized as a depressant of property values as compared to what they would be without the tax. But we don't say the same about individual income taxes and we don't know how to distinguish between properties affected by the two taxes. So we are pretty badly mixed up on the subject and I was hoping that some folks like yourselves might give us some enlightenment on it.

Vickrey: Well, just off-hand there is a kind of differentiation that occurs, because of the corporate income tax, between those properties that need to be financed as corporate equities and those properties financed largely by debt and mortage. In addition, since the corporate income tax suppresses investment in the equity finance area and directs investment to the mortgage and debt finance area, it in effect offsets the property tax.

Welch: I have always felt that the corporate income tax ought to be structured differently. It is not a return to equity, but a return to capital. I don't know if you endorse it, but that is the way I feel about it.

Vickrey: I would say that this is one of the defects of the corporate income tax.

Lynn: Other comments along that line? Well, one TRED conference kind of weaves into another.

Gaffney: May I have one more comment along that line? Recently there is a very strong movement to modify the income tax drastically in order to encourage capital formation. In the process it will probably end up encouraging land speculation, whatever that is, in terms of the way people use it, but we will undoubtedly exempt a lot of land income in the process of trying to encourage capital formation. This, I submit, is another reason for having a conference on the income tax and the distinction between the taxation of the income from capital and the income from land.

Becker: A few years ago when we had a conference, somebody gave a paper which I have always remembered. It referred to the taxable income on farmland in various states, and, as I recall, the average taxable income in California between 1969 and 1973 was $20 million or so. Wisconsin had average taxable income of $400 million. Apparently, there wasn't much taxable income arising from farmland in California under the federal income tax. This certainly must have had some influence on the price of farmland in California. I don't believe California needs to do anymore to exempt farmland income from the income tax in order to favor investment in land. Maybe it has already gone too far in this direction.

Lynn: Any other comments? I kind of sense the beginning of the end. Arthur, as chairman of the innertube or inner tread or whatever, do you have any words of wisdom?

Becker: No, I don't have anything at all. I think the digestive process has already begun.

Index

Land value taxation *(continued)*
85–87, 92; opposition to, 86; in New Zealand, 221; in Pennsylvania, 86; in Australia, 221–22; and multiple regression analysis, 100–103
Layfield, Sir Frank, 140
Layfield Committee, 140, 146, 148
Lent, George, 63
Lindholm, Richard W., 39, 110, 113, 115, 118—19, 173, 230–32; and Oregon land tax, 83–94
Local government taxes, 62
Local rates, 135
Location theorist, 169
Location value, 12–13, 14, 102, 170
Lynn, Arthur D., 231

Malthers, Thomas, 6
Manvel, Allen O., 45–48
Mapping land value, 70, 106
Marshall, Alfred, 83, 131, 132, 136, 140, 164, 166–68
Marx, Karl, 6–8, 16, 157–58, 205–220
Melville, Alexander J., 202
Mill, John Stuart, 41, 144, 156, 174, 207
McCall, Tom, 85
McGuire, Carl W., 118
MacKinnon, James G., 57
McLure, Charles E., 52
Mineral rights, 176, 183
Monopoly power, 85, 209, 212, 216
Multiple Regression Analysis, 100–103, 118

Nationalization of land, 146
Negative taxes, 10
Netzer, Dick, 33–34, 106, 112–15, 118, 161, 184—85
New Zealand: use of land tax, 64, 221

Oldman, Oliver, 69
OPEC, 162
Oregon: Eugene land tax, 87–92
Ownership of land, 165–66

Pigou, A. C., 144–45, 168
Planning: usefulness of, 10
Police power, 180
Polinsky, Mitchell, A., 57
Premature conversion, 162
Prest, Alan R., 113, 116, 139–49, 162, 168, 226, 231

Private appeal hearings, 76–78
Private property, 6–7
Production, 12, 158, 209, 210, 211, 212–13, 217–18, 228–29; effects of taxes, 24–25
Products: speculation in, 23
Profits: role of, 209–10, 212
Proposition 13, 110–11, 112, 114, 122, 129, 134, 157, 181
Property: 13–14; ownership, 13; moral basis of, 25–27; tax, 112, 114, 119, 135, 139, 159, 165; in land, 166
Public hearings, 73–80
Public lands, 178

Quesnay, François, 179–82

Rating system, 140
Real Estate Research Corporation, 91
Reeves, H. Clyde, 106, 111, 118, 226, 231–32
Reformers, 8
Rent levels, 201
Rents: city, 172
Rent taxation, 177–79, 185
Resource rent, 176–79
Revenue potential, 42, 64, 164
Ricardo, David, 6, 11, 41, 84, 155, 169, 185, 208
Richman, R. L., 64
Rubinfeld, Daniel L., 66

Sales: bare land, 98–99, 115–16, 121
Samuelson, Paul, 170
San Francisco, 8
Scarf, H. E., 57
Schroeder, Larry D., 53, 86
Seligman, E. R. A., 164–65, 69; doctrine, 159–60
Shaw, George Bernard, 6
Shifting of taxes, 169–71
Shoven, J. B., 55, 57
Simon, Herbert, 170
Simpson, Herbert D., 170
Single tax, 3, 10, 11, 17, 20, 28, 159; in New York City, 110; implications of, 29–30
Single taxers, 197, 198
Site value, 70–72, 147
Site value taxation: revenue potential of, 41–42; partial equilibrium approach, 42–52, 229; general equilibrium approach, 52–58; Harberger model, 53; dynamic equilibrium

COMPOSED BY LANDMANN ASSOCIATES, INC., MADISON, WISCONSIN
MANUFACTURED BY INTER-COLLEGIATE PRESS, INC., SHAWNEE MISSION, KANSAS
TEXT AND DISPLAY LINES ARE SET IN TIMES ROMAN

Library of Congress Cataloging in Publication Data
Main entry under title:
Land value taxation.
(Publications of the Committee on Taxation,
Resources, and Economic Development; 11)
Proceedings of a symposium sponsored by the
Committee on Taxation, Resources, and Economic
Development at the Lincoln Institute of Land Policy,
Cambridge, Mass., 1978.
Includes bibliographies and index.
1. Land value taxation—Congresses. 2. George,
Henry, 1839–1897. Progress and poverty—
Congresses. 3. Economics—Congresses. 4. Single
tax—Congresses. I. Lindholm, Richard Wadsworth,
1914–   . II. Lynn, Arthur D., 1921–
III. Committee on Taxation, Resources and Economic
Development. IV. Series.
HJ4165.L37   336.22′2   80-52299
ISBN 0-299-08520-1   AACR2